MAN DOES, WOMAN IS

# Man Does, Woman Is

## AN ANTHOLOGY OF WORK AND GENDER

*Edited by*
*Marion Shaw*

*faber and faber*

LONDON · BOSTON

First published in 1995
by Faber and Faber Limited
3 Queen Square London WC1N 3AU

Photoset by Intype Ltd, London
Printed in England by Clays Ltd, St Ives plc

© Marion Shaw, 1994

A CIP record for this book is available from the British
Library
ISBN 0–571–16558–3

# Contents

*For Liz*

# Introduction

Next to sleeping, work is what we spend most of our lives doing. Those who do not work, like invalids or the very rich or the very old, seem to belong to the margins of life, an impression shared most bitterly by the reluctantly unemployed. Work gives us social status as well as the means to live. This is true whether the work is enjoyable or not. To work is to own a place in the world, however modest, and to be deprived of work is to be exiled, punished. Work also creates our identity. Because it is categorized according to class, race, gender, status and remuneration, it constructs our notions of ourselves as people, as men and women. We may not like doing 'women's work', or we may relish being 'a woman in a man's world', but the boundaries these categories imply are important in establishing a sense of self.

In spite of its centrality to what we do and are, work has never seemed to feature visibly as a literary idea, certainly not as far as anthologies are concerned. Perhaps this is because work is not leisure, and anthologies are thought of as leisured and leisurely reading. The impression may also be that work is simply not written about very much, at least not in imaginative literature; it is difficult, for instance, to think of a novel which is 'about' work rather than about love or community or national feeling. Yet, work is everywhere in literature, perhaps not often as the dominant narrative or theme but omnipresent nevertheless. Work exists in the interstices of other plots as a cause of joy or despair, as a determinant of character and setting, an economic dynamic, a source of and a foil to the aesthetics of leisure, and a condition of the forms literature takes. This anthology seeks to bring to the surface some of this submerged writing about work in poetry and novels, and occasionally in non-fiction writing also. It thus acknowledges one of the great commonplaces of our lives, and one of the necessary although often unrecognized presences in literature.

There are problems of definition. In a broad sense, to work can mean to be busy, to do things, actively to occupy the time, to expend physical or mental effort in making something, and is used with these meanings when we talk about working in the garden, or working on the car. In a narrower sense, work means paid employment, what is done to earn a living, and this is a definition most people would accept. One might take a cue here from Philip Larkin who, on being asked by *Who's Who* what his occupation was, replied, 'Librarian;

a man is what he is paid to do.' One might also take note of Tom Sawyer's realization that an element of compulsion is involved, that 'Work consists of whatever the body is *obliged* to do, and that Play consists of whatever a body is not obliged to do. And this would help him to understand why constructing artificial flowers or performing on a treadmill is work, while rolling tenpins or climbing Mont Blanc is only amusement.'

So work comprises payment and obligation, and usually each involves the other. But there are people who are obliged to work although they receive no pay. Slaves provide an extreme example. Numerous others also do not receive direct remuneration for their labour, or reward is given 'in kind' and is dependent on the goodwill of someone else. The largest group of workers of this kind are those who work in the home and, although their condition may range from luxury to abject deprivation, the value of their work has never been satisfactorily calculated as financial reward. The married man's tax allowance, the extra (but not equal) amount paid to a pensionable man for his wife, divorce settlements, and various family supplements are public recognition that work in the home exists but either impracticability or a failure of will have meant that this is an imprecise and often token recognition, calibrated according neither to need nor to the value of the work done.

The difficulty of defining work is related to beliefs about the right to work. Who has this right and whether it extends to work of all kinds is contentious and unequally decided. Many societies by law reserve certain occupations, usually high-status ones, for their privileged members, and in effect the lowliest jobs are also reserved for those who, because of class, caste, colour or ethnicity, can never easily qualify for work of higher standing. It is a complex chicken-and-egg question of whether the work of a lowly person is inevitably of low status, or the low-status job defines a person as lowly. Perhaps there are no absolute categories of 'superior' and 'inferior' work but only a complex interaction between what is done and who does it.

Probably most far-reaching and deeply ingrained in matters of the right to work and the value of that work are the divisions according to gender. Throughout history, and probably in pre-history too, the idea that there is a natural division of labour, dependent on the biological differences of the two sexes, has structured work patterns in the fields, in the workshops and the factories, and in the home. What is known as 'men's' or 'women's' work may not be the same in all parts of the world but the gender distinctions will still be present and will be both biologically explained and culturally inscribed. Whatever its geographical or historical location, 'women's work' has tended to be of low regard and lowly paid. Only notions about race, where differences are likewise perceived as biologically determined, approach in depth of conviction this belief that there is a fitness for women and men to do certain kinds of work, which cannot or should not be done by the other sex.

In part the notions of separate work spheres according to sex derive from differences in physical prowess, the greater muscular strength of men and the relative weakness of women, particularly when burdened by pregnancy or the care of infants. But this is only partially the explanation, otherwise women would not have been barred from employment where little muscular strength is required. It has more to do with status, with power, and with a sense of the appropriate position of men and women relative to each other. Countless arguments have been adduced to prove that women should be denied access to areas of employment which might make them equal to and independent of men: they are not responsible for families, they only work for pin money, work of a taxing nature will impair their reproductive faculties, men will not want to marry them if they earn an equal or superior income, they are unsuited biologically to strenuous physical labour and psychologically to creative and ratiocinative endeavour. To have to disprove or counter any or all of these arguments has always been an exhausting addition to women's attempts to enter the workforce on equal terms, or indeed on any terms at all. But of all arguments, none has been more invidious – because it seeks to flatter – and pervasive – because it enters into the emotional relations between men and women – than the notion that women do not really have to do anything but should just simply *be*. They are the inspirers not the inspired, the muse and not the poet, the presence and not the activity.

The effect of this has been twofold. It has been to prescribe passivity as an ideal for women and it has also served to disguise just how much work women actually do, even though it may not be thought of as 'work' but as something else, like looking after the children or cooking the dinner. How many women, when asked what their work is, say, with a slightly self-deprecating smile, 'Oh, I'm only a housewife'?

The title proposition of this anthology, 'Man Does, Woman Is', which is taken from a volume of Robert Graves's poems, summarizes a sense of difference which stresses the passivity of woman's identity and its inactive relation to man's. Her work is therefore seen either as not really work at all, but as a mixture of a gift and a duty (child-bearing, for example), or, if she works outside the home, as exceptional, outrageous even, or valid only inasmuch as it mimics or leads to the service she gives within the home. Yet as United Nations statistics make clear, there are few countries where women make up less than 30 per cent of the workforce and many where the percentage is much higher, although women own only 2 per cent of the wealth of the world.

In literature, as Virginia Woolf pointed out in 1929 in *A Room of One's*

*Own*, the invisibility of women's work meant that they had been tied to the love and marriage plot. But a change was occurring:

> ... it is becoming evident that women, like men, have other interests besides the perennial interests of domesticity. 'Chloe liked Olivia. They shared a laboratory together . . .' I read on and discovered that these two young women were engaged in mincing liver, which is, it seems, a cure for pernicious anaemia.

Until that change, all the work that women did had had to be left out so that 'the splendid portrait of the fictitious woman is much too simple and much too monotonous'. Pointedly relevant, therefore, is the conversation Woolf's working woman, Peggy, the doctor in *The Years*, has with a fine-browed, pale and pasty young man at a party:

> 'I'm tired,' she apologized,'I've been up all night,' she explained. 'I'm a doctor . . .' The fire went out of his face when she said 'I'. That's done it – now he'll go, she thought. He can't be 'you' – he must be 'I'. She smiled. For up he got and off he went.

Woolf offers an explanation of why this should be in her comment in *A Room of One's Own* that 'Women have served all these centuries as looking-glasses possessing the magic and delicious power of reflecting the figure of man at twice his natural size.' She goes on to acknowledge that this magnified and illusory mirroring has powered men to clear swamps and jungles, fight wars, write books, and make laws: 'under the spell of that illusion [men] are striding to work.' If women also stride to work on a (more or less) equal footing with men, then what will become of the looking-glass?

*Man Does, Woman Is* is an anthology of writings about the work men and women do and their perceptions of that work, particularly in relation to gender differences. The selection is drawn mostly from English literature, and therefore inevitably mainly from a Protestant culture with its strong association of work with moral worth. To have gone beyond these limits to attempt a world view of attitudes to work would have been beyond the scope of a single anthology and also beyond my competence as an anthologist. As it is, the anthology both proves and disproves 'Man Does, Woman Is' in that it demonstrates man's dominion over the world and the literature of work while illustrating how much work women actually do in spite of *being* just women. It also, in some of its extracts, shows how venerable and persistent is the belief that when women are acknowledged as working it must be in their own sphere, that, in fact, the division of labour according to gender is both inevitable and desired.

The first section of the anthology, 'The Pen Has Been in Their Hands', comprises pronouncements, maxims and injunctions, largely by men because, as Jane Austen saw, the pen has been theirs inasmuch as historically their ownership of writing has been greater than women's, and theirs also has been the right, from Genesis onwards, to define and allocate work. Even when women have been literate enough to write about their own lives, they have been reluctant to write about their work for its own sake. To be busy in the service of others has been permitted and praised but to call this busy-ness work, or be paid for it, would not have been respectable. So women's work has often gone under the guise of duty, sacrifice to the good of others or mere obedience to authority. Men's centuries-old authority has curbed women's independence as workers and also their freedom to name and delineate their work. This male authority over the language of work has not entirely yielded with the coming of the twentieth century; there still seem to be more men than women writing about work, and this continues to contribute to the relative invisibility of women in the labour force.

The second and third sections, 'Man's Toil' and 'Woman's Labour', are concerned straightforwardly with the work that men and women do but with an underlying recognition that the gender of the worker is significant. There is a presupposition that only a man could be, for instance, a wheelwright or a harpooner, and only a woman a prostitute or a seamstress. The next section, 'Girls and Boys', shows how this gendering of adult duties and employment begins in childhood. Rousseau's holy child is, of course, male and while he works at his play, his future mate, Sophie, is trimming her existence and her employment in order to *be* for Emile whatever will magnify him into the citizen of the new age.

In some respects the next two sections, 'The Division of Labour' and 'Working Together', are the most illuminating in that they illustrate the relations between men's and women's work, those of both opposition and co-operation. But even in the co-operative activity of work, the separate spheres seem to be preserved and it is complementarity which produces results, not competition nor even similar or equally shared endeavour.

The final section, 'Engendering Idleness', could have been expanded to provide a whole anthology, so prevalent is the need to talk about not working and the reasons for this. One of the chief of these is sexual excess, where women are the tempters and a major cause of idleness. Even where women are absent, laziness in men is seen as a kind of effeminacy: a state of *being* rather than *doing*, the body overpowering the mind, as Keats says, and as Charlotte Brontë's Cleopatra grossly exemplifies. Idleness is gendered particularly for men if only by reference to what they ought to be doing; if they are not working their manhood is impugned and their lives cast to the margins. The entropic decadence of the lotos island of Tennyson's mariners gains emphasis from the memory of their wives and the world of work they have left behind.

Many of the extracts here are from the nineteenth century or later. Work has always been done, and done according to the division of labour by gender, and it was described before the nineteenth century but not with the philosophic intensity that it attracts from the Age of Reason onwards. In early societies – Greek or Anglo-Saxon, for instance – perhaps because they were fairly homogeneous and poetry served many cultural purposes, including instruction in practical skills, work featured matter-of-factly beside other activities so that *The Odyssey*, for example, has descriptions of building a boat, fishing, washing clothes (women's work then, as later), and butchering a pig, and these artisan activities are given credit in the poem alongside what we now think of as the truly epic accounts of battles and gods. But in more diversified and commercially sophisticated societies, work seems to have become relegated to a menial status, written about, if at all, in training manuals, while imaginative literature, usually the literature of the court or an élite, has turned its attention to less material concerns. By the time of the Renaissance, work as a literary topic lacks the glamour of love, nationhood or kingship so that when it occurs in Shakespeare it does so contingently, as a metaphor (in the garden scene in *Richard II*, for example) or as part of a comic or debased world which is present as a foil to the world of the court, as in *A Midsummer Night's Dream* or the history plays. The worker in Shakespeare, particularly the artisan, has little dignity; those who labour at being king or warlord have dignity but are not seen as workers, even though their toil is great. It is a state or condition they occupy and by contrast the worker, 'he whose brow with homely bigen bound / Snores out the watch of night', 'A wretch / Winding up days with toil and nights with sleep', is seen as having an easy, albeit brutalized, time of it in contrast with the 'hard condition' of being king.

This literary hierarchy in which work is, quite literally, in the servants' quarters begins to be challenged by writers of Puritan and then of bourgeois habits of mind. Reading the Bible to suit his notion of a prelapsarian state, Milton has Adam and Eve working in Paradise, 'our pleasant task enjoined'. (The exit from Paradise is because they divide their labour – Eve's fault – and ever afterwards their labour is divided by gender.) After the Fall, work is not newly introduced as a punishment; it is just that it is more laborious, harsher. But even then, as Adam says, 'what harm? Idleness had been worse.'

But it is really with the nineteenth century that work becomes theorized, its spiritual as well as its material values dwelt on, its ennobling qualities and the manner in which it marks out a man as honourable or otherwise. Also, the degradations of work, and the suffering it often entailed, are thought about more than in previous centuries and it is during this period that organized labour movements get under way. George Eliot's Caleb Garth is one emanation of the spirit of the age in his insistence that 'you must love your work [and] you must not be ashamed of your work', and another is the Blue Book description of the sweated trades which drive girls to prostitution, so badly are they paid and so inhuman the competitive operations they are caught up in.

It is also in the nineteenth century that the notion of separate spheres for men and women, and the effect of this on work opportunities for both sexes, becomes widespread in a population not only increasing rapidly in size but also living and therefore talking together more closely in the great conurbations. Even as the stereotypes harden, countermovements are under way whereby first one area of male prerogative – education, perhaps – and then others – medicine and the legislature – begin to fall to the women. By the time of Olive Schreiner, writing in 1911, a woman can reap the legacy of the nineteenth century to say 'We claim all labour for our province.' Towards the end of the twentieth century in the western world this claim has not been fully realized but nearly so. Women enter the professions, manage businesses, occasionally drive trains, fight on the front line, even become prime ministers, and although overall they still earn on average only two-thirds of the male rate, at least they do so in a greater variety of occupations than used to be open to them. Women have always been workers even though the myth of their *Being* has sought to disguise it. Perhaps now, in the face of their manifest activity in the workplace, the myth is being dismantled: *Woman Does* – not an antithesis to Man, not his mirror and negative, but an active and equal protagonist in her own right.

# THE PEN HAS BEEN
# IN THEIR HANDS

# Working and Weeping

'We certainly do not forget you, so soon as you forget us. It is, perhaps, our fate rather than our merit. We cannot help ourselves. We live at home, quiet, confined, and our feelings prey upon us. You are forced on exertion. You have always a profession, pursuits, business of some sort or other, to take you back into the world immediately, and continual occupation and change soon weaken impressions . . . Nay, it would be too hard upon you, if it were otherwise. You have difficulties, and privations, and dangers enough to struggle with. You are always labouring and toiling, exposed to every risk and hardship. Your home, country, friends, all quitted. Neither time, nor health, nor life, to be called your own. It would be too hard indeed' (with a faltering voice) 'if woman's feelings were to be added to all this.' . . .

'But let me observe [said Captain Harville] that all histories are against you, all stories, prose and verse. If I had such a memory as Benwick, I could bring you fifty quotations in a moment on my side the argument, and I do not think I ever opened a book in my life which had not something to say upon woman's inconstancy. Songs and proverbs, all talk of woman's fickleness. But perhaps you will say, these were all written by men.'

'Perhaps I shall. – Yes, yes, if you please, no reference to examples in books. Men have had every advantage of us in telling their own story. Education has been theirs in so much higher a degree; the pen has been in their hands. I will not allow books to prove any thing.'

'But how shall we prove any thing?'

'We never shall. We never can expect to prove any thing upon such a point. It is a difference of opinion which does not admit of proof.'

Jane Austen, from *Persuasion*, 1818

Unto the woman he said, I will greatly multiply thy sorrow and thy conception; in sorrow thou shalt bring forth children; and thy desire shall be to thy husband, and he shall rule over thee.

And unto Adam he said, Because thou hast hearkened unto the voice of thy wife, and hast eaten of the tree, of which I commanded thee, saying, Thou shalt not eat of it: cursed is the ground for thy sake; in sorrow shalt thou eat of it all the days of thy life.

Thorns also and thistles shall it bring forth to thee; and thou shalt eat the herb of the field;

In the sweat of thy face shalt thou eat bread, till thou return unto the ground; for out of it wast thou taken; for dust thou art, and unto dust shalt thou return.

Genesis 3:16–19

### The Three Fishers

Three fishers went sailing out into the West,
   Out into the West as the sun went down;
Each thought on the woman who loved him the best;
   And the children stood watching them out of the town;
For men must work, and women must weep,
And there's little to earn, and many to keep,
   Though the harbour bar be moaning.

Three wives sat up in the light-house tower,
   And they trimmed the lamps as the sun went down;
They looked at the squall, and they looked at the shower,
   And the night rack came rolling up ragged and brown!
But men must work, and women must weep,
Though storms be sudden, and waters deep,
   And the harbour bar be moaning.

Three corpses lay out on the shining sands
   In the morning gleam as the tide went down,
And the women are weeping and wringing their hands
   For those who will never come back to the town;
For men must work, and women must weep,
And the sooner it's over, the sooner to sleep –
   And good-bye to the bar and its moaning.

Charles Kingsley, 1851

## Poor Richard Says

But do thou be ever mindful of our injunction, and work, noble Perses, that hunger may abhor thee, but worshipful Demeter of the fair crown love thee and fill thy barn with livelihood. For hunger is altogether meet companion of the man who will not work. At him are gods and men wroth, whoso liveth in idleness, like in temper to the stingless drones, which in idleness waste and devour the labour of the bees. Be it thy choice to order the works which are meet, that thy

4

barns may be full of seasonable livelihood. By works do men wax rich in flocks and gear: yea, and by work shalt thou be far dearer to immortals and to mortals: for they utterly abhor the idle. Work is no reproach: the reproach is idleness. But if thou wilt work, soon shall the idle man envy thee thy wealth: on wealth attend good and glory. And whatever be thy lot, work is best, if thou wilt turn thy foolish mind from the goods of other men to work and study livelihood as I bid thee. Ill shame attendeth the needy man: shame which greatly harmeth men or greatly helpeth. Shame goeth with unweal: boldness with weal . . . The idle man filleth not his barn, neither he that putteth off. Diligence prospereth work, but the man who putteth off ever wrestleth with ruin.

Hesiod, eighth century BC, from *Works and Days*

*Industry need not wish*, as *Poor Richard* says, and *He that lives upon Hope will die fasting. There are no Gains without Pains*: then *Help Hands, for I have no Lands*, or if I have, they are smartly taxed. And, as *Poor Richard* likewise observes, *He that hath a Trade hath an Estate*, and *He that hath a Calling, hath an Office of Profit and Honour*, but then the *Trade* must be worked at, and the *Calling* well followed, or neither the *Estate*, nor the *Office*, will enable us to pay our Taxes. If we are industrious we shall never starve; for, as *Poor Richard* says, *At the working Man's House Hunger looks in, but dares not enter*. Nor will the Bailiff or the Constable enter, for *Industry pays Debts, while Despair encreaseth them*, says *Poor Richard*. What though you have found no Treasure, nor has any rich Relation left you a Legacy, *Diligence is the Mother of Good luck*, as *Poor Richard* says, and *God gives all Things to Industry*. Then *plough deep, while Sluggards sleep, and you shall have Corn to sell and to keep*, says *Poor Dick*. Work while it is called To-day, for you know not how much you may be hindered To-morrow, which makes *Poor Richard* say, *One To-day is worth two To-morrows*; and farther, *Have you somewhat to do To-morrow, do it To-day*. If you were a Servant, would you not be ashamed that a good Master should catch you idle? Are you then your own Master, *be ashamed to catch yourself idle*, as *Poor Dick* says. When there is so much to be done for yourself, your Family, your Country, and your gracious King, be up by Peep of Day; *Let not the Sun look down and say, Inglorious here he lies*. Handle your Tools without Mittens; remember that *the Cat in Gloves catches no Mice*, as *Poor Richard* says. 'Tis true there is much to be done, and perhaps you are weak-handed, but stick to it steadily, and you will see great Effects, for *constant Dropping wears away Stones*, and *by Diligence and Patience the Mouse ate in two the Cable*; and *little Strokes fell great Oaks*, as *Poor Richard* says in his Almanack, the Year I cannot just now remember.

Benjamin Franklin, from the Preface to *Poor Richard's Almanack*, 1757

No man is born into the world whose work
Is not born with him; there is always work,
And tools to work withal, for those who will;
And blessëd are the horny hands of toil!
The busy world shoves angrily aside
The man who stands with arms akimbo set,
Until occasion tells him what to do;
And he who waits to have his task marked out
Shall die and leave his errand unfulfilled.
Our time is one that calls for earnest deeds:
Reason and government, like two broad seas,
Yearn for each other with outstretchëd arms
Across this narrow isthmus of the throne,
And roll their white surf higher every day.
One age moves onward, and the next builds up
Cities and gorgeous palaces, where stood
The rude log huts of those who tamed the wild,
Rearing from out the forests they had felled
The goodly framework of a fairer state;
The builder's trowel and the settler's axe
Are seldom wielded by the selfsame hand;
Ours is the harder task, yet not the less
Shall we receive the blessing for our toil
From the choice spirits of the aftertime.

James Russell Lowell, from 'A Glance Behind the Curtain', 1890

I grew up in the Thirties with our unemployed father. He did not riot, he got
on his bike and looked for work.

Norman Tebbit, in a speech at the Conservative Party Conference, 1981

## Ease of Mind and a Full Belly

As there is watchinge, so is there sleepe; as there is warre, so is there peace:
as there is winter, so is there Summer: as there be many working dayes, so is
there also many holy-dayes: and if I may speak as in one worde, ease is the
sauce of labour, which is plainly to be seene, not onely in lyving thinges, but
also in thinges without life. Wee unbend the bowe that wee maye the better
bend him, we unloose the Harpe, that we may the sooner tune him, the body

6

is kept in health as well with fasting as eating, the minde healed with ease, as wel with labour.

John Lyly, from *Euphues: The Anatomy of Wit*, 1579

It may be proved, with much certainty, that God intends no man to live in this world without working: but it seems to me no less evident that He intends every man to be happy in his work. It is written, 'in the sweat of thy brow', but it was never written, 'in the breaking of thine heart', thou shalt eat bread: and I find that, as on the one hand, infinite misery is caused by idle people, who both fail in doing what was appointed for them to do, and set in motion various springs of mischief in matters in which they should have had no concern, so on the other hand, no small misery is caused by over-worked and unhappy people, in the dark views which they necessarily take up themselves, and force upon others, of work itself. Were it not so, I believe the fact of their being unhappy is in itself a violation of divine law, and a sign of some kind of folly or sin in their way of life. Now in order that people may be happy in their work, these three things are needed: They must be fit for it: They must not do too much of it: and they must have a sense of success in it – not a doubtful sense, such as needs some testimony of other people for its confirmation, but a sure sense, or rather knowledge, that so much work has been done well, and fruitfully done, whatever the world may say or think about it. So that in order that a man may be happy, it is necessary that he should not only be capable of his work, but a good judge of his work.

John Ruskin, from *Pre-Raphaelitism*, 1851

## Short Work

The continuous labour of life is to build the house of death.

Montaigne, from *Essays*, I, xx, *c.* 1571

All men for Honor hardest work
But are not known to earn –
Paid after they have ceased to work
In Infamy or Urn –

Emily Dickinson, 1871

I have seen the future, and it works.
    Lincoln Steffens, 1866–1936, after a visit to Moscow in 1919


*Arbeit Macht Frei* (Work liberates)
    Slogan above the gate of Dachau, 1933


Work expands so as to fill the time available for its completion.
    C. Northcote Parkinson, from *Parkinson's Law*, 1958


*The Peter Principle: In a Hierarchy Every Employee Tends to rise to His Level of Incompetence* ... Work is accomplished by those employees who have not yet reached their level of incompetence.
    Laurence Peter, from *The Peter Principle*, 1969


## Working in the Garden

'You must have a magnificent estate,' said Candide to the Turk.

'Only twenty acres,' replied the Turk. 'My children help me to farm it, and we find that the work banishes those three great evils, boredom, vice, and poverty.'

As he walked back to the farm, Candide reflected on what the Turk had said. 'That old fellow,' said he, turning to Pangloss and Martin, 'seemed to me to have done much better for himself than those six kings we had the honour of supping with.'

'High estate,' said Pangloss, 'is always dangerous, as every philosopher knows. For Eglon, King of Moab, was assassinated by Ehud, and Absalom was hanged by his hair and stabbed with three spears; King Nadab, the son of Jeroboam was killed by Baasha; King Elah by Zimri; Joram by Jehu; Athaliah by Jehoiada; and King Jehoiakin, King Jehoiachin, and King Zedekiah all became slaves. You know the miserable fate of Croesus, Astyages, Darius, Dionysius of Syracuse, Pyrrhus, Perseus, Hannibal, Jugurtha, Ariovistus, Caesar, Pompey, Nero, Otho, Vitellius, Domitian, Richard II of England, Edward II, Henry VI, Richard III, Mary Queen of Scots, Charles I, the three Henrys of France, and the Emperor Henry IV? You know ... ?'

'I also know,' said Candide, 'that we must go and work in the garden.'

'You are quite right,' said Pangloss. 'When man was placed in the Garden of Eden, he was put there "to dress it and to keep it", to work, in fact; which proves that man was not born to an easy life.'

'We must work without arguing,' said Martin; 'that is the only way to make life bearable.'

The entire household agreed to this admirable plan, and each began to exercise his talents. Small as the estate was, it bore heavy crops. There was no denying that Cunégonde was decidedly ugly, but she soon made excellent pastry. Pacquette was clever at embroidery, and the old woman took care of the linen. No one refused to work, not even Brother Giroflée, who was a good carpenter, and thus became an honest man. From time to time Pangloss would say to Candide:

'There is a chain of events in this best of all possible worlds; for if you had not been turned out of a beautiful mansion at the point of a jackboot for the love of Lady Cunégonde, and if you had not been involved in the Inquisition, and had not wandered over America on foot, and had not struck the Baron with your sword, and lost all those sheep you brought from Eldorado, you would not be here eating candied peel and pistachio nuts.'

'That's true enough,' said Candide; 'but we must go and work in the garden.'

Voltaire, from *Candide, or Optimism*, 1759,
tr. John Butt, 1947

## When Earth's Last Picture is Painted

When Earth's last picture is painted and the tubes are
    twisted and dried,
When the oldest colours have faded, and the youngest critic
    has died,
We shall rest, and, faith, we shall need it – lie down for an
    aeon or two,
Till the Master of All Good Workmen shall put us to work
    anew.

And those that were good shall be happy: they shall sit in a
    golden chair;
They shall splash at a ten-league canvas with brushes of
    comets' hair.
They shall find real saints to draw from – Magdalene, Peter,
    and Paul;
They shall work for an age at a sitting and never be tired at
    all!

> And only the Master shall praise us, and only the Master
>     shall blame;
> And no one shall work for money, and no one shall work for
>     fame,
> But each for the joy of the working, and each, in his separate
>     star,
> Shall draw the Thing as he sees It for the God of Things as
>     They are!
>
> Rudyard Kipling, 1892

## Work

There is no point in work
unless it absorbs you
like an absorbing game.

If it doesn't absorb you
if it's never any fun,
don't do it.

When a man goes out into his work
he is alive like a tree in spring,
he is living, not merely working.

When the Hindus weave thin wool into long, long lengths of stuff
with their thin dark hands and their wide dark eyes and their still souls
    absorbed
they are like slender trees putting forth leaves, a long white web of living
    leaf,
the tissue they weave,
and they clothe themselves in white as a tree clothes itself in its own foliage.

As with cloth, so with houses, ships, shoes, wagons or cups or loaves
men might put them forth as a snail its shell, as a bird that leans
its breast against its nest, to make it round,
as the turnip models his round root, as the bush makes flowers and
    gooseberries,
putting them forth not manufacturing them,
and cities might be as once they were, bowers grown out from the busy
    bodies of people.

And so it will be again, men will smash the machines.

At last, for the sake of clothing himself in his own leaf-like cloth
tissued from his life,
and dwelling in his own bowery house, like a beaver's nibbled mansion
and drinking from cups that came off his fingers like flowers off their five-
    fold stem,
he will cancel the machines we have got.

D. H. Lawrence, from *Pansies*, 1929

## Toads

Why should I let the toad *work*
    Squat on my life?
Can't I use my wit as a pitchfork
    And drive the brute off?

Six days of the week it soils
    With its sickening poison –
Just for paying a few bills!
    That's out of proportion.

Lots of folk live on their wits:
    Lecturers, lispers,
Losels, loblolly-men, louts –
    They don't end as paupers;

Lots of folk live up lanes
    With fires in a bucket,
Eat windfalls and tinned sardines –
    They seem to like it.

Their nippers have got bare feet,
    Their unspeakable wives
Are skinny as whippets and yet
    No one actually starves.

Ah, were I courageous enough
    To shout *Stuff your pension!*
But I know, all too well, that's the stuff
    That dreams are made on:

11

For something sufficiently toad-like
   Squats in me too;
Its hunkers are as heavy as hard luck,
   And cold as snow.

And will never allow me to blarney
   My way to getting
The fame and the girl and the money
   All at one sitting.

I don't say, one bodies the other
   One's spiritual truth;
But I do say it's hard to lose either,
   When you have both.

           Philip Larkin, from *The Less Deceived*, 1955

## A Great Law of Human Action

He took up his brush and went tranquilly to work. Ben Rogers hove in sight presently – the very boy, of all boys, whose ridicule he had been dreading. Ben's gait was the hop-skip-and-jump – proof enough that his heart was light and his anticipations high. He was eating an apple, and giving a long, melodious whoop, at intervals, followed by a deep-toned ding-dong-dong, ding-dong-dong, for he was personating a steamboat. As he drew near, he slacked speed, took the middle of the street, leaned far over to starboard and rounded to ponderously and with laborious pomp and circumstance – for he was personating the *Big Missouri*, and considered himself to be drawing nine feet of water. He was boat and captain and engine-bells combined, so he had to imagine himself standing on his own hurricane-deck giving the orders and executing them . . .

Tom went on whitewashing – paid no attention to the steamboat. Ben stared a moment and then said:

'Hi-*yi! You're* up a stump, ain't you!'

No answer. Tom surveyed his last touch with the eye of an artist, then he gave his brush another gentle sweep and surveyed the result, as before. Ben ranged up alongside of him. Tom's mouth watered for the apple, but he stuck to his work. Ben said:

'Hello, old chap, you got to work, hey?'

Tom wheeled suddenly and said:

'Why, it's you, Ben! I warn't noticing.'

'Say – *I*'m going in a-swimming, *I* am. Don't you wish you could? But of course you'd druther *work* – wouldn't you? Course you would!'

Tom contemplated the boy a bit, and said:

'What do you call work?'

'Why, ain't *that* work?'

Tom resumed his whitewashing, and answered carelessly:

'Well, maybe it is, and maybe it ain't. All I know, is, it suits Tom Sawyer.'

'Oh come, now, you don't mean to let on that you *like* it?'

The brush continued to move.

'Like it? Well, I don't see why I oughtn't to like it. Does a boy get a chance to whitewash a fence every day?'

That put the thing in a new light. Ben stopped nibbling his apple. Tom swept his brush daintily back and forth – stepped back to note the effect – added a touch here and there – criticized the effect again – Ben watching every move and getting more and more interested, more and more absorbed. Presently he said:

'Say, Tom, let *me* whitewash a little.'

Tom considered, was about to consent; but he altered his mind:

'No – no – I reckon it wouldn't hardly do, Ben. You see, Aunt Polly's awful particular about this fence – right here on the street, you know – but if it was the back fence I wouldn't mind and *she* wouldn't. Yes, she's awful particular about this fence; it's got to be done very careful; I reckon there ain't one boy in a thousand, maybe two thousand, that can do it the way it's got to be done.'

'No – is that so? Oh come, now – lemme just try. Only just a little – I'd let *you*, if you was me, Tom.'

'Ben, I'd like to, honest injun; but Aunt Polly – well, Jim wanted to do it, but she wouldn't let him; Sid wanted to do it, and she wouldn't let Sid. Now don't you see how I'm fixed? If you was to tackle this fence and anything was to happen to it – '

'Oh, shucks, I'll be just as careful. Now lemme try. Say – I'll give you the core of my apple.'

'Well, here – No, Ben, now don't. I'm afeard – '

'I'll give you *all* of it!'

Tom gave up the brush with reluctance in his face, but alacrity in his heart. And while the late steamer *Big Missouri* worked and sweated in the sun, the retired artist sat on a barrel in the shade close by, dangled his legs, munched his apple, and planned the slaughter of more innocents. There was no lack of material; boys happened along every little while; they came to jeer, but remained to whitewash. By the time Ben was fagged out, Tom had traded the next chance to Billy Fisher for a kite, in good repair; and when *he* played out,

Johnny Miller bought in for a dead rat and a string to swing it with – and so on, and so on, hour after hour. And when the middle of the afternoon came, from being a poor poverty-stricken boy in the morning, Tom was literally rolling in wealth. He had beside the things before mentioned, twelve marbles, part of a jews'-harp, a piece of blue bottle-glass to look through, a spool cannon, a key that wouldn't unlock anything, a fragment of chalk, a glass stopper of a decanter, a tin soldier, a couple of tadpoles, six firecrackers, a kitten with only one eye, a brass door-knob, a dog-collar – but no dog – the handle of a knife, four pieces of orange-peel, and a dilapidated old window-sash.

He had had a nice, good, idle time all the while – plenty of company – and the fence had three coats of whitewash on it! If he hadn't run out of whitewash, he would have bankrupted every boy in the village.

Tom said to himself that it was not such a hollow world, after all. He had discovered a great law of human action, without knowing it – namely, that in order to make a man or a boy covet a thing, it is only necessary to make the thing difficult to attain. If he had been a great and wise philosopher, like the writer of this book, he would now have comprehended that Work consists of whatever the body is *obliged* to do, and that Play consists of whatever a body is not obliged to do. And this would help him to understand why constructing artificial flowers or performing on a treadmill is work, while rolling tenpins or climbing Mont Blanc is only amusement. There are wealthy gentlemen in England who drive four-horse passenger-coaches twenty or thirty miles on a daily line, in the summer, because the privilege costs them considerable money; but if they were offered wages for the service, that would turn it into work and then they would resign.

Mark Twain, from *The Adventures of Tom Sawyer*, 1875

## Advice to Daughters

... but this is fixt
As are the roots of earth and base of all;
Man for the field and woman for the hearth:
Man for the sword and for the needle she:
Man with the head and woman with the heart:
Man to command and woman to obey;
All else confusion.

Alfred Tennyson, from *The Princess*, 1847

I must tell you that no respect is lasting but that which is produced by our being in some degree useful to those that pay for it. Where that faileth, the homage and the reverence go along with it, and fly to otheres where something may be expected in exchange for them. And upon this principle the respects even of the children and the servants will not stay with one that doth not think them worth their care, and the old housekeeper shall make a better figure in the family than the lady with all her fine clothes, if she wilfully relinquishes her title to the government. Therefore take heed of carrying your good breeding to such a height as to be good for nothing, and to be proud of it. Some think it hath a great air to be above troubling their thoughts with such ordinary things as their house and family; others dare not admit cares for fear they should hasten wrinkles. Mistaken pride makest some think they must keep themselves up and not descend to these duties, which do not seem enough refined for great ladies to be employed in; forgetting all this while that it is more than the greatest princes can do at once to preserve respect and to neglect their business. No age ever erected altars to insignificant gods; they had all some quality applied to them to draw worship from mankind; this makest it the more unreasonable for a lady to expect to be considered and at the same time resolve not to deserve it. Good looks alone will not do; they are not such a lasting tenure as to be relied upon; and if they should stay longer than they usually do, it will by no means be safe to depend upon them; for when time hath abated the violence of the first liking, and that the nap is a little worn off, though still a good degree of kindness may remain, men recover their sight which before might be dazzled, and allow themselves to object as well as to admire.

In such a case, when a husband seeth an empty airy thing sail up and down the house to no kind of purpose, and look as if she came thither only to make a visit; when he findeth that after her emptiness hath been extreme busy about some very senseless thing, she eats her breakfast half an hour before dinner, to be at greater liberty to afflict the company with her discourse, then calleth for her coach, that she may trouble her acquaintance, who are already cloyed with her; and having some proper dialogues ready to display her foolish eloquence at the top of the stairs, she setteth out like a ship out of the harbour laden with trifles, and cometh back with them. At her return she repeateth to her faithful waiting-woman the triumphs of that day's impertinence; then, wrapped up in flattery and clean linen, goeth to bed so satisfied that it throweth her into pleasant dreams of her own felicity. Such a one is seldom serious but with her tailor; her children and family may now and then have a random thought, but she never taketh aim but at something very impertinent.

I say, when a husband, whose province is without doors, and to whom the economy of the house would be in some degree indecent, findeth no order

15

nor quiet in his family, meeteth with complaints of all kinds springing from this root, the mistaken lady, who thinketh to make amends for all this by having a well-chosen petticoat, will at last be convinced of her error, and with grief be forced to undergo the penalties that belong to those who are wilfully insignificant. When this scurvy hour cometh upon her she first groweth angry, then when the time of it is past, would perhaps grow wiser, not remembering that we can no more have wisdom than grace whenever we think fit to call for it. There are times and periods fixed for both; and when they are too long neglected, the punishment is that they are irrecoverable, and nothing remaineth but a useless grief for the folly of having thrown them out of our power. You are to think what a mean figure a woman maketh when she is so degraded by her own fault; whereas there is nothing in those duties which are expected from you that can be lessening to you, except your want of conduct makes it so.

The Marquess of Halifax, 'Advice to a Daughter', 1700

Dear Patsy:

After four days' journey, I arrived here without any accident, and in as good health as when I left Philadelphia. The conviction that you would be more improved in the situation I have placed you than if still with me, has solaced me on my parting with you, which my love for you has rendered a difficult thing. The acquirements which I hope you will make under the tutors I have provided for you will render you more worthy of my love, and if they cannot increase it, they will prevent its diminution . . . With respect to the distribution of your time, the following is what I should approve:

From 8 to 10, practice music.
From 10 to 1, dance one day and draw another.
From 1 to 2, draw on the day you dance, and write a letter next day.
From 3 to 4, read French.
From 4 to 5, exercise yourself in music.
From 5 till bed-time, read English, write, etc.

. . . I have placed my happiness on seeing you good and accomplished; and no distress this world can now bring on me equal that of disappointing my hopes. If you love me, then strive to be good under every situation and to all living creatures, and to acquire those accomplishments which I have put in your power, and which will go far towards ensuring you the warmest love of your affectionate father.

Thomas Jefferson, Letter to his daughter, 1783

May she become a flourishing hidden tree
That all her thoughts may like the linnet be,
And have no business but dispensing round
Their magnanimities of sound.
Nor but in merriment begin a chase,
Nor but in merriment a quarrel.
O may she live like some green laurel
Rooted in one dear perpetual place . . .

So let her think opinions are accursed.
Have I not seen the loveliest woman born
Out of the mouth of Plenty's horn,
Because of her opinionated mind
Barter that horn and every good
By quiet natures understood
For an old bellows full of angry wind? . . .

And may her bridegroom bring her to a house
Where all's accustomed, ceremonious . . .
Ceremony's a name for the rich horn,
And custom for the spreading laurel tree.
　　W. B. Yeats, from 'A Prayer for My Daughter', 1921

## The Daughter's Reply

I know I have the body of a weak and feeble woman, but I have the heart and stomach of a king, and of a king of England too.
　　　　　　　　　　　　Queen Elizabeth I, 1533–1603

In missing men we three visitors to a female utopia had naturally missed the larger part of life, and had unconsciously assumed that they must miss it too. It took me a long time to realize – Terry never did realize – how little it meant to them. When we say *men, man, manly, manhood*, and all the other masculine derivatives, we have in the background of our minds a huge vague crowded picture of the world and all its activities. To grow up and 'be a man', to 'act like a man' – the meaning and connotation is wide indeed. That vast background is full of marching columns of men, of changing lines of men, of long processions of men; of men steering their ships into new seas, exploring unknown mountains, breaking horses, herding cattle, ploughing and sowing and reaping, toiling at the forge and furnace, digging in the mine, building roads and bridges and high cathedrals, managing great businesses, teaching in all the colleges, preaching in all the churches; of men everywhere, doing everything – 'the world'.

And when we say *women*, we think *female* – the sex.

But to these women, in the unbroken sweep of this two-thousand-year-old feminine civilization, the word *woman* called up all that big background, so far as they had gone in social development; and the word *man* meant to them only *male* – the sex.

Of course we could *tell* them that in our world men did everything; but that did not alter the background of their minds. That man, 'the male', did all these things was to them a statement, making no more change in the point of view than was made in ours when we first faced the astounding fact – to us – that in Herland women were 'the world'.

We had been living there more than a year. We had learned their limited history, with its straight, smooth, upreaching lines, reaching higher and going faster up to the smooth comfort of their present life. We had learned a little of their psychology, a much wider field than the history, but here we could not follow so readily. We were now well used to seeing women not as females but as people; people of all sorts, doing every kind of work.

Charlotte Perkins Gilman, from *Herland*, 1915

We, to-day, take all labour for our province! We seek to enter the non-sexual fields of intellectual or physical toil, because we are unable to see to-day, with regard to them, any dividing wall raised by sex which excludes us from them. We are yet equally determined to enter those in which sex difference does play its part, because it is here that woman, the bearer of the race, must stand side by side with man, the begetter; if a completed human wisdom, an insight that misses no aspect of human life, and an activity that is in harmony with the entire knowledge and the entire instinct of the entire human race, is to exist. It is here that the man cannot act for the woman nor the woman for the man; but both must interact. It is here that each sexual half of the race, so closely and indistinguishably blended elsewhere, has its own distinct contribution to make to the sum total of human knowledge and human wisdom. Neither is the woman without the man, nor the man without the woman, the completed human intelligence.

Therefore; – *We claim, to-day, all labour for our province!* Those large fields in which it would appear sex plays no part, and equally those smaller in which it plays a part.

Olive Schreiner, from *Woman and Labour*, 1911

### 'Ain't I A Woman?'

That man over there say
   a woman needs to be helped into carriages
and lifted over ditches
   and to have the best place everywhere.
Nobody ever helped me into carriages
   or over mud puddles
      or gives me a best place . . .

And ain't I a woman?
   Look at me
Look at my arm!
   I have plowed and planted
and gathered into barns
   and no man could head me . . .
And ain't I a woman?
   I could work as much
and eat as much as a man –
   when I could get to it –
and bear the lash as well
   and ain't I a woman?
I have born 13 children
   and seen most all sold into slavery
and when I cried out a mother's grief
   none but Jesus heard me . . .
and ain't I a woman?
   that little man in black there say
a woman can't have as much rights as a man
   cause Christ wasn't a woman
Where did your Christ come from?
   From God and a woman!
Man had nothing to do with him!
   If the first woman God ever made
was strong enough to turn the world
   upside down, all alone
together women ought to be able to turn it
   rightside up again.
                Sojourner Truth, 1797–1883

(There is no exact copy of this speech, which was given at the Women's Rights Convention in Akron, Ohio in 1852 and has been adapted to the poetic format by

Erlene Stetson from the copy found in *Sojourner, God's Faithful Pilgrim* by Arthur Huff Fauset.)

Young women, I would say, and please attend, for the peroration is beginning, you are, in my opinion, disgracefully ignorant. You have never made a discovery of any sort of importance. You have never shaken an empire or led an army into battle. The plays of Shakespeare are not by you, and you have never introduced a barbarous race to the blessings of civilization. What is your excuse? It is all very well for you to say, pointing to the streets and squares and forests of the globe swarming with black and white and coffee-coloured inhabitants, all busily engaged in traffic and enterprise and love-making, we have had other work on our hands. Without our doing, those seas would be unsailed and those fertile lands a desert. We have borne and bred and washed and taught, perhaps to the age of six or seven years, the one thousand six hundred and twenty-three million human beings who are, according to statistics, at present in existence, and that, allowing that some had help, takes time.

There is truth in what you say – I will not deny it. But at the same time may I remind you that there have been at least two colleges for women in existence in England since the year 1866; that after the year 1880 a married woman was allowed by law to possess her own property; and that in 1919 – which is a whole nine years ago – she was given a vote? . . . When you reflect upon these immense privileges and the length of time during which they have been enjoyed . . . you will agree that the excuse of lack of opportunity, training, encouragement, leisure and money no longer holds good . . .

Thus, with some time on your hands and with some book-learning in your brains . . . surely you should embark upon another stage of your very long, very laborious and highly obscure career. A thousand pens are ready to suggest what you should do and what effect you will have. My own suggestion is a little fantastic, I admit; I prefer, therefore, to put it in the form of fiction.

I told you in the course of this paper that Shakespeare had a sister. . . She died young – alas, she never wrote a word. She lies buried where the omnibuses now stop, opposite the Elephant and Castle. Now my belief is that this poet who never wrote a word and was buried at the cross-roads still lives. She lives in you and in me, and in many other women who are not here to-night, for they are washing up the dishes and putting the children to bed. But she lives; for great poets do not die; they are continuing presences; they need only the opportunity to walk among us in the flesh . . . Drawing her life from the lives of the unknown who were her forerunners, as her brother did before her, she will be born. As for her coming without that preparation, without that effort on our part, without that determination that when she is born again she shall find it possible to live and write her poetry, that we cannot expect, for that would be impossible. But I maintain that she would come if we worked for her, and that so to work, even in poverty and obscurity, is worth while.

Virginia Woolf, from *A Room of One's Own*, 1928

# MAN'S TOIL

## Sons of the Soil

His name was Lycidas; he was a goatherd.
Just one look, and there was no mistaking that:
before all else, he was every inch goatherd.
He wore on his shoulders a heavy goatskin,
shaggy, brownish and reeking of goatsmilk;
across his chest was an ample belt
holding together his timeworn shirt;
his right hand carried a wild-olive crook.

Theocritus, *c.* 308–240 BC, from *The Idylls*,
tr. Anthony Holden, 1974

With hym ther was a PLOWMAN, was his brother,
That hadde ylad of dong ful many a fother;
A trewe swynkere and a good was he,
Lyvynge in pees and parfit charitee.
God loved he best with al his hoole herte
At alle tymes, thogh him gamed or smerte,
And thanne his neighebor right as hymselve.
He wolde thresshe, and therto dyke and delve,
For Cristes sake, for every povre wight,
Withouten hire, if it lay in his myght.
His tithes payde he ful faire and wel,
Bothe of his propre swynk and his catel.
In a tabard he rood upon a mere.

*fother* – cartload
*swynkere* – worker
*thogh him gamed or smerte* – whether it pleased or pained him
*wight* – person
*tabard* – tunic

Geoffrey Chaucer, from the Prologue to *The Canterbury Tales*, *c.* 1390


I am living on my farm, and since I had my last bad luck, I have not spent twenty days, putting them all together, in Florence. I have until now been snaring thrushes with my own hands. I got up before day, prepared birdlime, went out with a bundle of cages on my back, so that I looked like Geta when he was returning from the harbour with Amphitryo's books. I caught at least two thrushes and at most six. And so I did all September. Later this pastime, pitiful and strange as it is, gave out, to my displeasure. And of what sort my life is, I shall tell you.

I get up in the morning with the sun and go into a grove I am having cut down, where I remain two hours to look over the work of the past day and kill some time with the cutters, who have always some bad-luck story ready, about either themselves or their neighbours.

Leaving the grove, I go to a spring, and thence to my aviary. I have a book in my pocket, either Dante or Petrarch, or one of the lesser poets, such as Tibullus, Avod, and the like. I read of their tender passions and their lives, remember mine, enjoy myself a while in that sort of dreaming. Then I move along the road to the inn; I speak with those who pass, ask news of their villages, learn various things, and note the various tastes and different fancies of men. In the course of these things comes the hour for dinner, where with my family I eat such food as this poor farm of mine and my tiny property allow. Having eaten, I go back to the inn; there is the host, usually a butcher, a miller, two furnace tenders. With these I sink into vulgarity for the whole day, playing at *cricca* and trich-trach, and then these games bring on a thousand disputes and countless insults with offensive words, and usually we are fighting over a penny, and nevertheless we are heard shouting as far as San Casciano. So, mixed up with these lice, I keep my brain from growing mouldy, and satisfy the malice of this fate of mine, being glad to have her drive me along this road, to see if she will be ashamed of it.

On the coming of evening, I return to my house and enter my study; and at the door I take off the day's clothing, covered with mud and dust, and put on garments regal and courtly; and reclothed appropriately, I enter the ancient courts of ancient men, where, received by them with affection, I feed on that food which only is mine and which I was born for, where I am not ashamed to speak with them and to ask them the reason for their actions; and they in their kindness answer me; and for four hours of time I do not feel boredom, I forget every trouble, I do not dread poverty, I am not frightened by death; entirely I give myself over to them.

And because Dante says it does not produce knowledge when we hear but do not remember, I have noted everything in their conversation which has profited me, and have composed a little work *On Princedoms*, where I go as deeply as I can into considerations on this subject, debating what a princedom is, of what kinds they are, how they are gained, how they are kept, why they are lost. If ever you can find any of my fantasies pleasing, this one should not displease you; and by a prince, and especially by a new prince, it ought to be welcomed. Hence I am dedicating it to His Magnificence Giuliano.

Niccolò Machiavelli, Letter to his benefactor Francesco Vettori, 1513,

tr. Allan Gilbert, 1965

### Harry Ploughman

Hard as hurdle arms, with a broth of goldish flue
Breathed round; the rack of ribs; the scooped flank; lank
Rope-over thigh; knee-nave; and barrelled shank –
    Head and foot, shoulder and shank –
By a grey eye's heed steered well, one crew, fall to;
Stand at stress. Each limb's barrowy brawn, his thew
That onewhere curded, onewhere sucked or sank –
        Soared or sank –,
Though as a beechbole firm, finds his, as at a rollcall, rank
And features, in flesh, what deed he each must do –
    His sinew-service where do.

He leans to it, Harry bends, look. Back, elbow, and liquid waist
In him, all quail to the wallowing o' the plough: 's cheek crimsons; curls
Wag or crossbridle, in a wind lifted, windlaced –
    See his wind-lilylocks-laced;
Churlsgrace too, child of Amansstrength, how it hangs or hurls
Them – broad in bluff hide his frowning feet lashed! raced
With, along them, cragiron under and cold furls –
    With-a-fountain's shining-shot furls.

Gerard Manley Hopkins, 1887

        We raise de wheat,
        Dey gib us de corn;
        We bake de bread,
        Dey gib us de crust;
        We sif de meal,
        Dey gib us de huss;

        We peel de meat,
        Dey gib us the skin;
        And dat's de way
        Dey take us in;

We skim de pot,
Dey gib us de liquor,
And say dat's good enough for nigger.

from *Life and Times of Frederick Douglass,* 1892

## Hay for the Horses

He had driven half the night
From far down San Joaquin
Through Mariposa, up the
Dangerous mountain roads,
And pulled in at eight a.m.
With his big truckload of hay
          behind the barn.
With winch and ropes and hooks
We stacked the bales up clean
To splintery redwood rafters
High in the dark, flecks of alfalfa
Whirling through shingle-cracks of light,
Itch of haydust in the
          sweaty shirt and shoes.
At lunchtime under Black oak
Out in the hot corral,
– The old mare nosing lunchpails
Grasshoppers crackling in the weeds –
'I'm sixty-eight,' he said,
'I first bucked hay when I was seventeen.
I thought, that day I started,
I sure would hate to do this all my life.
And dammit, that's just what
I've gone and done.'

Gary Snyder, from *Riprap and Cold Mountain Poems,* 1980

## Old Shepherd's Prayer

Up to the bed by the window, where I be lyin',
Comes bells and bleat of the flock wi' they two children's clack.

Over, from under the eaves there's the starlings flyin',
And down in yard, fit to burst his chain, yapping out at Sue I do hear young
                                                                                Mac.

Turning around like a falled-over sack
I can see team ploughin' in Whithy-bush field and meal carts startin' up road
                                                                    to Church-Town;
Saturday arternoon the men goin' back
And the women from market, trapin' home over the down.

Heavenly Master, I wud like to wake to they same green places
Where I be know'd for breakin' dogs and follerin' sheep.
And if I may not walk in th' old ways and look on th' old faces
I wud sooner sleep.

Charlotte Mew, from The Rambling Shepherd, 1929

## Death of a Gardener

He rested through the winter, watched the rain
On his cold garden, slept, awoke to snow
Padding the window, thatching the roof again
With silence. He was grateful for the slow
Nights and undemanding days; the dark
Protected him; the pause grew big with cold.
Mice in the shed scuffled like leaves; a spark
Hissed from his pipe as he dreamed beside the fire.

All at once light sharpened; earth drew breath,
Stirred; and he woke to strangeness that was spring,
Stood on the grass, felt movement underneath
Like a child in the womb; hope troubled him to bring
Barrow and spade once more to the waiting soil.
Slower his lift and thrust; a blackbird filled
Long intervals with song; a worm could coil
To safety underneath the hesitant blade.
Hands tremulous as cherry branches kept
Faith with struggling seedlings till the earth
Kept faith with him, claimed him as he slept
Cold in the sun beside his upright spade.

Phoebe Hesketh, 1966

# Woodwork

But the new Dawn had scarcely touched the East with red before Odysseus put his cloak and tunic on. The Nymph dressed herself too in a long silvery mantle of a light material charming to the eye, with a splendid golden belt round her waist, and her veil over her head. Then she turned her thoughts to the problem of her noble guest's departure. First she gave him a great axe of bronze. Its double blade was sharpened well, and the shapely handle of olive-wood fixed firmly in its head was fitted to his grip. Next she handed him an adze of polished metal; and then led the way for him to the farthest part of the island, where the trees grew tall, alders and poplars and firs that shot up to the sky, all withered timber that had long since lost its sap and would make buoyant material for his boat. When she had shown him the place where the trees were tallest the gracious goddess left for home, and Odysseus began to cut the timber down. He made short work of the task. Twenty trees in all he felled, and lopped their branches with his axe; then trimmed them in a workmanlike manner and trued them to the line. Presently Calypso brought him augers. With these he drilled through all his planks, cut them to fit across each other, and fixed this flooring together by means of dowels driven through the interlocking joints, giving the same width to his boat as a skilled shipwright would choose in designing the hull for a broad-bottomed trading vessel. He next put up the decking, which he fitted to ribs at short intervals, finishing off with long gunwales down the sides. He made a mast to go in the boat, with a yard-arm fitted to it; and a steering-oar too, to keep her on her course. And from stem to stern he fenced her sides with plaited osier twigs and a plentiful backing of brushwood, as some protection against the heavy seas. Meanwhile the goddess Calypso had brought him cloth with which to make the sail. This he manufactured too; and then lashed the braces, halyards, and sheets in their places on board. Finally he dragged her down on rollers into the tranquil sea.

Homer, *Odyssey*, Book V, *c.* 800 BC,
tr. E. V. Rieu, 1946


I went to work upon this Boat the most like a Fool that ever Man did, who had any of his Senses awake. I pleas'd my self with the Design, without determining whether I was ever able to undertake it; not but that the Difficulty of launching my Boat came often into my Head; but I put a stop to my own Enquiries into it, by this foolish Answer which I gave my self, *Let's first make it, I'll warrant I'll find some Way or other to get it along, when 'tis done.*

This was a most preposterous Method; but the Eagerness of my Fancy prevail'd, and to work I went. I fell'd a Cedar Tree: I question much whether *Solomon* ever had such a One for the Building of the Temple at *Jerusalem*. It was five Foot ten Inches Diameter at the lower Part next the Stump, and four Foot eleven Inches Diameter at the End of twenty two Foot, after which it lessen'd for a while, and then parted into Branches: It was not without infinite Labour that I fell'd this Tree: I was twenty Days hacking and hewing at it at the Bottom. I was fourteen more getting the Branches and Limbs, and the vast spreading Head of it cut off, which I hack'd and hew'd through with Axe and Hatchet, and inexpressible Labour: After this, it cost me a Month to shape it, and dub it to a Proportion, and to something like the Bottom of a Boat, that it might swim upright as it ought to do. It cost me near three Months more to clear the In-side, and work it so, as to make an exact Boat of it: This I did indeed without Fire, by mere Mallet and Chisel, and by the dint of hard Labour, till I had brought it to be a very handsome *Periagua*, and big enough to have carried six and twenty Men, and consequently big enough to have carried me and all my Cargo.

When I had gone through this Work, I was extremely delighted with it. The Boat was really much bigger than I ever saw a *Canoe*, or *Periagua*, that was made of one Tree, in my Life. Many a weary Stroke it had cost, you may be sure; and there remained nothing but to get it into the Water; and had I gotten it into the Water, I make no question but I should have began the maddest Voyage, and the most unlikely to be perform'd, that ever was undertaken.

But all my Devices to get it into the Water fail'd me, though they cost me infinite Labour too. It lay about one hundred Yards from the Water, and not more: But the first Inconvenience was, it was up Hill towards the Creek; well, to take away this Discouragement, I resolv'd to dig into the Surface of the Earth, and so make a Declivity: This I began, and it cost me a prodigious deal of Pains; but who grudges Pains, that have their Deliverance in View? But when this was work'd through, and this Difficulty manag'd, it was still much at one; for I could no more stir the *Canoe*, than I could the other Boat.

Then I measur'd the Distance of Ground, and resolv'd to cut a Dock, or Canal, to bring the Water up to the *Canoe*, seeing I could not bring the *Canoe* down to the Water: Well, I began this Work, and when I began to enter into it, and calculate how deep it was to be dug, how broad, how the Stuff to be thrown out, I found, that by the Number of Hands I had, being none of my own, it must have been ten or twelve Years before I should have gone through with it; for the Shore lay high, so that at the upper End it must have been at least twenty Foot deep; so at length, tho' with great Reluctancy, I gave this Attempt over also.

This griev'd me heartily, and now I saw, tho' too late, the Folly of beginning a Work before we count the Cost, and before we judge rightly of our own Strength to go through with it.

Daniel Defoe, from *Robinson Crusoe*, 1719

And now – how dare I go on to describe that swinging drive of the wheel-wright's action, fixing the spokes into the stock? Prose has no rhythm for it – the spring, the smashing blow recurrent at just the right time and place. The stock is to be imagined, ready at last, clamped down across the wheel-pit. From the front of it the gauge slants up; the dozen or fourteen spokes are near at hand, each with its tenon or 'foot' numbered (in scribbled pencilling) to match the number scribbled against its own place in the stock. For although uniformity has been aimed at throughout, still every mortise has been chiselled to receive its own special spoke, lest the latter should by chance have had any small splinter broken away after all. The true wheelwright would not take that chance. He intended that every spoke should really fit tight; and there he has the spokes all numbered, to his hand.

He picks up one in one hand, and with sledge-hammer in the other, lightly taps the spoke into its own mortise. Then he steps back, glancing behind him belike to see that the coast is clear; and, testing the distance with another light tap (a two-handed tap this time) suddenly, with a leap, he swings the sledge round full circle with both hands, and brings it down right on the top of the spoke – bang. Another blow or so, and the spoke is far enough into the mortise to be gauged. Is it leaning forward a little too much, or not quite enough? It can be corrected, with batterings properly planted on front or back of top, and accordingly the wheelwright aims his sledge, swinging it round tremen-dously again and again, until the spoke is indeed 'driven' into the stock. It is battered over on the top, but the oak stands firm in the mortise, to stay for years.

George Sturt, from *The Wheelwright's Shop*, 1923

## Hedger

To me the A Major Concerto has been dearer
Than ever before, because I saw one weave
Wonderful patterns of bright green, never clearer
Of April; whose hand nothing at all did deceive
Of laying right
The stakes of bright
Green lopped-off spear-shaped, and stuck notched, crooked-up;

Wonder was quickened at workman's craftsmanship
But clumsy were the efforts of my stiff body
To help him in the laying of bramble, ready
Of mind, but clumsy of muscle in helping; rip
Of clothes unheeded, torn hands. And his quick moving
Was never broken by any danger, his loving
Use of the bill or scythe was most deft, and clear –
Had my piano-playing or counterpoint
Been so without fear
Then indeed fame had been mine of most bright outshining;
But never had I known singer or piano-player
So quick and sure in movement as this hedge-layer
This gap-mender, of quiet courage unhastening.

> Ivor Gurney, from *Collected Poems*, 1982

## Hunting, Fishing and Shooting

Then they slit open the slot, seized the second stomach,
Cut it away with a keen knife, and cleared it of flesh.
Next they hacked off all the legs, the hide was stripped,
The belly broken open and the bowels removed,
Carefully, lest they loosen the ligature of the knot.
Then they gripped the gullet, disengaged deftly
The wezand from the windpipe and whipped out the guts.
Then their sharp knives shore through the shoulder-bones,
Which they slid out of a small hole, leaving the sides intact.
Then they cleft the chest clean through, cutting it in two.
Then again at the gullet they began to work,
And rapidly rived it, right to the fork,
Flicked out the shoulder-fillets, and faithfully thereafter
They rapidly ripped free the rib-fillets.
Similarly, as is seemly, the spine was cleared
All the way to the haunch, which hung from it;
And they heaved up the whole haunch and hewed it off;
And that is named the numbles, in nature, or so
              I find.
        At the thigh-forks then they strain
        And free the folds behind,

> Hurrying to hack all in twain,
> The backbone to unbind.

Then they hewed off the head and also the neck,
And after sundered the sides swiftly from the chine,
And into the foliage they flung the fee of the raven.
Then each fellow, for his fee, as it fell to him to have,
Skewered through the stout flanks beside the ribs,
And then by the hocks of the haunches they hung up their booty.
On one of the finest fells they fed their hounds,
And let them have the lights, the liver and the tripes,
With bread well imbrued with blood mixed with them.
Boldly they blew the kill amid the baying of hounds.
Then off they went homewards, holding their meat,
Stalwartly sounding many stout horn-calls.
As dark was descending, they were drawing near
To the comely castle where quietly our knight stayed.
> Fires roared,
> And blithely hearts were beating
> As into hall came the lord.
> When Gawain gave him greeting,
> Joy abounded at the board.

> from *Sir Gawain and the Green Knight*, fourteenth century,
> tr. Brian Stone, 1959

And first for Worms: Of these there be very many sorts; some breed only in the earth, as the *Earth-worms*; others of or amongst Plants, as the *Dug-worms*; and others breed either out of excrements, or in the bodies of living creatures, as in the horns of Sheep or Deer; or some of dead flesh, as the *Maggot* or *gentle*, and others . . .

And now, I shall shew you how to bait your hook with a worm, so as shall prevent you from much trouble, and the loss of many a hook too; when you Fish for a *Trout* with a running line: that is to say, when you fish for him by hand at the ground, I will direct you in this as plainly as I can, that you may not mistake.

*Suppose it be a big Lob-worm, put your hook into him somewhat above the middle, and out again a little below the middle: having so done, draw your worm above the arming of your hook, but note that at the entring of your hook it must not be at the head-end of the worm, but at the tail-end of him, (that the point of*

*your hook may come out toward the head-end) and having drawn him above the
arming of your hook, then put the point of your hook into the very head of
the worm, till it come near to the place where the point of the hook first came out:
and then draw back that part of the worm that was above the shank or arming of
your hook, and so fish with it. And if you mean to fish with two worms, then put
the second on before you turn back the hooks-head of the first worm; you cannot
lose above two or three worms before you attain to what I direct you; and having
attain'd it, you will find it very useful, and thank me for it: For you will run on
the ground without tangling.*

Izaak Walton, from *The Compleat Angler*, 1676

According to the invariable usage of the fishery, the whale boat pushes off
from the ship, with the headsman or whale-killer as temporary steersman, and
the harpooneer or whale-fastener pulling the foremost oar, the one known
as the harpooneer-oar. Now it needs a strong, nervous arm to strike the first
iron into the fish; for often, in what is called a long dart, the heavy implement
has to be flung to the distance of twenty or thirty feet. But however prolonged
and exhausted the chase, the harpooneer is expected to pull his oar meanwhile
to the uttermost; indeed, he is expected to set an example of superhuman
activity to the rest, not only by incredible rowing, but by repeated loud and
intrepid exclamations; and what it is to keep shouting at the top of one's
compass, while all the other muscles are strained and half started – what that
is none know but those who have tried it. For one, I cannot bawl very heartily
and work very recklessly at one and the same time. In this straining, bawling
state, then, with his back to the fish, all at once the exhausted harpooneer
hears the exciting cry – 'Stand up, and give it to him!' He now has to drop
and secure his oar, turn round on his centre half-way, seize his harpoon from
the crotch, and with what little strength may remain, he essays to pitch it
somehow into the whale. No wonder, taking the whole fleet of whalemen in a
body, that out of fifty fair chances for a dart, not five are successful: no wonder
that so many hapless harpooneers are madly cursed and disrated; no wonder
that some of them actually burst their blood vessels in the boat; no wonder that
some Sperm whalemen are absent four years with four barrels; no wonder
that to many ship owners, whaling is but a losing concern; for it is the
harpooneer that makes the voyage, and if you take the breath out of his body
how can you expect to find it there when most wanted!

Again, if the dart be successful, then at the second critical instant, that is,
when the whale starts to run, the boatheader and harpooneer likewise start to
running fore and aft to the imminent jeopardy of themselves and every one

else. It is then they change places; and the headsman, the chief officer of the little craft, takes his proper station in the bows of the boat.

Now, I care not who maintains the contrary, but all this is both foolish and unnecessary. The headsman should stay in the bows from first to last; he should both dart the harpoon and the lance, and no rowing whatever should be expected of him except under circumstances obvious to any fisherman. I know that this would sometimes involve a slight loss of speed in the chase; but long experience in various whalemen of more than one nation has convinced me that in the vast majority of failures in the fishery, it has not by any means been so much the speed of the whale as the before described exhaustion of the harpooneer that has caused them.

To ensure the greatest efficiency in the dart, the harpooneers of this world must start to their feet from out of idleness, and not from out of toil.

Herman Melville, from *Moby Dick; or The White Whale*, 1851

Having received the route for Birmingham, the precise date I do not now remember, we were all astir by the sound of early trumpets one morning, and marched out of the barrack gates; the band playing, horses prancing, crowds accompanying, with baggage piled upon waggons, followed by the hospital sergeant, orderlies, convalescents, tailors, shoemakers, saddlers, women and children, dismounted invalids, and unmounted recruits. I was an unmounted recruit, and with the other on foot formed the baggage guard.

Our march from Brighton to Birmingham occupied either nine or ten days. I had seen but little of rural England before that time; and though that was but a glimpse compared with what I have seen since, it was fresh, vivid, and impressive. I retain it to this day distinctly: and can at will, sitting by the hearth, looking dreamily into the fire, and vacantly upon a book, draw out the whole line of country before me: the villages, roadside inns, half-way houses where we halted to rest, swinging sign-boards, village greens, broad commons, cross roads, finger-posts, travellers journeying with us, and telling where a gibbet once was, or villagers shrinking out of sight with the recollection of the swing riots of 1830 and 1831 still fresh – with the dread still upon them of the special commission accompanied by soldiers, which had consigned a few to the gallows, many to the hulks, and had probably missed the chiefs who fired the rick yards or led the multitudes to break the thrashing mills – some of these chiefs now looking upon us from a distance, without any desire to come nearer. Other villages, where no riots nor Swing* fires had been, and no fears for troops of cavalry were felt, came out to be critical on the horses, and to approve of the long swords, the carbines, the bright scarlet, the black bear-skin on the men's heads, and the white feathers on the bear-skin. They stood, and I can see them standing now, on the play-worn ground beside the parish stocks, in front of the churchyard walls. Behind them the churches, venerable and grey, not always with lofty spires, conspicuously upraised to heaven, but oftener lowly and half-concealed among the trees, as if retreating there for humble worship; the trees with the dead of many generations under their roots, bearing on their branches, one might suppose as fruit, a young generation of miniature men in round white hats, smock frocks, leather leggings, and laced-up boots; the fathers and elder brothers of the miniature men thus clustered on the trees, standing on the ground in their round white hats, smock frocks, leather leggings, and laced-up boots, as if they had dropped from the trees when they grew large and heavy; all were out to look at the soldiers – who taking cross country roads went through villages where soldiers are seldom seen, and where a regiment mounted on grey horses was never before seen.

Women also and babies were out. And laughing little maids, the future brides and mothers of rural England, climbed on the gates and stiles to see; and hearing the boys in the trees call, 'Soldier, give I that long sword, wilt thee, soldier?' cried, 'Soldier, take I on that horse with the long white tail, wilt thee, soldier?'

And gentlemen and ladies from the mansions, that stood within the wooded parks, walked out to look upon the unusual sight. So did grave vicars, and rectors, and their servants from vicarage and rectory, look out when the trumpets or the band played. And when the rear came up, they inquired where we were going, was there swing rioters abroad again?

The village live-stock upon the commons – dogs, hogs, and asses; and old horses, which had once been in military service, now capered when they heard the trumpets, as if young again; all were set astir by the marching of a regiment among them. The cows hobbled to the farthest side of the common, having no sympathy for bright scarlet, or kettle drums. And the geese, which had survived the killing and the roasting at Christmas sheered off, and faced round at a distance to hiss us, as if they were disloyal geese, hissing a regiment of royal dragoons, or as if they knew that we, being Scotch dragoons, were ignorant of roast goose.

Alexander Somerville, from *The Autobiography of a Working Man*, 1848

---

* Peasant riots, usually involving rick-burning, and preceded by an anonymous letter signed 'SWING'.

We passed no one until we came to a bombing post – three serious-minded men who said that no one had been further than that yet. Being in an exploring frame of mind, I took a bag of bombs and crawled another sixty or seventy yards with Kendle close behind me. The trench became a shallow groove and ended where the ground overlooked a little valley along which there was a light railway line. We stared across at the Wood. From the other side of the valley came an occasional rifle-shot, and a helmet bobbed up for a moment. Kendle remarked that from that point anyone could see into the whole of our trench on the slope behind us. I said we must have our strong-post here and told him to go back for the bombers and a Lewis gun. I felt adventurous and it seemed as if Kendle and I were having great fun together. Kendle thought so too. The helmet bobbed up again. 'I'll just have a shot at him,' he said, wriggling away from the crumbling bank which gave us cover. At this moment Fernby appeared with two men and a Lewis gun. Kendle was half kneeling against some broken ground; I remember seeing him push his tin hat back from his forehead and then raise himself a few inches to take aim. After firing once he looked at us with a lively smile; a second later he fell sideways. A blotchy mark showed where the bullet had hit him just above the eyes.

The circumstances being what they were, I had no justification for feeling either shocked or astonished by the sudden extinction of Lance-Corporal Kendle. But after blank awareness that he was killed, all feelings tightened and contracted to a single intention – to 'settle that sniper' on the other side of the valley. If I had stopped to think, I shouldn't have gone at all. As it was, I discarded my tin hat and equipment, slung a bag of bombs across my shoulder, abruptly informed Fernby that I was going to find out who *was* there, and set off at a downhill double. While I was running I pulled the safety-pin out of a Mills bomb; my right hand being loaded, I did the same for my left. I mention this because I was obliged to extract the second safety-pin with my teeth, and the grating sensation reminded me that I was half way across and not so reckless as I had been when I started. I was even a little out of breath as I trotted up the opposite slope. Just before I arrived at the top I slowed up and threw my two bombs. Then I rushed at the bank, vaguely expecting some sort of scuffle with my imagined enemy. I had lost my temper with the man who had shot Kendle; quite unexpectedly I found myself looking down into a well-conducted trench with a great many Germans in it. Fortunately for me, they were already retreating. It had not occurred to them that they were being attacked by a single fool; and Fernby, with presence of mind which probably saved me, had covered my advance by traversing the top of the trench with his Lewis gun. I slung a few more bombs, but they fell short of the clumsy field-grey figures, some of whom half turned to fire their rifles over the left shoulder as they ran across the open toward the wood, while a crowd of jostling helmets vanished along the trench. Idiotically elated, I stood there with my finger in my right ear and emitted a series of 'view-holloas' (a gesture which ought to win the approval of people who still regard war as a form of outdoor sport). Having thus failed to commit suicide, I proceeded to occupy the trench – that is to say I sat down on the fire-step, very much out of breath, and hoped to God the Germans wouldn't come back again.

Siegfried Sassoon, from *Memoirs of an Infantry Officer*, 1930

Their life was now one unresting struggle against the encroaching mud, which threatened to engulf roads and trenches in liquid ruin. Daily, when out of the line, they were sent off with shovels and brooms to sweep it off the roadway, and shovel it up as a kind of embankment against the barns and stables bordering the road. What was too liquid to heap up, they trapped in sumps. A man pushing a broom through it would find two converging streams closing behind him. A train of limbers or lorries passing seemed to squeeze it up out of the road-metalling. Earth exuded mud. Most of it had the consistency of thin cream, and threatened, if it were neglected for a moment, to become tidal. They had to scrape it from their puttees and trousers with their jack-knives, and what was left hardened the serge to cardboard. When they became dry they were beaten against the corner of a hut, and the dust flew from them; but that was seldom. In the line there were trenches which could only be kept clear by pumping. Sometimes frost would congeal the mud, and then a quick thaw would cause part of a trench to slide in, and it had to be built up again: sand-bagged and revetted. They became almost indistinguishable from the mud in which they lived.

The weather grew colder too, and they wore their cardigans; then leather jerkins, lined with fleeces or thick serge, were issued to them, and in the resulting warmth the lice increased and multiplied beyond imagining. It was some weeks before they could get a bath; and then necessarily it was make-shift. Half a company stood under trickling showers, while the other half-company pumped up water outside and when the men were covered with a lather of soap the water invariably failed.

The strange thing was that the greater the hardships they had to endure, for wet and cold bring all kinds of attendant miseries in their train, the less they grumbled. They became a lot quieter, and more reserved in themselves, and yet the estaminets would be swept by roaring storms of song. It may have been a merely subjective impression, but it seemed that once they were in the front line, men lost a great deal of their individuality; their characters, even

39

their faces, seemed to become more uniform; they worked better, the work seeming to take some of the strain off their minds, the strain of waiting. It was, perhaps, that they withdrew more into themselves, and became a little more diffident in the matter of showing their feelings. Actually, though the pressure of external circumstances seemed to wipe out individuality, leaving little if any distinction between man and man, in himself each man became conscious of his own personality as of something very hard, and sharply defined against a background of other men, who remained merely generalized as 'the others'. The mystery of his own being increased for him enormously; and he had to explore that doubtful darkness alone, finding a foothold here, a handhold there, grasping one support after another and relinquishing it when it yielded, crumbling; the sudden menace of ruin, as it slides into the unsubstantial past, calling forth another effort, to gain another precarious respite. If a man could not be certain of himself, he could be certain of nothing. The problem which confronted them all equally, though some were unable or unwilling to define it, did not concern death so much as the affirmation of their own will in the face of death; and once the nature of the problem was clearly stated, they realized that its solution was continuous, and could never be final. Death set a limit to the continuance of one factor in the problem, and peace to that of another; but neither of them really affected the nature of the problem itself.

Frederic Manning, from Her Privates We, 1930

# The Literary Life

## The Literary Life, a Scrapbook

My photo: I before I was I, or a book;
inch-worm! A cheekbone gumballs out my cheek;
too much live hair. My wife caught in that eye blazes,
an egg would boil in the tension of that hand,
my untied shoestrings write my name in the dust . . .
I rest on a tree, and try to sharpen bromides
to serve the great, the great God, the New Critic,
who loves the writing better than we ourselves . . .
In those days, if I pressed an ear to the earth,
I heard the bass growl of Hiroshima. No!
In the *Scrapbook*, it's the old who die classics:

one foot in the grave, two in books – one of the living!
Who wouldn't rather be his indexed correspondents
than the boy Keats spitting out blood for time to breathe?
                    Robert Lowell, from *Notebook*, 1970


## I Am Raftery

I am Raftery, hesitant and confused among
the cold-voiced graduate students and inter-
changeable instructors. Were it not for the
nice wives who do the talking I would have
run out of hope some time ago, and of love.
I have traded-in the 'simplistic maunderings'
that made me famous, for a wry dissimulation,
an imagery of adventitious ambiguity dredged
from God knows what polluted underground spring.
Death is near, I have come of age, I doubt if
I shall survive another East Anglian winter.
Scotch please, plenty of water. I am reading
Joyce by touch and it's killing me. Is it
empty pockets I play to? Not on your life,
they ring with a bright inflationary music –
two seminars a week and my own place reserved
in the record library. Look at me now,
my back to the wall, taking my cue
from an idiot disc-jockey between commercials.
                    Derek Mahon, from *Poems 1962–78*


## The Novelist

Encased in talent like a uniform,
The rank of every poet is well known;
They can amaze us like a thunderstorm,
Or die so young, or live for years alone.

They can dash forward like hussars: but he
Must struggle out of his boyish gift and learn
How to be plain and awkward, how to be
One after whom none think it worth to turn.

For, to achieve his lightest wish, he must
Become the whole of boredom, subject to
Vulgar complaints like love, among the Just

Be just, among the Filthy filthy too,
And in his own weak person, if he can,
Dully put up with all the wrongs of Man.

W. H. Auden, 1939

4 Sunday [June 1826]*   I wrote a good task yesterday and to-day a great one, scarce stirring from the desk the whole day except a few minutes when Lady Rae calld. I was glad to see my wife's old friend with whom in early life we had so many *liaisons*. I am not sure it is right to work so hard. But a man must take himself as well as other people when he is in the humour. A man will do twice as much at one time and in half the time and twice as well that he will be able to do in another. People are always crying out about method and in some respects it is good and shows to great advantage among men of business. But I doubt if men of method who can lay aside or take up the pen just at the hour appointed will ever be better than poor creatures. L. L. S-t used to tell me of Mr Hoole the translator of Tasso and Ariosto, and in that capacity a noble transmuter of gold into lead, that he was a clerk in the India House with long rufles and a snuffcoloured suit of clothes who occasionally visited her father. She sometimes conversed with him and was amused to find that he *did* exactly so many couplets day by day neither more nor less and habit had made it light to him however heavy it might seem to the reader.

Well but if I lay down the pen as the pain in my breast hints that I should what am I to do? If I think – why I shall weep – and that's nonsense – and I have no friend now – none – to receive my tediousness for half an hour of the gloaming – Let me be grateful – I have good news from Abbotsford . . .

12 Monday   Finishd Vol. III of *Napoleon*. I resumed it on the 1st of June, the earliest period that I could bend my mind to it after my great loss. Since that time I have lived to be sure the life of a hermit except at attending the court five times in the week for about three hours on an average. Except at that time I have been reading or writing on the subject of Boney and have finish[d] last night and sent to printer this morning the last sheets of fifty two written since first June. It is an awful creed but grief makes me a house keeper and to labour is my only resource. Ballantyne thinks well of the work – very

* At the time of these Journal entries, Scott was writing *The Life of Napoleon*. He had been made bankrupt in January 1826, with debts of £120,000, and his wife had died in May 1826.

well – But I shall [expect] inaccuracies. An it were to do again I would get some one to look it over. But who could that some one be? Whom is there left of human race that I could hold such close intimacy with? No one . . .

14 Wednesday   In the morning I began wt. a page and a half before breakfast – This is always the best way. You stand like a child going to be bathed shivering and shaking till the first pitcherfull is flung about your ears and then are as blythe as a water-wag-tail. I am just come home from P. House and now, my friend Nap – have at you with a downright blow – Methinks I would fain [make] peace with my conscience by doing six pages to-night. Bought a little bit of Gruyere cheeze instead of our domestic choak-dog concern. When did I ever purchase any thing for my own eating? – But I will say no more of that – and now to the tread Mill. Cheeze 6/-.

from The Journal of Sir Walter Scott

To Louise Colet

[Croisset] Saturday night [24 April 1852]
If I haven't written sooner in reply to your sad, discouraged letter, it's because I have been in a great fit of work. The day before yesterday I went to bed at five in the morning and yesterday at three. Since last Monday I have put everything else aside, and have done nothing all week but sweat over my *Bovary*, disgruntled at making such slow progress. I have now reached my ball, which I will begin Monday. I hope that may go better. Since you last saw me I have written 25 pages in all (25 pages in six weeks). They were rough going. Tomorrow I shall read them to Bouilhet. I have gone over them so much myself, copied them, changed them, shuffled them, that for the time being I see them very confusedly. But I think they will stand up. You speak of your discouragements: if you could see mine! Sometimes I don't understand why my arms don't drop from my body with fatigue, why my brain doesn't melt away. I am leading an austere life, stripped of all external pleasure, and am sustained only by a kind of permanent frenzy, which sometimes makes me weep tears of impotence but never abates. I love my work with a love that is frantic and perverted, as an ascetic loves the hair shirt that scratches his belly.

Sometimes, when I am empty, when words don't come, when I find I haven't written a single sentence after scribbling whole pages, I collapse on my couch and lie there dazed, bogged in a swamp of despair, hating myself and blaming myself for this demented pride that makes me pant after a chimera. A quarter of an hour later, everything has changed; my heart is pounding with joy. Last Wednesday I had to get up and fetch my handkerchief; tears were streaming down my face. I have been moved by my own writing:

43

the emotion I had conceived, the phrase that rendered it, and the satisfaction of having found the phrase – all were causing me the most exquisite pleasure.


To Louise Colet

[Croisset] Friday night, 2 o'clock. [23 December 1853]
I must love you to write you tonight, for I am *exhausted*. My skull feels encased in an iron helmet. Since two o'clock yesterday afternoon (except for about twenty-five minutes for dinner), I have been writing *Bovary*. I am in full fornication, in the very midst of it: my lovers are sweating and gasping. This has been one of the rare days of my life passed completely in illusion, from beginning to end. At six o'clock tonight, as I was writing the word 'hysterics', I was so swept away, was bellowing so loudly and feeling so deeply what my little Bovary was going through, that I was afraid of having hysterics myself. I got up from my table and opened the window to calm myself. My head was spinning. Now I have great pains in my knees, in my back, and in my head. I feel like a man who has been fucking too much (forgive the expression) – a kind of rapturous lassitude. And since I am in the midst of love it is only proper that I should not fall asleep before sending you a caress, a kiss, and whatever thoughts are left in me.

Will what I have written be good? I have no idea – I am hurrying a little, to be able to show Bouilhet a complete section when he comes. What is certain is that my book has been going at a lively rate for the past week. May it continue so, for I am weary of my usual snail's pace. But I fear the awakening, the disillusion that may come when the pages are copied. No matter: for better or worse, it is a delicious thing to write, to be no longer yourself but to move in an entire universe of your own creating. Today, for instance, as man and woman, both lover and mistress, I rode in a forest on an autumn afternoon under the yellow leaves, and I was also the horses, the leaves, the wind, the words my people uttered, even the red sun that made them almost close their love-drowned eyes.

Is this pride or piety? Is it a foolish overflow of exaggerated self-satisfaction, or is it really a vague and noble religious instinct? But when I brood over these marvellous pleasures I have enjoyed, I would be tempted to offer God a prayer of thanks if I knew he could hear me. Praised may he be for not creating me a cotton merchant, a vaudevillian, a wit, etc.! Let us sing to Apollo as in ancient days, and breathe deeply of the fresh cold air of Parnassus; let us strum our guitars and clash our cymbals, and whirl like dervishes in the eternal hubbub of Forms and Ideas.

from *The Letters of Gustave Flaubert 1830–1857*,
selected, ed. and tr. by Francis Steegmuller, 1980

## What The Chairman Told Tom

Poetry? It's a hobby.
I run model trains.
Mr Shaw there breeds pigeons.

It's not work. You dont sweat.
Nobody pays for it.
You *could* advertise soap.

Art, that's opera; or repertory –
The Desert Song.
Nancy was in the chorus.

But to ask for twelve pounds a week –
married, aren't you? –
you've got a nerve.

How could I look a bus conductor
in the face
if I paid you twelve pounds?

Who says it's poetry, anyhow?
My ten year old
can do it *and* rhyme.

I get three thousand and expenses,
a car, vouchers,
but I'm an accountant.

They do what I tell them,
my company.
What do *you* do?

Nasty little words, nasty long words,
it's unhealthy.
I want to wash when I meet a poet.

They're Reds, addicts,
all delinquents.
What you write is rot.

Mr Hines says so, and he's a schoolteacher,
he ought to know.
Go and find *work*.

Basil Bunting, 1965

The body of
Benjamin Franklin, printer,
(Like the cover of an old book,
Its contents worn out,
And stript of its lettering and gilding)
Lies here, food for worms!
Yet the work itself shall not be lost,
For it will, as he believed, appear once more
In a new
And more beautiful edition,
Corrected and amended
By its Author!
Benjamin Franklin, 1706–90, Epitaph for himself

## Dedicated Men

But to get down to Erasmus. No matter what his other characteristics may be, and they are splendid, as for his habit of roaming, which is the object of your rude attack, I would definitely not hesitate to prefer it to any one of your virtues, even one in which you take the greatest pride. I imagine that one who has a penchant for relaxation and shudders at hard work would rather squat with you than roam with him. If one looks at his hard work, he sometimes does more work in one day than your people do in several months; if one judges the value of his work, he sometimes has done more for the whole Church in one month than you have in several years, unless you suppose that anybody's fastings or pious prayers have as deep and wide an influence as his brilliant works, which are educating the entire world to the meaning of true holiness; or unless you suppose he is enjoying himself as he defies stormy seas and savage skies and all the scourges of land travel, provided it furthers the common cause. Possibly, it is not a pleasant experience to endure seasickness and the tortures of tossing waves and the threat of a deadly storm, and to stare at the ever-present menace of shipwreck. Possibly, it is not a keen delight to plod along through dense forest and wild woodland, over rugged hilltops and steep mountains, along roads beset with bandits, or to be battered by the winds, spattered with mud, drenched by rains, weary of travelling, exhausted from hardships, and then to receive a shabby welcome and be refused the sort of food and bed you are enjoying; and especially since all these many, many troubles, which would soon tire a healthy, sturdy young man, must be encountered and endured with a poor body that is growing old and has lost its strength from hard study and toil; and therefore, it is quite obvious that he would have had to succumb long ago to all these difficuties, had not God ('Who makes His sun to rise upon the good and the bad') preserved him for the benefit even of ungrateful people. No matter where his journeys take him, he always comes back loaded with wonderful gifts for everyone else, while the only returns for him are his shattered health and the insults from wicked men which have been occasioned by his kindly gifts.

Therefore these expeditions are so dear to his heart that he would be quick to drop them only at the demand of his studies, that is, for the cause of the common good, which he very often purchases at great expense to himself. On these trips, which are the target of your criticisms, he spends his time only with those men approved for learning and goodness, and, as a result, his mind is ever nurturing some unborn ideas, which eventually will be brought forth to the general profit of scholarship; but if he had preferred his own personal comfort, he would now be much healthier in body and also much richer in money, because rulers and leaders all over the world have been competing with one another to win him with their extraordinary offers. Since, wherever he is, he scatters abroad, as the sun its rays, his wonderful riches, it was only a matter of justice that comparable returns be made to him from all sides. Because he dedicates himself completely to the service of others and expects no personal reward in this life, I am sure that the all-kind God will repay him in that place where he would rather receive his reward; and when I compare you with him, who is the object of your contempt, and when I contrast your services with his, then, to the extent that a human being may make a conjecture from that comparison, I feel confident that when the day dawns on which the merits of each of you will be recompensed, while I hope your reward will be high and pray it will be extremely high, God, however, the just dispenser for both of you, will prefer his travelling to your squatting, and this He will do without any offence to you, in fact, in keeping with your disposition then, even with your compliance; I feel confident too that, since all things work together unto good, God will prefer his use of the tongue to your silence, his silence to your prayers, his eating to your fasting, his sleeping to your vigils, and, in a word, everything you haughtily disdain in him, God will esteem much more than all the things that fascinate you in your way of life.

Sir Thomas More (1478–1535), Letter to a monk

To his son Louis

Paris, 9 February 1858

I'm working as hard as I can to finish my score, and gradually it's getting done. At the moment I am at Dido's final monologue ('Je vais mourir'). I am

47

more pleased with what I have just written than with anything I've done so far. I believe that the music of these terrible scenes of the fifth act will carry heartrending conviction. Once again I have altered this act: I have made a large cut, and added a character piece which is intended to contrast with the epic, passionate style of the rest. It's a sailor's song: I thought of you, dear Louis, when I wrote it, and I send you the words. It is night, the Trojan ships lie at anchor in the port. Hylas, a young Phrygian sailor, sings as he rocks at the masthead . . .

To Adolphe Samuel [Professor of Harmony at the Brussels Conservatoire]

Paris, 26 February 1858

I have worked at the poem with extreme patience, and will not have to make major changes. Why should we not have patience? I was reading yesterday in a life of Virgil that he took eleven years to write the *Aeneid*, yet to him it seemed so unfinished that on his death-bed he ordered his heirs to burn it . . .

I think you will be satisfied with my score. You can easily guess what the scenes of passion, of tenderness or of nature, whether calm or stormy, must be like: but there are other scenes of which you cannot as yet have an idea. It no longer matters to me what happens to the work – whether it is produced or not produced. My musical and Virgilian passion has been sated. Farewell, dear Friend, Patience and Perseverance! I may even add Indifference: what does anything matter?

To Richard Pohl [music critic]

[Paris] April 1858

Are you going to the Prague Festival? Count Nostiz has invited me. Are you going to the Cologne Festival? The committee and our good friend Hiller have invited me. I have refused both invitations. I am too absorbed in my great affair to leave Paris.

I am in the middle of reducing for piano my score of *The Trojans*, which has been completely finished, as you no doubt know, for a month. This labour has made me see a lot of little faults which the most assiduous reading of the work hadn't made clear: and I'm correcting them as best I can. If later God wills that I can let you hear it, I hope you will be pleased with it. In any case I can do no better, and I am putting all my efforts and all my concentration into removing the blemishes which I find. What I can promise you is that there is great truth of expression and that the work is music. If a Cassandra or a Dido or an order from the Emperor come my way I can produce the work.

But there is another person who could well come first, that is Death.

Farewell: until that horrible hag presents herself, let us live and always frankly love what is beautiful, it's the only way of laughing at her . . .

Hector Berlioz, from *A Selection from His Letters*,
tr. Humphrey Searle, 1966

You complain that you find it difficult to write and have to sit quite a long time over every sentence. What else did you expect? Did you imagine that one can do things without any effort or hard work? I often sit for two long hours biting my pen and not knowing how to begin my article, then, quite unexpectedly, others praise it and discover it to have been written easily and spontaneously. Remember how difficult I used to find it to do my work for Zaremba. Just think how I ruined my nerves in 1866 at Miatlev's dacha, sweating over my symphony which would not come out properly, however hard I tried. Even now, when composing, I have to bite my nails sometimes, smoke an enormous amount of cigarettes, and walk up and down the room before discovering the main theme. Sometimes, on the other hand, everything is easy and thoughts are born and push each other out as fast as they can. Everything depends on the mood and humour you are in. But even if you are not in the proper mood you have to force yourself to work. You will never succeed otherwise. You write that you are in a bad mood. Believe me it is not worse than mine. All to do with my accursed nerves.

Piotr Tchaikovsky, Letter to his brother, 6 January 1875,
tr. Galina von Meck, 1973

And now to the matter for precepts, for observations or directions to the art of limning, which you require as briefly and as plainly as I can, concerning the best way and means to practice and attain to skill in limning. In a word before, I exhorted such to temperance; I mean sleep not much, watch not much, eat not much, sit not long, use not violent exercise in sports, nor earnest for your recreation, but dancing or bowling or little of either. Then the first and chiefest precept which I give is cleanliness, and therefore fittest for gentlemen; that the practicer of limning be precisely pure and cleanly in all his doings: as in grinding his colours in a place where there is neither dust nor smoke; the water well chosen, or distilled most pure, as the water distilled from the water of some clear spring, or from black cherries, which is the cleanest that ever I could find, and keepeth longest sweet and clear; the gum to be gum arabic of the whitest and brittlest, broken into white powder on a fair and clean grinding stone; and white sugar candy in like sort to be kept dry in boxes of ivory; the grinding stone of fine crystal, serpentine, jasper or hard porphyry at the least. Let your apparel be silk, such as sheddeth least dust or hairs; wear nothing straight. Beware you touch not your work with your fingers, or any hard thing, but with a clean pencil brush it, or with a white feather; neither breathe on it, especially in cold weather. Take heed of the dandruff of the head shedding from the hair, and of speaking over your work for sparkling, for the least sparkling of spittle will never be helped if it light in the face, or any part of the naked.

Nicholas Hilliard, from *A Treatise Concerning the Arte of Limning, c.* 1600


They went to work, and Fred helped vigorously. His spirits had risen, and he heartily enjoyed a good slip in the moist earth under the hedgerow, which soiled his perfect summer trousers. Was it his successful onset which had elated him, or the satisfaction of helping Mary's father? Something more. The accidents of the morning had helped his frustrated imagination to shape an employment for himself which had several attractions . . . But they went on in silence except when their business demanded speech. At last, when they had finished and were walking away, Mr Garth said –

'A young fellow needn't be a B.A. to do this sort of work, eh, Fred?'

'I wish I had taken to it before I had thought of being a B.A. ,' said Fred. He paused a moment, and then added, more hesitatingly, 'Do you think I am too old to learn your business, Mr Garth?'

'My business is of many sorts, my boy,' said Mr Garth, smiling. 'A good deal of what I know can only come from experience: you can't learn it off as you learn things out of a book. But you are young enough to lay a foundation yet.' Caleb pronounced the last sentence emphatically, but paused in some uncertainty. He had been under the impression lately that Fred had made up his mind to enter the Church.

'You do think I could do some good at it, if I were to try?' said Fred, more eagerly.

'That depends,' said Caleb, turning his head on one side and lowering his voice, with the air of a man who felt himself to be saying something deeply religious. 'You must be sure of two things; you must love your work, and not be always looking over the edge of it, wanting your play to begin. And the other is, you must not be ashamed of your work, and think it would be more honourable to you to be doing something else. You must have a pride in your own work in learning to do it well, and not be always saying, There's this and there's that – if I had this or that to do, I might make something of it. No matter what a man is – I wouldn't give twopence for him' – here Caleb's mouth looked bitter, and he snapped his fingers – 'whether he was the prime minister or the rick-thatcher, if he didn't do well what he undertook to do.'

'I can never feel that I should do that in being a clergyman,' said Fred, meaning to take a step in argument.

'Then let it alone, my boy,' said Caleb, abruptly, 'else you'll never be easy. Or if you *are* easy, you'll be a poor stick.'

George Eliot, from *Middlemarch*, 1872

Sherlock Holmes was transformed when he was hot upon such a scent as this. Men who had only known the quiet thinker and logician of Baker Street would have failed to recognize him. His face flushed and darkened. His brows were drawn into two hard, black lines, while his eyes shone out from beneath them with a steely glitter. His face was bent downwards, his shoulders bowed, his lips compressed, and the veins stood out like whip-cord in his long, sinewy neck. His nostrils seemed to dilate with a purely animal lust for the chase, and his mind was so absolutely concentrated upon the matter before him, that a question or remark fell unheeded upon his ears, or at the most only provoked a quick, impatient snarl in reply. Swiftly and silently he made his way along the track which ran through the meadows, and so by way of the woods to the Boscombe Pool. It was damp, marshy ground, as is all that district, and there were marks of many feet, both upon the path and amid the short grass which bounded it on either side. Sometimes Holmes would hurry on, sometimes stop dead, and once he made quite a little *détour* into the meadow. Lestrade and I walked behind him, the detective indifferent and contemptuous, while I watched my friend with the interest which sprang from the conviction that every one of his actions was directed towards a definite end.

Sir Arthur Conan Doyle, from 'The Boscombe Valley Mystery',
*The Adventures of Sherlock Holmes*, 1892

## Working in Darkness

We understand nothing of the works of God unless we understand that God desires to enlighten some and leave others in darkness.

Blaise Pascal, from *Pensées*, 1670

### *Eu sou carvão*

Eu sou carvão!
E tu arrancas-me brutalmente do chão
e fazes-me tua mina, patrão.

Eu sou carvão!
E tu acendes-me, patrão
para te servir eternamente como força motriz
mas eternamente não, patrão.
Eu sou carvão
e tenho que arder, sim
e queimar tudo com a força da minha combustão.
Eu sou carvão
tenho que arder na exploração
arder até às cinzas da maldição
arder vivo como alcatrão, meu irmão
até não ser mais a tua mina, patrão.
Eu sou carvão
Tenho que arder
queimar tudo com o fogo da minha combustão.
Sim!
Eu serei o teu carvão, patrão!

(I am coal! / And you tear me brutally from the ground / and you make me your source of wealth, boss. / I am coal! / And you ignite me, boss / in order to serve you eternally as motive force / but not eternally, boss. / I am coal / and I must blaze, yes / and burn all with the force of my combustion. / I am coal / I must blaze in exploitation / blaze into ashes of malediction / blaze live like tar, my brother / until I am no longer your wealth, boss. / I am coal / I must blaze / burn all with the fire of my combustion. / Yes! / I will be your coal, boss!)

José Craveirinha (Mozambique), 1964,
tr. Russell G. Hamilton

### *Working*

Among stooped getters, grimy, knacker-bare,
head down thrusting a 3 cwt corf
turned your crown bald, your golden hair
chafed fluffy first and then scuffed off,

chick's back, then eggshell, that sunless white.
You strike sparks and plenty but can't see.
You've been underneath too long to stand the light.
You're lost in this sonnet for the bourgeoisie.

Patience Kershaw, bald hurryer, fourteen,
this workshift and inwit's a load of crap
for dumping on a slagheap, I mean
*th'art nobbut summat as wants raking up.*

I stare into the fire. Your skinned skull shines.
I close my eyes. That makes a dark like mines.

Wherever hardship held its tongue the job
's breaking the silence of the worked-out gob.*
                    Tony Harrison, from *Continuous*, 1981


All forty-six men woke to rifle shot. All forty-six. Three whitemen walked along the trench unlocking the doors one by one. No one stepped through. When the last lock was opened, the three returned and lifted the bars, one by one. And one by one the black men emerged – promptly and without the poke of a rifle butt if they had been there more than a day; promptly with the butt if, like Paul D, they had just arrived. When all forty-six were standing in a line in the trench, another rifle shot signaled the climb out and up to the ground above, where one thousand feet of the best hand-forged chain in Georgia stretched. Each man bent and waited. The first man picked up the end and threaded it through the loop in his leg iron. He stood up then, and, shuffling a little, brought the chain tip to the next prisoner, who did likewise. As the chain was passed on and each man stood in the other's place, the line of men turned around, facing the boxes they had come out of. Not one spoke to the other. At least not with words. The eyes had to tell what there was to tell: 'Help me this mornin; 's bad'; 'I'm a make it'; 'New man'; 'Steady now steady.'

Chain-up completed, they knelt down. The dew, more likely than not, was mist by then. Heavy sometimes and if the dogs were quiet and just breathing you could hear doves. Kneeling in the mist they waited for the whim of a guard, or two, or three. Or maybe all of them wanted it. Wanted it from one prisoner in particular or none – or all.

* 'gob': an old Northern coal-mining word for the space left after the coal has been extracted. Also, of course, the mouth, and speech.

'Breakfast? Want some breakfast, nigger?'

'Yes, sir.'

'Hungry, nigger?'

'Yes, sir.'

'Here you go.'

Occasionally a kneeling man chose gunshot in his head as the price, maybe, of taking a bit of foreskin with him to Jesus. Paul D did not know that then. He was looking at his palsied hands, smelling the guard, listening to his soft grunts so like the doves', as he stood before the man kneeling in mist on his right. Convinced he was next, Paul D retched – vomiting up nothing at all. An observing guard smashed his shoulder with the rifle and the engaged one decided to skip the new man for the time being lest his pants and shoes got soiled by nigger puke.

'Hiii!'

It was the first sound, other than 'Yes, sir' a black man was allowed to speak each morning, and the lead chain gave it everything he had. 'Hiii!' It was never clear to Paul D how he knew when to shout that mercy. They called him Hi Man and Paul D thought at first the guards told him when to give the signal that let the prisoners rise up off their knees and dance two-step to the music of hand-forged iron. Later he doubted it. He believed to this day that the 'Hiii!' at dawn and the 'Hoooo!' when evening came were the responsibility Hi Man assumed because he alone knew what was enough, what was too much, when things were over, when the time had come.

They chain-danced over the fields, through the woods to a trail that ended in the astonishing beauty of feldspar, and there Paul D's hands disobeyed the furious rippling of his blood and paid attention. With a sledge hammer in his hands and Hi Man's lead, the men got through. They sang it out and beat it up, garbling the words so they could not be understood; tricking the words so their syllables yielded up other meanings. They sang the women they knew; the children they had been; the animals they had tamed themselves or seen others tame. They sang of bosses and masters and misses; of mules and dogs and the shamelessness of life. They sang lovingly of graveyards and sisters long gone. Of pork in the woods; meal in the pan; fish on the line; cane, rain and rocking chairs.

And they beat. The women for having known them and no more, no more; the children for having been them but never again. They killed a boss so often and so completely they had to bring him back to life to pulp him one more time. Tasting hot mealcake among pine trees, they beat it away. Singing love songs to Mr Death, they smashed his head. More than the rest, they killed the flirt whom folks called Life for leading them on. Making them think the next sunrise would be worth it; that another stroke of time would do it at last.

54

Only when she was dead would they be safe. The successful ones – the ones who had been there enough years to have maimed, mutilated, maybe even buried her – kept watch over the others who were still in her cock-teasing hug, caring and looking forward, remembering and looking back. They were the ones whose eyes said, 'Help me, 's bad'; or 'Look out' meaning *this might be the day I bay or eat my own mess or run,* and it was this last that had to be guarded against, for if one pitched and ran – all, all forty-six, would be yanked by the chain that bound them and no telling who or how many would be killed. A man could risk his own life, but not his brother's. So the eyes said, 'Steady now', and 'Hang by me.'

Eighty-six days and done. Life was dead. Paul D beat her butt all day every day till there was not a whimper in her. Eighty-six days and his hands were still, waiting serenely each rat-rustling night for 'Hiiii!' at dawn and the eager clench on the hammer's shaft. Life rolled over dead. Or so he thought.

Toni Morrison, from *Beloved*, 1988

## Unlocking Nature's Secrets

I thought that if I could bestow animation upon lifeless matter, I might in process of time (although I now found it impossible) renew life where death had apparently devoted the body to corruption.

These thoughts supported my spirits, while I pursued my undertaking with unremitting ardour. My cheek had grown pale with study, and my person had become emaciated with confinement. Sometimes, on the very brink of certainty, I failed; yet still I clung to the hope which the next day or the next hour might realize. One secret which I alone possessed was the hope to which I had dedicated myself; and the moon gazed on my midnight labours, while, with unrelaxed and breathless eagerness, I pursued nature to her hiding-places. Who shall conceive the horrors of my secret toil as I dabbled among the unhallowed damps of the grave or tortured the living animal to animate the lifeless clay? My limbs now tremble, and my eyes swim with the remembrance; but then a resistless and almost frantic impulse urged me forward; I seemed to have lost all soul or sensation but for this one pursuit. It was indeed but a passing trance, that only made me feel with renewed acuteness so soon as, the unnatural stimulus ceasing to operate, I had returned to my old habits. I collected bones from charnel-houses and disturbed, with profane fingers, the tremendous secrets of the human frame. In a solitary chamber, or rather cell, at the top of the house, and separated from all the other apartments by a gallery and staircase, I kept my workshop of filthy creation: my eyeballs were starting from their sockets in attending to the details of my employment. The dissecting room and the slaughter-house furnished many of my materials; and often did my human nature turn with loathing from my occupation, whilst, still urged on by an eagerness which perpetually increased, I brought my work near to a conclusion.

The summer months passed while I was thus engaged, heart and soul, in one pursuit. It was a most beautiful season; never did the fields bestow a more plentiful harvest, or the vines yield a more luxuriant vintage: but my eyes were insensible to the charms of nature. And the same feeling which made me neglect the scenes around me caused me also to forget those friends who were so many miles absent, and whom I had not seen for so long a time. I knew my silence disquieted them; and I well remembered the words of my father: 'I know that while you are pleased with yourself, you will think of us with affection, and we shall hear regularly from you. You must pardon me if I regard any interruption in your correspondence as a proof that your other duties are equally neglected.'

I knew well therefore what would be my father's feelings; but I could not tear my thoughts from my employment, loathsome in itself, but which had taken an irresistible hold of my imagination. I wished, as it were, to procrastinate all that related to my feelings of affection until the great object, which swallowed up every habit of my nature, should be completed ...

The leaves of that year had withered before my work drew near to a close; and now every day showed me more plainly how well I had succeeded. But my enthusiasm was checked by my anxiety, and I appeared rather like one doomed by slavery to toil in the mines, or any other unwholesome trade, than an artist occupied by his favourite employment. Every night I was oppressed by a slow fever, and I became nervous to a most painful degree; the fall of a leaf startled me, and I shunned my fellow creatures as if I had been guilty of a crime. Sometimes I grew alarmed at the wreck I perceived that I had become; the energy of my purpose alone sustained me: my labours would soon end, and I believed that exercise and amusement would then drive away incipient disease; and I promised myself both of these when my creation should be complete.

Mary Shelley, from *Frankenstein, or the Modern Prometheus*, 1818

As a man who has become alive to the primacy of work leans over his retorts or microscope, he sees, intensely illuminated, the potential significance and value of the particle of intelligence and activity he has at his disposal. It is his function to complete cosmic evolution by making the inexhaustible energies at the heart of which he is born 'work' as though with a leaven, until all the promise they hold is realized. Who could number the still dormant seeds, the rich potentialities, hidden in matter? The dullest, most inert object, once the appropriate stimulant has been applied to it, and it has been given the sort of complement or contact it needs and awaits, is capable of exploding into irresistible effects or of transforming itself into a nature that is prodigiously active.

As a result of natural contacts or of an instinctive, hidden work, the Cosmos has already realized one part of its capabilities, giving us the world we know, with its individual substances and shades of life. But how many valuable properties are still to be discovered, that will perfect and transform the present picture of things? For too long, in seeking for health and growth, mankind has confined itself to docile empiricism and patient resignation ... The time has now come to master nature, to make it unlock its secrets, to dominate it, to inaugurate a new phase; in that phase intelligence, which emerged from the universe, will turn back to it, to readjust and rejuvenate it, and make it provide its conscious portion with the full contribution it can make of growth in joy and activity.

We may ask what term is held out as the fruit of such efforts. The scientist's answer may still be vague, but he has behind him discoveries that have enabled him enormously to increase his power, to transform bodies and methodically to overcome disease. He can envisage a new era in which suffering is effectively alleviated, well-being is assured, and – who knows? – our organs are perhaps rejuvenated and even artificially developed. It is dangerous to challenge science and set a limit to its victories, for the hidden energies it summons from the depths are unfathomable. May it not even become possible to cultivate the brain itself, and intensify at will the power and keenness of thought?

Borne up by this vast hope of indefinitely increasing his stature and of achieving his own beatification by using matter as a firm purchase-point, man devotes himself with new fervour to an impassioned study of the powers of the universe and becomes absorbed in the quest for the Great Secret. His austere task is enveloped in the mystical glow that lit up the anxious faces of the alchemists, haloed the brow of the Magi, and divinized the bold theft of Prometheus; and, before each new property that is revealed to him, each a new window on the Promised Land, the scientist falls on his knees, almost as though to the revelation of an attribute to God.

Pierre Teilhard de Chardin, from *Writings in Time of War*,

tr. René Hague, 1968

## All Trades Agoing

A cook they hadde with hem for the nones
To boille the chiknes with the marybones,
And poudre-marchant tart and galyngale.
Wel koude he knowe a draughte of Londoun ale.
He koude rooste, and sethe, and broille, and frye,
Maken mortreux, and wel bake a pye.
But greet harm was it, as it thoughte me,
That on his shyne a mormal hadde he.
For blankmanger, that made he with the beste.

*marybones* – marrowbones
*poudre-marchant tart and galyngale* – piquant spices
*mortreux* – stews
*mormal* – gangrenous ulcer
*blankmanger* – a chicken or fish stew

Geoffrey Chaucer, from Prologue to *The Canterbury Tales*, c. 1390


*Die ganzen Zahlen hat der liebe Gott gemacht, alles andere ist Menschenwerk.*
(God made the integers; and all the rest is the work of man.)

Leopold Kronecker, statement made at a meeting in Berlin in 1886


### How the First Hielandman of God was made of ane Horse Turd in Argyll as is said

God and Sanct Peter
    Was gangand be the way
Heich up in Argyll
    Where their gait lay.

Sanct Peter said to God
    In a sport word,
Can ye not mak a Hielandman
    Of this horse turd?

God turn'd owre the horse turd
    With his pykit staff
And up start a Hielandman
    Blak as ony draff.

Quod God to the Hielandman,
   Where wilt thow now?
I will doun in the Lawland, Lord,
   And there steill a cow.

And thou steill a cow, cairle,
   Than they will hang thee.
What rack, Lord, of that,
   For anis mon I die.

God then he leuch
   And owre the dyke lap,
And out of his sheath
   His gully outgat.

Sanct Peter socht this gully
   Fast up and doun,
Yet could not find it
   In all that braid roun.

Now, quod God, here a marvel,
   How can this be,
That I suld want my gully,
   And we here bot three?

Humff, quod the Hielandman,
   And turn'd him about,
And at his plaid neuk
   The gully fell out.

Fy, quod Sanct Peter,
   Thou will never do weill,
And thou bot new made
   And sa soon gais to steill.

Umff, quod the Hielandman,
   And sware be yon kirk,
Sa lang as I may gear get to steill
   Will I never work.

pykit] pointed   anis] once   leuch] laughed   lap] leapt   gully] large knife
outgat] disappeared   fast] carefully   braid roun] space around   his
plaid neuk] corner of his plaid

                           Anon., sixteenth century

[23 June 1652] The morning growing excessively hot, I sent my footman some hours before, and so rod negligently, under favour of the shade, 'til being now come to within three miles of *Bromely*, at a place calld the procession *Oake*, started out two Cutt-throates, & striking with their long staves at the horse, taking hold of the reignes, threw me downe, & immediately tooke my sword, & haled me into a deepe Thickett, some quarter of a mile from the high-way, where they might securely rob me, as they soon did; what they got of mony was not considerable, but they tooke two rings, the one an Emrald with diamonds, an [Onyx], & a pair of boucles set with rubies & diamonds which were of value, and after all, barbarously bound my hands behind me, & my feete, having before pull'd off my bootes: & then set me up against an *Oake*, with most bloudy threatnings to cutt my throat, if I offerd to crie out, or make any noise, for that they should be within hearing, I not being the person they looked for: I told them, if they had not basely surpriz'd me, they should not have made so easy a prize, & that it should teach me hereafter never to ride neere an hedge; since had I ben in the mid way, they durst not have adventur'd on me, at which they cock'd their pistols, & told me they had long guns too, & were 14 companions, which all were lies: I begg'd for my *Onyx* & told them it being engraven with my armes, would betray them, but nothing prevaild: My horses bridle they slipt, & search'd the saddle which they likewise pull'd off, but let the horse alone to grace, & then turning againe bridld him, & tied him to a Tree, yet so as he might graze, & so left me bound: The reason they tooke not my horse, was I suppose, because he was mark'd, and cropt on both Eares, & well known on that roade, & these rogues were lusty foote padders, as they are cald: Well, being left in this manner, grievously was I tormented with the flies, the ants, & the sunn, so as I sweate intollerably, no little was my anxiety how I should get loose in that solitary place, where I could neither heare or see any creature but my poore horse & a few sheepe stragling in the Coppse; til after neere two houres attempting I got my hands to turne paulme to paulme, whereas before they were tied back to back, and then I stuck a greate while ere' I could slip the cord over my wrist to my thumb, which at last I did, & then being quite loose soone unbound my feete, & so sadling my horse, and roaming a while about, I at last perceiv'd a dust to rise, & soone after heard the rattling of a Cart, towards which I made, and by the help of two Country fellows that were driving it, got down a steepe bank, into the highway againe; but could heare nothing of the Villains: So I rod to *Colonel Blounts* a greate justiciarie of the times, who sent out *hugh & Crie* immediately: and 25, The next morning weary & sore as I was at my wrists & armes, I went from *Deptford* to *Lond*, got 500 ticketts, printed & dispers'd, by an officer of *Gould Smiths-hall*, describing what I had lost, and within two daies after had tidings of all I lost, except my Sword

which was a silver hilt, & some other trifles: These *rogues* had paund my
Rings &c for a trifle to a Goldsmiths Servant, before the tickets came to the
shop, by which meanes they scap'd, the other ring was bought by a Victualer,
who brought it to a Goldsmith, that having seene the ticket, seiz'd upon him;
but whom I afterwards discharg'd upon the mediation of friends & protestation
of his innocency: Thus did God deliv[e]r me from these villains, & not onely
so, but restor'd to me what they tooke, as twise before he had graciously don,
both at sea & land, I meane, when I had ben rob'd by *Pyrates* and was in
danger of a considerable losse at *Amsterdam*, for which & many, many signal
preservations I am eternaly obligd to give thanks to God my Saviour.

from *The Diary of John Evelyn*

### The Happy Beggarman

Of all trades agoing, begging it is my delight;
My rent it is paid and I lay down my bags ev'ry night;
I'll throw away care and take a long staff in my hand,
And I'll flourish each day courageously looking for chance.

With my belt round my shoulder and down my bags they do hang;
With a push and a joult it's quickly I'll have them yoked on;
With my horn by my side, likewise my skiver and can;
With my staff and long pike to fight the dogs as I gang.

To patterns and fairs I'll go round for collection along,
I'll seem to be lame and quite useless of one of my hands;
Like a pilgrim I'll pray each day with my hat in my hand,
And at night in the alehouse I'll stay and pay like a man.

Anon., *c.* 1820

'Oh dear me, dear me!' sighs Mr Venus, heavily, snuffing the candle, 'the
world that appeared so flowery has ceased to blow! You're casting your eye
round the shop, Mr Wegg. Let me show you a light. My working bench. My
young man's bench. A Wice. Tools. Bones, warious. Skulls, warious. Preserved
Indian baby. African ditto. Bottled preparations, warious. Everything within
reach of your hand, in good preservation. The mouldy ones a-top. What's in
those hampers over them again, I don't quite remember. Say, human warious.
Cats. Articulated English baby. Dogs. Ducks. Glass eyes, warious. Mummied
bird. Dried cuticle, warious. Oh dear me! That's the general panoramic view.'
Having so held and waved the candle as that all these heterogeneous objects

seemed to come forward obediently when they were named, and then retire again, Mr Venus despondently repeats, 'Oh dear me, dear me!' resumes his seat, and with drooping despondency upon him, falls to pouring himself out more tea . . .

'You seem very low, Mr Venus. Is business bad?'

'Never was so good.'

'Is your hand out at all?'

'Never was so well in. Mr Wegg, I'm not only first in the trade, but I'm *the* trade. You may go and buy a skeleton at the West End if you like, and pay the West End price, but it'll be my putting together. I've as much to do as I can possibly do, with the assistance of my young man, and I take a pride and a pleasure in it.' . . .

'That ain't a state of things to make you low, Mr Venus.'

'Mr Wegg, I know it ain't. Mr Wegg, not to name myself as workman without an equal, I've gone on improving myself in my knowledge of Anatomy, till both by sight and by name I'm perfect. Mr Wegg, if you was brought here loose in a bag to be articulated, I'd name your smallest bones blindfold equally with your largest, as far as I could pick 'em out, and I'd sort 'em all, and sort your wertebrae, in a manner that would equally surprise and charm you.'

'Well,' remarks Silas (though not quite so readily as last time), '*that* ain't a state of things to be low about. – Not for *you* to be low about, leastways.'

'Mr Wegg, I know it ain't; Mr Wegg, I know it ain't. But it's the heart that lowers me, it is the heart! Be so good as take and read the card out loud.'

Silas receives one from his hand, which Venus takes from a wonderful litter in a drawer, and putting on his spectacles, reads:

' "Mr Venus," '

'Yes. Go on.'

' "Preserver of Animals and Birds," '

'Yes. Go on.'

' "Articulator of human bones." '

'That's it,' with a groan. 'That's it! Mr Wegg, I'm thirty-two, and a bachelor. Mr Wegg, I love her. Mr Wegg, she is worthy of being loved by a Potentate!' Here Silas is rather alarmed by Mr Venus springing to his feet in the hurry of his spirits, and haggardly confronting him with his hand on his coat collar; but Mr Venus, begging pardon, sits down again, saying, with the calmness of despair, 'She objects to the business.'

'Does she know the profits of it?'

'She knows the profits of it, but she don't appreciate the art of it, and she objects to it. "I do not wish", she writes in her own handwriting, "to regard myself, nor yet to be regarded, in that bony light." '

Mr Venus pours himself out more tea, with a look and in an attitude of the deepest desolation.

'And so a man climbs to the top of the tree, Mr Wegg, only to see that there's no look-out when he's up there! I sit here of a night surrounded by the lovely trophies of my art, and what have they done for me? Ruined me. Brought me to the pass of being informed that "she does not wish to regard herself, nor yet to be regarded, in that bony light!" ' Having repeated the fatal expressions, Mr Venus drinks more tea by gulps, and offers an explanation of his doing so.

'It lowers me. When I'm equally lowered all over, lethargy sets in. By sticking to it till one or two in the morning, I get oblivion. Don't let me detain you, Mr Wegg. I'm not company for any one.'

Charles Dickens, from Our Mutual Friend, 1865

He spent the afternoon exploring the premises of the Potwell Inn and learning the duties that might be expected of him, such as Stockholm tarring fences, digging potatoes, swabbing out boats, helping people land, embarking, landing, and time-keeping for the hirers of two rowing boats and one Canadian canoe, bailing out the said vessels and concealing their leaks and defects from prospective hirers, persuading inexperienced hirers to start down-stream rather than up, repairing row-locks and taking inventories of returning boats with a view to supplementary charges, cleaning boots, sweeping chimneys, house painting, cleaning windows, sweeping out and sanding the Tap and Bar, cleaning pewter, washing glasses, turpentining woodwork, whitewashing generally, plumbing and engineering, repairing locks and clocks, waiting and tapster's work generally, beating carpets and mats, cleaning bottles and saving corks, taking into the cellar, moving, tapping, and connecting beer-casks with their engines, blocking and destroying wasps' nests, doing forestry with several trees, drowning superfluous kittens, dog-fancying as required, assisting in the rearing of ducklings and the care of various poultry, bee-keeping, stabling, baiting and grooming horses and asses, cleaning and 'garing' motor-cars and bicycles, inflating tyres and repairing punctures, recovering the bodies of drowned persons from the river as required, and assisting people in trouble in the water, first aid and sympathy, improvising and superintending a bathing station for visitors, attending inquests and funerals in the interest of the establishment, scrubbing floors and all the ordinary duties of a scullion, the Ferry, chasing hens and goats from the adjacent cottages out of the garden, making up paths and superintending drainage, gardening generally, delivering bottled beer and soda-water siphons in the neighbourhood, running miscellaneous errands, removing drunken and offensive persons from the premises by tact or muscle, as occasion required, keeping in with the local policeman, defending the premises in general and the orchard in particular from nocturnal depredators . . .

'Can but try it,' said Mr Polly towards tea-time. 'When there's nothing else on hand I suppose I might do a bit of fishing.'

H. G. Wells, from *The History of Mr Polly*, 1910

# WOMAN'S LABOUR

# Woman's Labour

Take notice that all women do not keep the same posture in their delivery; some lye on their beds, being very weak, some sit in a stool or chair, or rest upon the side of the bed, held by other women that come to the Labor.

If the Woman that lyeth in be very fat, fleshy, or gross, let her ly groveling on the place, for that opens the womb, and thrusts it downwards. The Midwife must annoint her hands with Oyl of Lillies, and the Womans Secrets, or with Oyl of Almonds, and so with her hands handle and unloose the parts, and observe how the Child lyeth, and stirreth, and so help as time and occasion direct. But above all take heed you force not the birth till the time be come, and the Child come forward and appears ready to come forth.

Now the danger were much to force delivery, because when the woman hath laboured sore, if she rest not a while, she will not be able presently to endure it, her strength being spent before.

Also when you see the after-buthen, then be sure the Birth is at hand; but if the coats be so strong that they will not break to make way for the Child to come forth, the Midwife must gently and prudently break and rend it with her nails, if she can raise it, she may cut a piece of it with a knife or pair of Scissers, but beware of the infant.

Then follows presently a flux of humours and the Child after that, but if all the humours that should make the place slippery chance to run forth by this means before the child come, the parts within and without must be annointed with Oyl of Almonds, or Lillies, and a whole Egg Yelk and white beaten, and poured into the privy passage to make it glib, instead of the waters that are run forth too soon.

If the child have a great head and stick by the way, the Midwife must annoint the place with Oyl as before, and enlarge the part as much as may be; the like must be done when Twins offer themselves; if the head comes first, the birth is natural, but if it comes any other way, the Midwife must do what she can to bring it to this posture.

Jane Sharp, from *The Midwives Book Or the Whole Art of Midwifry Discovered*, 1671

The machine is bleeping. Someone's calling for help. It's late, it's evening, electric light is prising her eyes, it's late, it's time. The mass forces downwards, jammed between her bones, rupturing through the peeling tissues of her body. She must push.

'No, no, stop that!' Their voices are urgent: 'It's not time, control it!' They are shouting: 'For heaven's sake, girl, remember your breathing – quick breaths, quick breaths!'

She does it, she gets control – snip, cuts her head and shoulders away from the rest of her body, lifts them floating on shallow dog-pants. 'Good girl, well done.' She's their baby, their goody, their Frankenstein beauty. Oh, no, she's not, there's the urge: her body gels, gathers, and now she's her very own monster, wolf-mouth howling, frog-legs flexing: they flinch back. She can make them flinch back, hold them off from her own magic circle. She laughs, wild strangled laughter, coiling helter-skelter inside the huge knot of her, she sees them looking from one to the other. In spite of their magic, in spite of their enemas, she squirts shit in their faces.

The head smashes down through the bag of her abdomen. It won't come. It won't come out. Skull like a turnip, the enormous great big turnip that the farmer couldn't pull from the cold black earth. He pulled and pulled, but it wouldn't come up. The farmer called his wife. Sister calls Doctor. Doctor hears, Doctor sees. 'Foetal distress,' says Doctor; *Foetal distress*, said the textbook in its outdated type on good old-fashioned paper; 'Foetal distress,' calls the nurse. Sister calls the hospital porter. The farmer's wife called the boy. The doctor raises a syringe and plunges the needle into Zelda's arm.

They lift her over. The ceiling slips, she's slipping, losing grip, losing substance, a soul that doesn't need feeding, falling like a parachute over the skull and round it and away, and for a moment she thinks she's free, that she's left it behind, bloody skull floating away above her. But then she sees the wild roses, coming towards her, a bank of pink roses, she's falling towards it, nearer and nearer, so close she can see the individual blossoms, five petals each, each petal shaped like a heart, pink at the outer edge, icy-white in the centre, the stamens bristling like unknown insects, and then she knows the time has come . . .

The surgeon pauses; looks up at Roland, his surgical scissors poised. 'We are doing a transverse incision.'

'Oh,' says Roland. 'Good.'

Oh, good. A transverse incision. More commonly known as a bikini-line incision. Performed on those patients the obstetrician considers would otherwise suffer a reduction in their sexual viability. Oh, good. Now Zelda will be able to wander half-clad on beaches, her sexual viability intact. No one need know. No one will guess she's been through all this.

The surgeon goes on: 'We often don't bother in such cases, when it's a question of urgency, but we've managed this time.'

'Oh,' says Roland. 'Marvellous.' Marvellous. Specially for Roland.

'We're getting it nice and low, below the pubic hair-line.' Oh, good. This surgeon must consider she wears very brief bikinis. This patient is a very sexy patient. Or so he flatters Roland.

He busies himself cutting.

The attendant clips the blood off, clamps the vessels. They've worked right across; now the surgeon must lean a little, and the attendant no longer has to. Someone's stomach rumbles. It's getting late. Someone needs their supper.

'Nearly there,' says the surgeon.

The attendant stands back. Now it's up to the chief, to put his hand in and deliver. 'Oh!' he says, conversationally, just before he pulls, 'I can see it's a boy!'

A boy. Good Lord, a boy. She hadn't imagined the possibility of a boy.

The boy. Who would have guessed it would be the boy, under the pink and white skin of roses?

A sluther. Pop. He pulls it out, like a rabbit from a hat.

A purple corkscrew baby.

'There we are, it's a boy!' He holds it up for all to see, in his two plastic hands: bent and raw, the scrotum hanging like a prune. It blinks and stares, black currants of surprise.

'Here, Dad!' says the surgeon, and hands the baby to Roland.

Roland holds out his arms, stiff, bent in the middle – meccano arms. Be careful, Roland, the baby will drop out of them. 'Hello,' says Roland. To the baby, experimentally. 'Hello,' in a strange, thin, puppet-on-a-string voice, looking up briefly, aware of people watching him. 'Hello.'

The baby stares, shocked.

'All right, Dad,' says a nurse, coming up behind Roland, 'we mustn't let him get cold.' Dad must be quickly relieved of the baby. Dad is overwhelmed, as Dads can be expected to be on such occasions. Roland tries to hand the baby over. There's a struggle, arms tangled – should he straighten or bend them? Then the nurse gets the baby and bears it away.

'Right!' says the surgeon, and begins quickly sewing up the incision. Zelda looks down. Her stomach has gone flat. Back to normal. Transformed. Abracadabra. Good as new. He sews quickly, magic stitches that disappear all by themselves in a week. Invisible mending. No one will know.

Elizabeth Baines, from *The Birth Machine*, 1983

## Lullaby

you're the night watchman, fingers swimming
cloaked along dark streets, you spill
lantern light on flesh, slow

guardian of my city's
deepest cellars, round and round you go
you're familiar with my doorway
every hour this summer night
my cones of lilac burn, and drip
like candles, you call out
all's well, all's well

you're the nightingale
you're the cock at dawn

you're the bruiser, boy, you lust and leap
you scale your mother's lap
like hills in el dorado, leave
home for ever till tomorrow
when she lets you slip, and slaps
you swarm up apple trees, steal fruit
rip legs off flies

you're the pirate baby
you're the mouth at the sweet wine

you're the night fisherman, you push
long finger boats along canals
you slide, exploring, in between the river's lips

and you're the man
who pleasures all my locks with oil
who has the key, who knows the way
in, and who hears me call
all's well, all's well

    Michèle Roberts, from *The Mirror of the Mother*, 1986

---

I contemplated the work of all the blessed Trinity, in which contemplation I saw and understood these three properties: the property of the fatherhood, and the property of the motherhood, and the property of the lordship in one God. In our almighty Father we have our protection and our bliss, as regards our natural substance, which is ours by our creation from without beginning; and in the second person, in knowledge and wisdom we have our perfection, as regards our sensuality, our restoration and our salvation, for he is our Mother, brother and saviour; and in our good Lord the Holy Spirit we have our reward and our gift for our living and our labour, endlessly surpassing all that we desire in his marvellous courtesy, out of his great plentiful grace. For all our life consists of three: In the first we have our being, and in the second we have our increasing, and in the third we have our fulfilment. The first is nature, the second is mercy, the third is grace . . .

But now I should say a little more about this penetration, as I understood our Lord to mean: How we are brought back by the motherhood of mercy and grace into our natural place, in which we were created by the motherhood of love, a mother's love which never leaves us.

Our Mother in nature, our Mother in grace, because he wanted altogether to become our Mother in all things, made the foundation of his work most humbly and most mildly in the maiden's womb. And he revealed that in the first revelation, when he brought that meek maiden before the eye of my understanding in the simple stature which she had when she conceived; that is to say that our great God, the supreme wisdom of all things, arrayed and prepared himself in this humble place, all ready in our poor flesh, himself to do the service and the office of motherhood in everything. The mother's service is nearest, readiest and surest: nearest because it is most natural, readiest because it is most loving, and surest because it is truest. No one ever might or could perform this office fully, except only him. We know that all our mothers bear us for pain and for death. O, what is that? But our true Mother Jesus, he alone bears us for joy and for endless life, blessed may he be. So he carries us within him in love and travail, until the full time when he wanted to suffer the sharpest thorns and cruel pains that ever were or will be, and at the last he died. And when he had finished, and had borne us so for bliss, still all this could not satisfy his wonderful love. And he revealed this in these great surpassing words of love: If I could suffer more, I would suffer more. He could not die any more, but he did not want to cease working; therefore he must nourish us, for the precious love of motherhood has made him our debtor.

The mother can give her child to suck of her milk, but our precious Mother Jesus can feed us with himself, and does, most courteously and most tenderly, with the blessed sacrament, which is the precious food of true life; and with all the sweet sacraments he sustains us most mercifully and graciously, and so he meant in these blessed words, where he said: I am he whom Holy Church preaches and teaches to you. That is to say: All the health and the life of the sacraments, all the power and the grace of my word, all the goodness which is ordained in Holy Church for you, I am he.

The mother can lay her child tenderly to her breast, but our tender Mother Jesus can lead us easily into his blessed breast through his sweet open side, and show us there a part of the godhead and of the joys of heaven, with inner certainty of endless bliss. And that he revealed in the tenth revelation, giving

71

us the same understanding in these sweet words which he says: See, how I love you, looking into his blessed side, rejoicing.

Julian of Norwich, from Showings, fourteenth century

## The Wife's Tale

Who can find a virtuous woman? for her price is far above rubies.

The heart of her husband doth safely trust in her, so that he shall have no need of spoil.

She will do him good and not evil all the days of her life.

She seeketh wool, and flax, and worketh willingly with her hands.

She is like the merchants' ships: she bringeth her food from afar.

She riseth also while it is yet night, and giveth meat to her household, and a portion to her maidens.

She considereth a field, and buyeth it: with the fruit of her hands she planteth a vineyard.

She girdeth her loins with strength, and strengtheneth her arms.

She perceiveth that her merchandise is good; her candle goeth not out by night.

She layeth her hands to the spindle, and her hands hold the distaff.

She stretcheth out her hand to the poor; yea, she reacheth forth her hands to the needy.

She is not afraid of the snow for her household: for all her household are clothed with scarlet.

She maketh herself coverings of tapestry; her clothing is silk and purple.

Her husband is known in the gates, when he sitteth among the elders of the land.

She maketh fine linen, and selleth it; and delivereth girdles unto the merchant.

Strength and honour are her clothing; and she shall rejoice in time to come.

She openeth her mouth with wisdom; and in her tongue is the law of kindness.

She looketh well to the ways of her household, and eateth not the bread of idleness.

Her children arise up, and call her blessed; her husband also, and he praiseth her.

Proverbs 31: 10–28

> For though that evere vertuous was she,
> She was encressed in swich excellence
> Of thewes goode, yset in heigh bountee,

And so discreet and fair of eloquence,
So benigne and so digne of reverence,
And koude so the peples herte embrace,
That ech hire lovede that looked on hir face.

Noght oonly of Saluces in the toun
Publiced was the bountee of hir name,
But eek biside in many a regioun,
If oon seide wel, another seyde the same;
So spradde of hire heighe bountee the fame
That men and wommen, as wel yonge as olde
Goon to Saluce upon hire to biholde.

Thus Walter lowely – nay, but roially –
Wedded with fortunat honestetee,
In Goddes pees lyveth ful esily
At hoom, and outward grace ynogh had he;
And for he saugh that under low degree
Was ofte vertu hid, the peple hym heelde
A prudent man, and that is seyn ful seelde.

Nat oonly this Grisildis thurgh hir wit
Koude al the feet of wyfly hoomlinesse,
But eek, whan that the cas required it,
The commune profit koude she redresse.
Ther nas discord, rancour, ne hevynesse
In al that land that she ne koude apese,
And wisely brynge hem alle in reste and ese.

Though that hire housbonde absent were anon,
If gentil men or othere of hire contree
Were wrothe, she wolde bryngen hem aton;
So wise and rype wordes hadde she,
And juggementz of so greet equitee,
That she from hevene sent was, as men wende,
Peple to save and every wrong t'amende.

Nat longe tyme after that this Grisild
Was wedded, she a doghter hath ybore,
Al had hire levere have born a knave child;
Glad was this markys and the folk therfore,
For though a mayde child coome al bifore,
She may unto a knave child atteyne
By liklihede, syn she nys nat bareyne.

73

*thewes* – personal qualities
*Saluces* – Saluzzo, in Piedmont
*seelde* – seldom
*feet* – skills
*aton* – to agree
*knave* – boy

Geoffrey Chaucer, from 'The Clerk's Tale',
*The Canterbury Tales, c.* 1390

The Tsarina has the most elegant figure and, though she is excessively thin, I find her whole presence exudes an indefinable charm. Her appearance, far from arrogance, as I had been led to expect, expresses the habit of resignation in a proud soul. As she entered the chapel, she was overcome with emotion and looked as if she were about to die: a nervous convulsion passed across her whole face, at times making her head shake. Her eyes, deep-set, soft and blue, speak of profound suffering, borne with angelic calm. Her gaze, full of feeling, is all the more powerful in that she does not seek to make it so. Prematurely broken, she is ageless and it would not be possible, by looking at her, to guess how old she is. She is so weak that one would think she had not the strength to cling to life, she is wasting away, moribund, no longer of this earth – a shade. She has never recovered from the anguish she felt on the day of her accession to the throne; her conjugal duties consumed the remainder of her life.

She has given too many idols to Russia, too many children to the Tsar. 'Exhausted of Grand Dukes: what a fate!' remarked a Polish noblewoman, not feeling obliged to pay lip-service to what she hated in her heart.

Everyone sees the state of the Tsarina, but no one remarks on it. The Tsar loves her. Is she feverish? Confined to bed? He cares for her himself, watches at her bedside, prepares her drinks and gets her to take them, like a nurse. But as soon as she is on her feet, he kills her again with activity, entertainments, journeys, love-making. Certainly, as soon as any sign of danger appears, he abandons his plans; but he detests the precautions that would prevent harm; so, in Russia, wife, children, servants, relations, favourites, all must be drawn along with the imperial whirlwind, smiling unto death.

Marquis de Custine, from *Letters from Russia*, July 1839,
tr. Robin Buss, 1991

She rose to His Requirement – dropt
The Playthings of Her Life
To take the honorable Work
Of Woman, and of Wife –

If ought She missed in Her new Day,
Of Amplitude, or Awe –
Or first Prospective – Or the Gold
In using, wear away,

It lay unmentioned – as the Sea
Develop Pearl, and Weed,
But only to Himself – be known
The Fathoms they abide –

Emily Dickinson, c. 1863

I think you would be sorry if you began to feel that your desire to earn money, even for so laudable an object as to help your husband, made you unable to give your tender sympathy to your little ones in their small joys & sorrows; and yet, don't you know how you, – how every one, who tries to write stories *must* become absorbed in them, (fictitious though they be,) if they are to interest their readers in them. Besides viewing the subject from a solely artistic point of view a good writer of fiction must have *lived* an active & sympathetic life if she wishes her books to have strength & vitality in them. When you are forty, and if you have a gift for being an authoress you will write ten times as good a novel as you could do now, just because you will have gone through so much more of the interests of a wife and a mother . . .

Your MSS has not been forwarded to me along with your letter; so at present I have no opportunity of judging of its merits; when I have read it I will give you the best & truest opinion I can. I feel very sorry for you, for I think I can see that, at present, at least you are rather overwhelmed with all you have to do; and I think it possible that the birth of two children – one so close upon another may have weakened you bodily, and made you more unfit to cope with your many household duties. Try – even while waiting for my next letter, to strengthen yourself by every means in your power; by being very careful as to your diet; by cold-bathing, by resolute dwelling on the cheerful side of everything; and by learning to economize strength as much as possible in all your household labours; for I dare say you already know how much time may be saved, by beginning any kind of work in good time, and not driving all in a hurry to the last moment. I hope (for instance,) you soap & soak your dirty clothes well for some hours before beginning to wash; and that you understand the comfort of preparing a dinner & putting it on to cook *slowly*, early in the morning, as well as having *always* some kind of sewing ready arranged to your hand, so that you can take it up at any odd minute and do a few stitches. I dare say at present it might be difficult for you to procure the sum that is necessary to purchase a sewing machine; and indeed, unless you are a good workwoman to begin with, you will find a machine difficult to manage. But *try*, my dear, to conquer your 'clumsiness' in sewing; there are a thousand little bits of work, which no sempstress ever does so well as the wife or mother who knows how the comfort of those she loves depends on little peculiarities which no one but she cares enough for the wearers to attend to.

My first piece of advice to you would be *Get strong* – I am almost sure you are out of bodily health and that, if I were you, I would make it my first object to attain. Did you ever try a tea-cup full of *hop-tea* the first thing in the morning? It is a very simple tonic, and could do no harm. Then again try *hard* to arrange your work well. That is a regular piece of head-work and taxes a woman's powers of organization; but the reward is immediate and great. I have known well what it is to be both wanting money, & feeling weak in body and entirely disheartened. I do not think I ever cared for literary fame; nor do I think it *is* a thing that ought to be cared for. It comes and it goes. The exercise of a talent or power *is* always a great pleasure; but one should weigh well whether this pleasure may not be obtained by the sacrifice of some duty.

Elizabeth Gaskell, Letter to an unknown correspondent, 25 September 1862


When you see what some girls marry, you realize how much they must hate to work for a living.

Helen Rowland, from *Reflections of a Bachelor Girl*, 1909


For the majority of the 1,250 women under review the ordinary routine seems to be as follows. Most of them get up at 6.30. If their husband and/or sons are miners, or bakers, or on any nightshift, they may have to get up at 4 (possibly earlier), make breakfast for those members of the family, and then, if they feel disposed to further sleep, go back to bed for another hour's rest. The same woman who does this has probably got a young child or even a baby, who wakes up early, and sleeping in the same room will in no case give his mother much peace after 6 a.m. If there is a suckling baby as well, (and it must be remembered that the woman who has had seven or eight children before the age of 35 has never been without a tiny baby or very young child,) she will have had to nurse him at least as late as 10 the night before. There are many complaints of children who for some reason or other disturb the night's rest. Her bed is shared not only by her husband but, in all probability, by one *at least* of her young family. Sleeplessness is not often spoken of in this investigation, because it is not considered an ailment, but it is quite clear that a good night's rest in a well-aired, quiet room and in a comfortable, well-covered bed, is practically unknown to the majority of these mothers. A woman can become accustomed to very little sleep just as she can to very little food.

When once she is up there is no rest at all till after dinner. She is on her legs the whole time. She has to get her husband off to work, the children washed, dressed and fed and sent to school. If she has a large family, even if she has only the average family of this whole group, four or five children, she is probably very poor and therefore lives in a very bad house, or a house extremely inadequately fitted for her needs. Her washing up will not only therefore be heavy, but it may have to be done under the worst conditions. She may have to go down (or up) two or three flights of stairs to get her water, and again to empty it away. She may have to heat it on the open fire, and she may have to be looking after the baby and the toddler at the same time. When this is done, she must clean the house. If she has the average family, the rooms are very 'full of beds', and this will make her cleaning much more difficult than if she had twice the number of rooms with half the amount of furniture in each. She lacks the utensils too; and lacking any means to get hot water except by the kettle on the fire, she will be as careful as possible not to waste a drop. The school-children will be back for their dinner soon after 12, so she must begin her cooking in good time. Great difficulties confront her here. She has not got more than one or two sauce pans and a frying pan, and so even if she is fortunate in having some proper sort of cooking stove, it is impossible to cook a dinner as it should be cooked, slowly and with the vegetables separately; hence the ubiquitous stew, with or without the remains of the Sunday meat according to the day of the week. She has nowhere to store food, or if there is a cupboard room, it is inevitably in the only living room and probably next to the fireplace. Conditions may be so bad in this respect that she must go out in the middle of her morning's work to buy for dinner. This has the advantage of giving her and the baby a breath of fresh air during the morning; otherwise, unless there is a garden or yard, the baby, like herself is penned up in the 9 ft square kitchen during the whole morning.

Dinner may last from 12 till 3. Her husband or a child at work may have quite different hours from the school-children, and it is quite usual to hear this comment. Very often she does not sit down herself to meals. The serving of five or six other people demands so much jumping up and down that she finds it easier to take her meals standing. If she is nursing a baby, she will sit down for that, and in this way 'gets more rest'. She does this after the children have returned to school. Sometimes the heat and stuffiness of the kitchen in which she has spent all or most of her morning takes her off her food, and she does not feel inclined to eat at all, or only a bite when the others have all finished and gone away. Then comes the same process of washing up, only a little more difficult because dinner is a greasier meal than breakfast. After that, with luck at 2 or 2.30 but sometimes much later, if dinner for any reason has had to go on longer, she can tidy herself up and rest, or go out, or sit down.

Then comes tea, first the children's and then her husband's, when he comes home from work; and by the time that is all over and washed up it is time the children began to go to bed. If she is a good manager she will get them all into bed by 8, perhaps even earlier, and then at last, at last, 'a little peace and quietude!' She sits down again, after having been twelve or fourteen hours at work, mostly on her feet (and this means *standing* about, not *walking*,) and perhaps she then has a 'quiet talk with hubby', or listens to the wireless, 'our one luxury'. Perhaps her husband reads the paper to her. She has got a lot of sewing to do, so she doesn't read much to herself, and she doesn't go out because she can't leave the children unless her husband undertakes to keep house for one evening a week, while she goes to the pictures or for a walk. There is no money to spare anyhow for the pictures, or very seldom. She may or may not have a bite of supper with her husband, cocoa and bread and butter, or possibly a bit of fried fish. And so to bed – to her share of the bed, mostly at about 10.30 or 11 . . .

There is also no avoidance of the other great labour which is superimposed on the ordinary round, the labour of child-bearing. The work will have to be done in the same way for those nine months before the baby comes and for the two or three months after she is about again but still not feeling 'quite herself'. The baby will probably be born in the bed which has already been described, the bed shared by other members of the family, and in the room of the use of which, even if she can get the bed to herself for a week, she cannot possibly deprive the family for more than a few hours. It is out of the question, she thinks, to go to hospital, and to leave her husband and children either to fend for themselves – or to the care of a stranger, or of an already overworked but friendly neighbour. Even if she is in bed, she is at least in her own home; and can direct operations, even perhaps doing some of the 'smaller' jobs herself – like drying crockery, ironing, and of course the eternal mending. How is it possible that she should stay in bed for long enough to regain her full physical strength, the strength that has been taxed not only in the actual labour of child-birth, but in six or seven of the preceding months, when every household duty has been more difficult to accomplish and has involved a far greater strain than it does when she is in her 'normal' health?

Margery Spring Rice, from *Working-Class Wives*, 1939

## Portrait of a Nun

The smile folded as a marriage-veil
hoarded in heaven

Over her abdomen
the hands crossed: consequence
of a mystic conception

The nostril: arched for incense –

The mourning and the starching
of her body's concealing:
a cloth coffin

Her face wrapping: a white napkin –

The round halo rising
through her flesh shining:
virgin apple to angels' offering

The ascensional eyes:
pointed skyward as a crown
or now cast down.

A nun
seeing no one
but Jesus
is gentle to us

    Mina Loy, from *The Last Lunar Baedeker*, 1923


## Two Women

Daily to a profession – paid thinking
and clean hands – she rises,
unquestioning. It's second nature now.
The hours, though they're all of daylight, suit her.
The desk, typewriter, carpets, pleasantries
are a kind of civilization – built on money
of course, but money, now she sees, is human.
She has learnt giving from a bright new chequebook,
intimacy from absence. Coming home
long after dark to the jugular torrent

of family life, she brings,
tucked in her bag, the simple, cool-skinned apples
of a father's loving objectivity.
That's half the story. There's another woman
who bears her name, a silent, background face
that's always flushed with work, or swallowed anger.
A true wife, she picks up scattered laundry
and sets the table with warmed plates to feed
the clean-handed woman. They've not met.
If they were made to touch, they'd burn each other.

Carol Rumens, from *Selected Poems*, 1987

# Housework

## *Thoughts After Ruskin*

Women reminded him of lilies and roses.
Me they remind rather of blood and soap,
Armed with a warm rag, assaulting noses,
Ears, neck, mouth and all the secret places.

Armed with a sharp knife, cutting up liver,
Holding hearts to bleed under a running tap,
Gutting and stuffing, pickling and preserving,
Scalding, blanching, broiling, pulverizing,
– All the terrible chemistry of their kitchens.

Their distant husbands lean across mahogany
And delicately manipulate the market,
While safe at home, the tender and the gentle
Are killing tiny mice, dead snap by the neck,
Asphyxiating flies, evicting spiders,
Scrubbing, scouring aloud, disturbing cupboards,
Committing things to dustbins, twisting, wringing,
Wrists red and knuckles white and fingers puckered,
Pulpy, tepid. Steering screaming cleaners
Around the nags of furniture, they straighten
And haul out sheets from under the incontinent

And heavy old, stoop to importunate young,
Tugging, folding, tucking, zipping, buttoning,
Spooning in food, encouraging excretion,
Mopping up vomit, stabbing cloth with needles,
Contorting wool around their knitting needles,
Creating snug and comfy on their needles.

Their huge hands! their everywhere eyes! their voices
Raised to convey across the hullabaloo,
Their massive thighs and breasts dispensing comfort,
Their bloody passages and hairy crannies,
Their wombs that pocket a man upside down!

And when all's over, off with overalls,
Quickly consulting clocks, they go upstairs,
Sit and sigh a little, brushing hair,
And somehow find, in mirrors, colours, odours,
Their essences of lilies and of roses.

    Elma Mitchell, from *The Poor Man in the Flesh*, 1976

## Woman Work

I've got the children to tend
The clothes to mend
The floor to mop
The food to shop
Then the chicken to fry
The baby to dry
I got company to feed
The garden to weed
I've got the shirts to press
The tots to dress
The cane to be cut
I gotta clean up this hut
Then see about the sick
And the cotton to pick.

Shine on me, sunshine
Rain on me, rain
Fall softly, dewdrops
And cool my brow again.

Storm, blow me from here
With your fiercest wind
Let me float across the sky
'Til I can rest again.

Fall gently, snowflakes
Cover me with white
Cold icy kisses and
Let me rest tonight.

Sun, rain, curving sky
Mountain, oceans, leaf and stone
Star shine, moon glow
You're all that I can call my own.
  Maya Angelou, from *And Still I Rise*, 1986


## Dusting

Every day a wilderness – no
shade in sight. Beulah
patient among knicknacks,
the solarium a rage
of light, a grainstorm
as her gray cloth brings
dark wood to life.

Under her hand scrolls
and crests gleam
darker still. What
was his name, that
silly boy at the fair with
the rifle booth? And his kiss and
the clear bowl with one bright
fish, rippling
wound!

Not Michael –
something finer. Each dust
stroke a deep breath and
the canary in bloom.
Wavery memory: home
from a dance, the front door

blown open, and the parlor
in snow, she rushed the bowl to the stove, watched
as the locket of ice
dissolved and he
swam free.

That was years before
Father gave her up
with her name, years before
her name grew to mean
Promise, then
Desert-in-Peace.
Long before the shadow and
sun's accomplice, the tree.

Maurice.

Rita Dove, from *Thomas and Beulah*, 1986

# Washing Day

### *The Shirt of a Lad*

As I did the washing one day
Under the bridge at Aberteifi,
And a golden stick to drub it,
And my sweetheart's shirt beneath it –
A knight came by upon a charger,
Proud and swift and broad of shoulder,
And he asked if I would sell
The shirt of the lad that I loved well.

No, I said, I will not trade –
Not if a hundred pounds were paid;
Not if two hillsides I could keep
Full with wethers and white sheep;
Not if two fields full of oxen
Under yoke were in the bargain;
Not if the herbs of all Llanddewi,
Trodden and pressed, were offered to me –

Not for the likes of that, I'd sell
The shirt of the lad that I love well.

Anon., sixteenth century<br>
tr. from the Welsh by Anthony Conran, 1967

## Washing Day

Come, Muse, and sing the dreaded Washing-Day.
Ye who beneath the yoke of wedlock bend,
With bowed soul, full well ye ken the day
Which week, smooth sliding after week, brings on
Too soon – for to that day nor peace belongs
Nor comfort; ere the first gray streak of dawn,
The red-armed washers come and chase repose.
Nor pleasant smile, nor quaint device of mirth,
E'er visited that day: the very cat,
From the wet kitchen scared and reeking hearth,
Visits the parlour – an unwonted guest.
The silent breakfast-meal is soon dispatched;
Uninterrupted, save by anxious looks
Cast at the lowering sky, if sky should lower.
From that last evil, O preserve us, heavens!
For should the skies pour down, adieu to all
Remains of quiet: then expect to hear
Of sad disasters – dirt and gravel stains
Hard to efface, and loaded lines at once
Snapped short – and linen-horse by dog thrown down,
And all the petty miseries of life.
Saints have been calm while stretched upon the rack,
And Guatimozin smiled on burning coals;
But never yet did housewife notable
Greet with a smile a rainy washing-day.

– But grant the welkin fair, require not thou
Who call'st thyself perchance the master there,
Or study swept, or nicely dusted coat,
Or usual 'tendance; ask not, indiscreet,
Thy stockings mended, though the yawning rents
Gape wide as Erebus; nor hope to find

Some snug recess impervious; shouldst thou try
The 'customed garden walks, thine eye shall rue
The budding fragrance of thy tender shrubs,
Myrtle or rose, all crushed beneath the weight
Of coarse checked apron – with impatient hand
Twitched off when showers impend: or crossing lines
Shall mar thy musings, as the wet cold sheet
Flaps in thy face abrupt . . .

I well remember, when a child, the awe
This day struck into me; for then the maids,
I scarce knew why, looked cross, and drove me from them:
Nor soft caress could I obtain, nor hope
Usual indulgences; jelly or creams,
Relic of costly suppers, and set by
For me their petted one; or buttered toast,
When butter was forbid; or thrilling tale
Of ghost or witch, or murder – so I went
And sheltered me beside the parlour fire:
There my dear grandmother, eldest of forms,
Tended the little ones, and watched from harm,
Anxiously fond, though oft her spectacles
With elfin cunning hid, and oft the pins
Drawn from her ravelled stocking, might have soured
One less indulgent.
At intervals my mother's voice was heard,
Urging dispatch: briskly the work went on,
All hands employed to wash, to rinse, to wring,
To fold, and starch, and clap, and iron, and plait.

Then would I sit me down, and ponder much
Why washings were. Sometimes through hollow bowl
Of pipe amused we blew, and sent aloft
The floating bubbles; little dreaming then
To see, Montgolfier, thy silken ball
Ride buoyant through the clouds – so near approach
The sports of children and the toils of men.
Earth, air, and sky, and ocean, hath its bubbles,
And verse is one of them – this most of all.

Anna Laetitia Barbauld, 1797

The workhouse was about halfway up the street, just where the road began to go uphill . . . It was an immense shed with a flat roof, exposed beams supported by cast-iron pillars, and enclosed by clear glass windows. A wan daylight penetrated the hot steam hanging like a milky fog. Clouds rising here and there spread out and veiled the background in a bluish haze. Everywhere a heavy moisture rained down, laden with the smell of soap, a persistent, stale, dank aroma sharpened at times by a whiff of bleach. A row of women stretched along the washing-boards down each side of the central passage; their arms were bare up to the shoulders, dresses turned down at the neck, skirts caught up, showing their coloured stockings and heavy laced boots. They were all banging furiously, laughing, leaning back to bawl through the din, bending forwards into their washtubs, a foul-mouthed, rough, ungainly looking lot, sopping wet as though they had been rained on, with red, steaming flesh. All round and underneath them water was slopping about, from pails of hot water being carried along and shot straight at their target, taps of cold water left on and piddling down, splashes from beaters, drips from washing already rinsed, and the pools they were standing in wandered off in streamlets over the uneven flagstones. And amid the shouting, the rhythmical beating, the swishing of the downpour, amid this storm of noise muffled by the damp ceiling, the steam engine over on the right-hand side, white with a fine dew of condensation, chuffed and snorted away without respite, and its dancing flywheel seemed to be regulating the outrageous din . . .

. . . the vibration and snorting of the steam engine went on and on, without rest or pause, and seemed to emerge louder and louder until it filled the immense hall. But not one of the women noticed it, for it was like the very breathing of the washhouse, a fiery breath blowing the eternal floating mist upwards to collect among the rafters. The heat was becoming unbearable; the rays of light, striking in through the high windows to the left, turned the steamy vapour into opalescent streaks of the softest rosy-grey and grey-blue . . . It was the uphill part of the afternoon and washing was being banged for dear life. In the vast shed the steam took on a ruddy hue, broken here and there by circles of sunlight, golden globules coming through holes in the blinds. The very air you breathed was stifling hot and smelt of soap. All of a sudden the shed was filled with white vapour; the huge lid of the copper in which the washing was boiled was raised mechanically on its ratchet, and the gaping hole in its setting of brickwork belched forth clouds of steam with the sickly smell of potash. And to one side were working the driers in which bundles of washing were spun round in cast-iron cylinders, shooting out all their water as the machine turned its flywheel, puffing and blowing and making the whole place vibrate with the ceaseless plunging of its steel arms.

Emile Zola, from *L'Assommoir*, 1876,

tr. L. W. Tancock, 1970

My grandmother was a dear old dame, whose chief consolations in her last days were a pinch of snuff and half a glass of gin before bedtime. At that period the snuff-box was always in her hand, but the glass was never seen except late in the evening. Anne Morris, to give her her maiden name, had a couple of personal peculiarities: she had only one leg, but, to make up for it, two eyes of different colours – one hazel, the other blue. The leg which she had not had been lost in a Worcestershire nail factory, where she had been employed as a girl, and where the constant standing on a damp floor had induced a disease that necessitated amputation. I well remember another feature too – the hard and unsightly corns on the old lady's knuckles, which were almost as large as the knuckles themselves. When she was left with a family of five girls, she and they set up a laundry – not a laundry in the modern, but in the ancient acceptation of the term. The corns were the result of the hard scrubbing and rubbing she used to bestow on the shirts and skirts of her patrons. It came to pass in her closing days, when her daughters, having embarked on other enterprises, were able to relieve her of the drudgery of the washtub, that her hands became as white and soft as a baby's . . .

Concerning this laundry business, allusion to it would not have been introduced if there hadn't been a lesson to be drawn. It was an honest occupation – as honest, say, as stock-jobbing.

There was nothing in the whole episode of which any mortal need be ashamed. Yet dainty people would perhaps consider that it was a fact to be concealed. Let us understand each other. Work of any sort is honourable. It is idleness, and especially that form of idleness which is called loafing, that is disgraceful. Dickens never appeared to me so snobbish and contemptible as when he whined and whimpered about the degradation of having as a boy to earn a few shillings a week by pasting labels on blacking bottles. The thing is, however, not only to work, but to work well – to put the best that is in us into everything we do. Theodore Parker in one of his powerful sermons tells us that Michael sweeping round a lamp-post or Bridget sweeping out a kitchen, assuming that the work is honestly done, is as meritorious as Paul preaching on Mars' Hill. 'Work is worship.' Honesty in work as in all things else. The same doctrine is taught by Emerson, Carlyle, Ruskin, and every great thinker who has expatiated on the subject. 'All service ranks the same with God,' writes Browning, whose ancestor was a footman. Well, the humble and industrious women who laboured amidst suds and steam carried into practice the precepts of the philosophers. The washtub and the mangle were dignified by what they did with them. As Cromwell's Ironsides put a conscience into marching and fighting, so did these poor women put a conscience into scrubbing and ironing. None of the gentry for whom they worked ever had reason to complain that their cuffs and collars, their flounces and their furbelows, were not returned without a sign of previous wear. Thus did widow and orphans earn the title to a place beside Paul on Mars' Hill. Mr Ruskin proudly described his father as 'an entirely honest merchant'. I say as proudly of my grandmother that she was 'an entirely honest washerwoman'.

W. E. Adams, from *Memoirs of a Social Atom*, 1903

# Churning Day

### *Charm of the Church*

Come will the free, come;
Come will the bond, come;
Come will the bells, come;
Come will the maers, come;
Come will the blade, come;
Come will the sharp, come;
Come will the hounds, come;
Come will the wild, come;
Come will the mild, come;
Come will the kind, come;
Come will the loving, come;
Come will the squint, come;
Come will he of the yellow cap,
That will set the churn a-running.

The free will come,
The bond will come,
The bells will come,
The maers will come,
The blades will come,
The sharp will come,
The hounds will come,
The wild will come,
The mild will come,
The kind will come,

The loving will come,
The devious will come,
The brim-full of the globe will come,
To set the churn a-running;
The kindly Columba will come in his array,
And the golden-haired Bride of the kine.

> Trad., from *Carmina Gadelica: Charms of the Gaels*, no. 191,
> collected and translated by Alexander Carmichael, 1992

### The Milk-Maid o' the Farm

O Poll's the milk-maïd o' the farm!
  An' Poll's so happy out in groun',
Wi' her white païl below her eärm
  As if she wore a goolden crown.

An' Poll don't zit up half the night,
  Nor lie vor half the day a-bed;
An' zoo her eyes be sparklen bright,
  An' zoo her cheäks be bloomen red.

In zummer mornens, when the lark
  Do rouse the litty lad an' lass
To work, then she's the vu'st to mark
  Her steps along the dewy grass.

An' in the evenen, when the zun
  Do sheen ageän the western brows
O' hills, where bubblen brooks do run,
  There she do zing bezide her cows.

An' ev'ry cow of hers do stand,
  An' never overzet her païl;
Nor try to kick her nimble hand,
  Nor switch her wi' her heavy taïl.

Noo leädy, wi' her muff an' vaïl,
  Do walk wi' sich a steätely tread
As she do, wi' her milken païl
  A-balanc'd on her comely head.

An' she, at mornen an' at night,
  Do skim the yollow cream, an' mwold

An' wring her cheeses red an' white,
  An' zee the butter vetch'd an' roll'd.

An' in the barken or the ground,
  The chaps do always do their best
To milk the vu'st their own cows round,
  And, then help her to milk the rest.

Zoo Poll's the milkmaïd o' the farm!
  An' Poll's so happy out in groun',
Wi' her white païl below her eärm,
  As if she wore a goolden crown.

William Barnes, 1879

## Churning Day

A thick crust, coarse-grained as limestone rough-cast,
hardened gradually on top of the four crocks
that stood, large pottery bombs, in the small pantry.
After the hot brewery of gland, cud and udder
cool porous earthenware fermented the buttermilk
for churning day, when the hooped churn was scoured
with plumping kettles and the busy scrubber
echoed daintily on the seasoned wood.
It stood then, purified, on the flagged kitchen floor.

Out came the four crocks, spilled their heavy lip
of cream, their white insides, into the sterile churn.
The staff, like a great whisky muddler fashioned
in deal wood, was plunged in, the lid fitted.
My mother took first turn, set up rhythms
that slugged and thumped for hours. Arms ached.
Hands blistered. Cheeks and clothes were spattered
with flabby milk.

          Where finally gold flecks
began to dance. They poured hot water then,
sterilized a birchwood-bowl
and little corrugated butter-spades.
Their short stroke quickened, suddenly
a yellow curd was weighting the churned up white,
heavy and rich, coagulated sunlight

that they fished, dripping, in a wide tin strainer,
heaped up like gilded gravel in the bowl.

The house would stink long after churning day,
acrid as a sulphur mine. The empty crocks
were ranged along the wall again, the butter
in soft printed slabs was piled on pantry shelves.
And in the house we moved with gravid ease,
our brains turned crystals full of clean deal churns,
the plash and gurgle of the sour-breathed milk,
the pat and slap of small spades on wet lumps.

Seamus Heaney, from *Death of a Naturalist*, 1966


# The Servant

*Saturday 7 March* [1863]   Got up early, for they all went to Temple Bar to
see the princess come through. They all got off in carriages before 9 o'clock
– Mary the housemaid & Sarah as well & I was left, & it was a first-rate
chance for me to get some cleaning done. I black'd the grates & that & clean'd
3 pairs of boots. Took the breakfast up & Mr Garle came down & ask'd me
to brush his trousers & I did 'em for him, kneeling on the floor & wi' him
putting his foot on a chair for the bottoms. I stood in the hall & watch'd 'em
off & then I had some breakfast. Clean'd away upstairs & wash'd the things
up. Put coals on the fire. Went up & made all the beds & emptied the slops.
Came down & swept the dining room all over & dusted it. Swept the hall &
steps & shook the mats & then I had a mutton chop & some beer for my
dinner. Clean'd the windows in the hall & passage & clean'd the hall & steps
on my knees, the back stairs, then I was got to the passage. I took the matting
out & shook it. Swept the passage & took the things out of the hole under
the stairs – Mary uses it for her dustpans & brushes. It's a dark hole & about
2 yards long & very low. I crawl'd in on my hands & knees & lay curl'd up in
the dirt for a minute or so & then I got the handbrush & swept the walls
down. The cobwebs & dust fell all over me & I had to poke my nose out o'
the door to get breath, like a dog's out of a kennel. Then I swept the floor of
it & got my pail & clean'd it out & put the things back in their places. I was
very black as I could be, but I didn't wash till I'd clean'd the passage & 'tatoe
hole out & the shelves & back cellar, & then I finish'd in the kitchen & made
the fires up & wash'd my face & hands. Shut the shutters & lit the lamp. Shut
all the windows upstairs, for it began to rain & was getting dusk & I saw the

people rushing home again as much as they did to *go* & see the procession, & there was hundreds went past young & old & some wi' children even.

The first part of the family came back at six & was ready for tea. The Mistress said she was very glad to be at home again, it'd been such a hard day for her. She said that as I carried the umbrella over her from the front gate. I carri'd the tea things up & all that & waited on them all they wanted, & then a lot more came in & I wash'd up & took up fresh tea. Clean'd away again & then laid the cloth for supper & cook'd the potatoes. Carried the supper up & waited on them. Clean'd more knives & wash'd plates. Clean'd away & laid the kitchen cloth for Mary & the waiter & us all. Had supper. Put away & then I went to bed very tired & in my dirt.

from *The Diaries of Hannah Cullwick*,
ed. Liz Stanley, 1984

### 'Au pair'

Home she went, to the big white house by the river. The middle of a weekday, and she felt guilty at returning to her own home when not expected. She stood unseen, looking in at the kitchen window. Mrs Parkes, wearing a discarded floral overall of Susan's, was stooping to slide something into the oven. Sophie, arms folded, was leaning her back against a cupboard and laughing at some joke made by a girl not seen before by Susan – a dark foreign girl, Sophie's visitor. In an armchair Molly, one of the twins, lay curled, sucking her thumb and watching the grownups. She must have some sickness, to be kept from school. The child's listless face, the dark circles under her eyes, hurt Susan: Molly was looking at the three grownups working and talking in exactly the same way Susan looked at the four through the kitchen window: she was remote, shut off from them.

But then, just as Susan imagined herself going in, picking up the little girl, and sitting in an armchair with her, stroking her probably heated forehead, Sophie did just that: she had been standing on one leg, the other knee flexed, its foot set against the wall. Now she let her foot in its ribbon-tied red shoe slide down the wall, stood solid on two feet, clapping her hands before and behind her, and sang a couple of lines in German, so that the child lifted her heavy eyes at her and began to smile. Then she walked, or rather skipped, over to the child, swung her up, and let her fall into her lap at the same moment she sat herself. She said: 'Hopla! Hopla! Molly . . .' and began stroking the dark untidy young head that Molly laid on her shoulder for comfort.

*Well* . . . Susan blinked the tears of farewell out of her eyes, and went quietly up the house to her bedroom. There she sat looking at the river through the trees. She felt at peace, but in a way that was new to her. She had no desire to move, to talk, to do anything at all. The devils that had haunted the house, the garden, were not there; but she knew it was because her soul was in Room 19 in Fred's Hotel; she was not really here at all. It was a sensation that should have been frightening: to sit at her own bedroom window, listening to Sophie's rich young voice sing German nursery songs to her child, listening to Mrs Parkes clatter and move below, and to know that all this had nothing to do with her: she was already out of it.

Later, she made herself go down and say she was home: it was unfair to be here unannounced. She took lunch with Mrs Parkes, Sophie, Sophie's Italian friend Maria, and her daughter Molly, and felt like a visitor.

Doris Lessing, 'To Room Nineteen', from *A Man and Two Women*, 1963

## Warming Her Pearls

Next to my own skin, her pearls. My mistress
bids me wear them, warm them, until evening
when I'll brush her hair. At six, I place them
round her cool, white throat. All day I think of her,

resting in the Yellow Room, contemplating silk
or taffeta, which gown tonight? She fans herself
whilst I work willingly, my slow heat entering
each pearl. Slack on my neck, her rope.

She's beautiful. I dream about her
in my attic bed; picture her dancing
with tall men, puzzled by my faint, persistent scent
beneath her French perfume, her milky stones.

I dust her shoulders with a rabbit's foot,
watch the soft blush seep through her skin
like an indolent sigh. In her looking-glass
my red lips part as though I want to speak.

Full moon. Her carriage brings her home. I see
her every movement in my head . . . Undressing,
taking off her jewels, her slim hand reaching
for the case, slipping naked into bed, the way

she always does . . . And I lie here awake,
knowing the pearls are cooling even now

in the room where my mistress sleeps. All night
I feel their absence and I burn.
        Carol Ann Duffy, from *Selling Manhattan*, 1987


## *Physick and Chirugery*

I have fpoken enough concerning your Cloaths, and Face and Hands; now I
will give you direction for to be your own Chirurgions and Phyficians, unlefs
the cafe be defperate: but before I begin to teach, be pleafed to take notice of
what Cures I have done, that you may be affured of my ability.

Firft, Take notice that my Mother and my Elder Sifters vvere very vvell
skilled in Phyfick and Chirurgery, from vvhom I learned a little, and at the
age of feventeen I had the fortune to belong to a Noble Lady in this Kingdom,
till I Married, which was at twenty four years (thofe feven years I was with
her) fhe finding my genius, and being of a Charitable temper to do good
amongft her poor Neighbours, I had her purfe at command to buy what
Ingredients might be required to make Balfoms, Salves, Oyntments, Waters
for Wounds, Oyls, Cordials and the like; befides fhe procured fuch knowledge for me from her Phyficians and Chirurgions (who were the beft that all
*England* could afford) and alfo bought many Books for me to read, that in
fhort time, with the help of thofe Worthy men before mentioned, I foon
became a Practitioner, and did begin with Cut fingers, Bruifes, Aches, Agues,
Head-ach, Bleeding at the Nofe, Felons, Whitloes on the Fingers, Sore Eyes,
Drawing of Blifters, Burnings, Tooth-ach, and any thing which is commonly
incident; and in all thofe Cures God was pleafed to give me good fuccefs.

When I was about the age of two and twenty years, I was fent by this Noble
Lady to a Woman in hard labour of Child, who being quite wearied out with
her pains, fhe fell into ftrong Convulfion fits, which greatly endangered
both her felf and her Child; but by Gods help thofe Remedies which I gave
her caufed her Fits to ceafe, and a fafe Delivery followed.

When I was Married to Mr *Wolley*, we lived together at *Newport Pond* in
Effex near *Saffron Walden* feven years; my Husband having been Mafter of
that Free-School fourteen years before; we having many Boarders my skill was
often exercifed amongft them, for oftentimes they got mifhaps when they
were playing, and oftentimes fell into diftempers; as Agues, Feavors, Meazles,
Small-pox, Confumptions, and many other Difeafes; in all which, unlefs they
were defperately ill, their Parents trufted me without the help of any Phyfician
or Chirurgion: likewife the Neighbours in eight or ten miles round came to
me for Cure.

A Woman vvho had had a fore Leg one and twenty years I quite Cured.

Another being kicked by a Churliſh Husband on her Leg, ſo that a Vein vvas burſt, whereby ſhe loſt at the leaſt a pottle [4 pints] of Blood; I ſtayed the Blood and cured her Leg.

A young Maid as ſhe vvas cutting Sticks vvith an Ax, by chance cut her Leg ſorely, ſhe having long time been afflicted vvith the Green-ſickneſs and Dropſie; I not only Cured her Leg, but alſo her other Diſtempers at the ſame time.

A Gentleman having got a bruiſe on his Leg by the laſh of a Whip, and being in a deſperate condition with it, ſo that he was in danger of his life, I in a competent time did Cure.

Many of the Convulſion-fits, and Rickets among Children I did Cure.

One being bitten with a Mad-Dog, I in very ſhort time did Cure him.

Several Women who had ſore Breaſts and ſore Nipples, I Cured.

Many who had violent fits of the Stone, I eaſed them.

A Man being much bruiſed with the fall of a Cart upon him, I cured.

One being much bruiſed by Rogues meeting him on the way, and after they had beaten him down, kicked him on one ſide of his Head, ſo that his Ear was ſwelled you could ſee no ſhape it had, and withal fell into a Feavor: I, by Gods help did Cure.

A Woman who for divers Months had a very great Flux upon her, I ſpeedily Cured.

A man lying ſick of the Meazles, and being all ſtruck in, ſo that it was thought he could not poſſibly have lived, I gave him a Cordial which brought them forth again and recovered him.

A Child of a year old being taken with the ſhaking Palſie, I Cured.

A Man having a Pitch-fork run into the Corner of his Eye, I cured.

A Woman having a Stick run into the corner of her Eye, I Cured.

A little Boy falling from a Bridge into a little River, cut his Head ſo with a ſtone, that while I had it in Cure there came forth a ſliver of the Skull; I cured.

A Man taken ſuddenly with an Apoplex, as he walked the Street, his Neighbours taking him into a Houſe, and as they thought he was quite dead, I being called unto him, chanced to come juſt when they had taken the Pillow from his Head, and were going to ſtrip him; but I cauſed him to be ſet upright, and his mouth to be open by force, then did I give him ſomething out of a little glaſs, and cauſed him to be rubbed and chaffed, and Air to be given him, ſo that in a little time he came to himſelf and knew every one: He lived about ten hours after, and gave God and me thanks, that he was not taken away in that condition, but gave him ſence to make his Peace with God and to order what he had left. I willed him to ſend for a Phyſician; which he did, who did approve of what I had done, but could not ſave his life.

95

A Woman being ſtruck with a ſtaff upon the Lip, ſo that it was cut aſunder with the blow: I in ſhort time Cured.

Many I did cure in that Town, which were burned with Fire, and ſome ſcalded, and none of them had a Scar.

A Girle about twelve years of Age being taken with a Lethargy, and after I had brought her out of it ſhe fell into ſtrong and ſtrange Convulſion-fits, which in few weeks I did perfectly Cure.

After theſe Seven years were paſt, we lived at *Hackney*, near *London*, where we had above threeſcore Boarders; and there I had many more Trials for my Skill both at home and abroad.

I Cured my own Son of an Impoſtume in the Head, and of a deep Conſumption, after the Phyſicians had given him over.

I Cured a Woman of Threeſcore years old, who had lyen Bed-ridden half a year of a Timpany, and was not able to help her ſelf: This Cure I did in three days.

I Cured a Man-ſervant to a Gentleman, who had a ſore Leg by a fall from an high place, and it was grown ſo dangerous, that it was thought incurable.

I Cured a Bricklayer who had a ſore Leg by the fall of Timber, and becauſe he was poor his Chirurgion gave it over.

I Cured a Shoe-maker of a ſore Leg, who had ſpent three pounds on it before he came to me.

I Cured a poor Woman of a ſore Leg, who was adviſed by a Chirurgion to have it cut off.

A Cancer in the Noſe I have Cured.

Cankers in the Mouth and Throat.

The Green-ſickneſs in many. Dropſie, Jaundies, Scurvy, Sciatica, Griping of the Guts, Vomiting and Looſneſs.

And for the Palſie, whether Dead or Shaking, I am ſure none can give better Remedies, nor know it better than I do, having bought my Experience at a dear rate; there is none who have been more afflicted with it than my ſelf, and (I humbly bleſs God for it) there is no Perſon more freer from it than my ſelf, nor from any other Diſeaſe, and that is very much, I being now in my Two and fiftieth year.

Much more I could ſay, but I think I need not; for they who do believe any thing I write, will, I hope, have confidence to make uſe of theſe Receipts I ſhall give them without any fear. It is altogether as neceſſary that you ſhould know how to keep your Bodies in health, to preſerve your Eye-ſight and your Limbs, as it is to Feed or Cloath your ſelf. Therefore the more fully to accompliſh you, let me perſwade you not to ſlight, but to value what I ſhall teach, and give God the glory; who out of ſo mean things as I ſhall name, he ſhould, of his goodneſs to us, create in them ſo great a vertue. I do not attribute any thing but to his alone power, and give him praiſe when he pleſeth to make me an Inſtrument of doing good.

Hanna Woolley, from *A Supplement to the Queen-Like Closet; or A Little of Everything Presented To all Ingenious Ladies, and Gentlewomen*, 1674

Twice a week, when there is a concert in the big hall, the officers and the VADs are divided, by some unspoken rule – the officers sitting at one side of the room, the VADs in a white row on the other.

When my eyes rest for a moment on the motley of dressing-gowns, mackintoshes, uniforms, I inevitably see in the line one face set on a slant, one pair of eyes forsaking the stage and fixed on me in a steady, inoffensive beam.

This irritates me. The very lack of offence irritates me. But one grows to look for everything.

Afterwards in the dining-room during Mess he will ask politely: 'What did you think of the concert, Sister? Good show . . .'

How wonderful to be called Sister! Every time the uncommon name is used towards me I feel the glow of an implied relationship, something which links me to the speaker.

My Sister remarked: 'If it's only a matter of that, we can provide thrills for you here very easily.'

The name of my . . . admirer . . . is, after all, Pettitt. The other nurse in the Mess, who is very grand and insists on pronouncing his name in the French way, says he is 'of humble origin'.

He seems to have no relations and no visitors.

Out in the corridor I meditate on love.

Laying trays soothes the activity of the body, and the mind works softly.

I meditate on love. I say to myself that Mr Pettitt is to be envied. I am still the wonder of the unknown to him: I exist, walk, talk, every day beneath the beam of his eye, impenetrable.

He fell down again yesterday, and his foot won't heal. He has time before him.

But in a hospital one has never time, one is never sure. He has perhaps been here long enough to learn that – to feel the insecurity, the impermanency.

At any moment he may be forced to disappear into the secondary stage of convalescent homes.

Yes, the impermanency of life in a hospital! An everlasting dislocation of combinations.

Like nuns, one must learn to do with no nearer friend than God.

Bolts, in the shape of sudden, whimsical orders, are flung by an Almighty whom one does not see.

The Sister who is over me, the only Sister who can laugh at things other than jokes, is going in the first week of next month. Why? Where? She doesn't know, but only smiles at my impatience. She knows life – hospital life.

It unsettles me as I lay my spoons and forks. Sixty-five trays. It takes an hour to do. Thirteen pieces on each tray. Thirteen times sixty-five ... eight hundred and forty-five things to collect, lay, square up symmetrically. I make little absurd reflections and arrangements – taking a dislike to the knives because they will not lie still on the polished metal of the tray, but pivot on their shafts, and swing out at angles after my fingers have left them.

I love the long, the dim and lonely, corridor; the light centred in the gleam of the trays, salt-cellars, yellow butters, cylinders of glass ...

Impermanency ... I don't wonder the Sisters grow so secret, so uneager. How often stifled! How often torn apart!

It's heaven to me to be one of such a number of faces.

To see them pass into Mess like ghosts – gentleman, tinker, and tailor; each having shuffled home from death; each having known his life rock on its base ... not talking much – for what is there to say? – not laughing much, for they have been here too long – is a nightly pleasure to me.

Creatures of habit! All the coloured dressing-gowns range themselves round the two long tables – this man in this seat, that man by the gas-fire; this man with his wheel-chair drawn up at the end, that man at the corner where no one will jostle his arm.

Curious how these officers leave the hospital, so silently. Disappearances ... One face after another slips out of the picture, the unknown heart behind the face fixed intently on some other centre of life.

I went into a soldiers' ward to-night to inquire about a man who has pneumonia.

Round his bed there stood three red screens, and the busy, white-capped heads of two Sisters bobbed above the rampart.

It suddenly shocked me. What were they doing there? Why the screens? Why the look of strain in the eyes of the man in the next bed who could see behind the screens?

I went cold and stood rooted, waiting till one of them could come out and speak to me.

Soon they took away the screen nearest to me; they had done with it.

The man I was to inquire for has no nostrils; they were blown away, and he breathes through two pieces of red rubber tubing: it gave a more horrible look to his face than I have ever seen.

98

The Sister came out and told me she thought he was 'not up to much'. I think she means he is dying.

I wonder if he thinks it better to die . . . But he was nearly well before he got pneumonia, had begun to take up the little habits of living. He had been out to tea.

Inexplicable, what he thinks of, lying behind the screen.

Enid Bagnold, from A Diary Without Dates, 1918

## The Money Got by Labour

'I make moleskin trowsers. I get 7*d*. and 8*d*. per pair. I can do two pairs in a day, and twelve when there is full employment, in a week. But some weeks I have no work at all. I work from six in the morning to ten at night; that is what I call my day's work. When I am fully employed I get from 7*s*. to 8*s*. a week. My expenses out of that for twist, thread, and candles are about 1*s*. 6*d*. a week, leaving me about 6*s*. per week clear. But there's coals to pay for out of this, and that's at the least 6*d*. more; so 5*s*. 6*d* is the very outside of what I earn when I'm in full work. Lately I have been dreadfully slack; so we are every winter, all of us "sloppers", and that's the time when we wants the most money. The week before last I had but two pair to make all the week; so that I only earnt 1*s*. clear. For this last month I'm sure I haven't done any more than that each week. Taking one week with another, all the year round I don't make above 3*s*. clear money each week. I don't work at any other kind of slop-work. The trowsers work is held to be the best paid of all. I give 1*s*. a week rent.

'My father died when I was five years of age. My mother is a widow, upwards of 66 years of age, and seldom has a day's work. Generally once in the week she is employed pot-scouring – that is, cleaning publicans' pots. She is paid 4*d*. a dozen for that, and does about four dozen and a half, so that she gets about 1*s*. 6*d*. in the day by it. For the rest she is dependent upon me. I am 20 years of age the 25th of this month. We earn together, to keep the two of us, from 4*s*. 6*d*. to 5*s*. each week. Out of this we have to pay 1*s*. rent, and there remains 3*s*. 6*d*. to 4*s*. to find us both in food and clothing. It is of course impossible for us to live upon it, and the consequences is I am obligated to go a bad way. I have been three years working at slop-work . . .

'Many young girls at the shop advised me to go wrong. They told me how comfortable they was off; they said they could get plenty to eat and drink, and good clothes. There isn't one young girl as can get her living by slop-work. The masters all know this, but they wouldn't own to it of course. It stands to reason that no one can live and pay rent, and find clothes, upon 3s. a week, which is the most they can make clear, even the best hands, at the moleskin and cord trowsers work. There's poor people moved out of our house that was making three-farthing shirts. I am satisfied there is not one young girl that works at slop-work that is virtuous, and there are some thousands in the trade. They may do very well if they have got mothers and fathers to find them a home and food, and to let them have what they earn for clothes; then they may be virtuous, but not without. I've heard of numbers who have gone from slop-work to the streets altogether for a living, and I shall be obliged to do the same thing myself unless something better turns up for me.

'If I was never allowed to speak no more, it was the little money I got by my labour that led me to go wrong. Could I have honestly earnt enough to have subsisted upon, to find me in proper food and clothing, such as is necessary, I should not have gone astray; no, never – As it was I fought against it as long as I could – that I did – to the last. I hope to be able to get a ticket for a midwife; a party has promised me as much, and, he says, if possible, he'll get me an order for a box of linen. My child will only increase my burdens, and if my young man won't support my child I must go on the streets altogether. I know how horrible all this is. It would have been much better for me to have subsisted upon a dry crust and water rather than be as I am now. But no one knows the temptations of us poor girls in want. Gentlefolks can never understand it. If I had been born a lady it wouldn't have been very hard to have acted like one. To be poor and to be honest, especially with young girls, is the hardest struggle of all. There isn't one in a thousand that can get the better of it. I am ready to say again, that it was want, and nothing more, that made me transgress. If I had been better paid I should have done better. Young as I am, my life is a curse to me. If the Almighty would please to take me before my child is born, I should die happy.'

Anon., 1849, from *The Unknown Mayhew*,
ed. Eileen Yeo and E. P. Thompson, 1971

The paintresses form the *noblesse* of the banks. Their task is a light one, demanding deftness first of all; they have delicate fingers, and enjoy a general reputation for beauty: the wages they earn may be estimated from their finery on Sundays. They come to business in cloth jackets, carry dinner in little satchels; in the shop they wear white aprons, and look startlingly neat and tidy. Across the benches over which they bend their coquettish heads gossip flies and returns like a shuttle; they are the source of a thousand intrigues, and one or other of them is continually getting married or omitting to get married. On the bank they constitute 'the sex'. An infinitesimal proportion of them, from among the branch known as ground-layers, die of lead-poisoning – a fact which adds pathos to their frivolous charm. In a subsidiary room off the painting-shop a single girl was seated at a revolving table actuated by a treadle. She was doing the 'band-and-line' on the rims of saucers. Mynors and Anna watched her as with her left hand she flicked saucer after saucer into the exact centre of the table, moved the treadle, and, holding a brush firmly against the rim of the piece, produced with infallible exactitude the band and the line. She was a brunette, about twenty-eight: she had a calm, vacuously contemplative face; but God alone knew whether she thought. Her work represented the summit of monotony; the regularity of it hypnotized the observer, and Mynors himself was impressed by this stupendous phenomenon of absolute sameness, involuntarily assuming towards it the attitude of a showman.

'She earns as much as eighteen shillings a week sometimes,' he whispered.

Arnold Bennett, from *Anna of the Five Towns*, 1902

## The Light of Intellect

Women often strive to live by intellect. The clear, brilliant, sharp radiance of intellect's moonlight rising upon such an expanse of snow is dreary, it is true, but some love its solemn desolation, its silence, its solitude – if they are but *allowed* to live in it; if they are not perpetually balked or disappointed. But a woman cannot live in the light of intellect. Society forbids it. Those conventional frivolities, which are called her 'duties', forbid it. Her 'domestic duties', high-sounding words, which, for the most part, are bad habits (which she has not the courage to enfranchise herself from, the strength to break through) forbid it. What are these duties (or bad habits)? – Answering a multitude of letters which lead to nothing, from her so-called friends, keeping herself up to the level of the world that she may furnish her quota of amusement at the breakfast-table; driving out her company in the carriage. And all these things are exacted from her by her family which, if she is good and affectionate, will have more influence with her than the world . . .

Women are never supposed to have any occupation of sufficient importance *not* to be interrupted, except 'suckling their fools'; and women themselves have accepted this, have written books to support it, and have trained themselves so as to consider whatever they do as *not* of such value to the world or to others, but that they can throw it up at the first 'claim of social life'. They have accustomed themselves to consider intellectual opposition as a merely selfish amusement, which it is their 'duty' to give up for every trifler more selfish than themselves.

A young man (who was afterwards useful and known in his day and generation) when busy reading and sent for by his proud mother to shine in some morning visit, came; but, after it was over, he said, 'Now, remember, this is not to happen again. I came that you might not think me sulky, but I shall not come again.' But for a young woman to send such a message to her mother and sisters, how impertinent it would be! A woman of great administrative powers said that she never undertook anything which she 'could not throw by at once, if necessary'.

How do we explain then the many cases of women who have distinguished themselves in classics, mathematics, even in politics?

Widowhood, ill-health, or want of bread, these three explanations or excuses are supposed to justify a woman taking up an occupation. In some cases, no doubt, an indomitable force of character will suffice without any of these three, but such are rare.

Florence Nightingale, from *Cassandra*, 1852

The days darkened. Through November rains and fogs Marian went her usual way to the Museum, and toiled there among the other toilers. Perhaps once a week she allowed herself to stray about the alleys of the Reading-room, scanning furtively those who sat at the desks, but the face she might perchance have discovered was not there.

One day at the end of the month she sat with books open before her, but by no effort could fix her attention upon them. It was gloomy, and one could scarcely see to read; a taste of fog grew perceptible in the warm, headachy air. Such profound discouragement possessed her that she could not even maintain the pretence of study; heedless whether anyone observed her, she let her hands fall and her head droop. She kept asking herself what was the use and purpose of such a life as she was condemned to lead. When already there was more good literature in the world than any mortal could cope with in his lifetime, here was she exhausting herself in the manufacture of printed stuff which no one even pretended to be more than a commodity for the day's market. What unspeakable folly! To write – was not that the joy and the privilege of one who had an urgent message for the world? Her father, she knew well, had no such message: he had abandoned all thought of original production, and only wrote about writing.

She herself would throw away her pen with joy but for the need of earning money. And all these people about her, what aim had they save to make new books out of those already existing, that yet newer books might in turn be made out of theirs? This huge library, growing into unwieldiness, threatening to become a trackless desert of print – how intolerably it weighed upon the spirit!

Oh, to go forth and labour with one's hands, to do any poorest, commonest work of which the world had truly need! It was ignoble to sit here and support the paltry pretence of intellectual dignity. A few days ago her startled eye had caught an advertisement in the newspaper, headed 'Literary Machine'; had it then been invented at last, some automaton to supply the place of such poor creatures as herself, to turn out books and articles? Alas! the machine was only one for holding volumes conveniently, that the work of literary manufacture might be physically lightened. But surely before long some Edison would make the true automaton; the problem must be comparatively such a simple one. Only to throw in a given number of old books, and have them reduced, blended, modernized into a single one for today's consumption.

The fog grew thicker; she looked up at the windows beneath the dome and saw that they were a dusky yellow. Then her eye discerned an official walking along the upper gallery, and in pursuance of her grotesque humour, her mocking misery, she likened him to a black, lost soul, doomed to wander in an eternity of vain research along endless shelves. Or again, the readers who sat here at these radiating lines of desks, what were they but hapless flies caught in a huge web, its nucleus the great circle of the Catalogue? Darker, darker. From the towering wall of volumes seemed to emanate visible motes, intensifying the obscurity; in a moment the book-lined circumference of the room would be but a featureless prison-limit.

But then flashed forth the sputtering whiteness of the electric light, and its ceaseless hum was henceforth a new source of headache. It reminded her how little work she had done to-day; she must, she must, force herself to think of the task in hand. A machine has no business to refuse its duty. But the pages were blue and green and yellow before her eyes; the uncertainty of the light was intolerable. Right or wrong she would go home, and hide herself, and let her heart unburden itself of tears.

George Gissing, from *New Grub Street*, 1891

The seventy young women, of ages varying in the main from nineteen to one-and-twenty, though several were older, who at this date filled the species of nunnery known as the Training-School at Melchester, formed a very mixed community which included the daughters of mechanics, curates, surgeons, shopkeepers, farmers, dairymen, soldiers, sailors, and villagers. They sat in the large school-room of the establishment on the evening previously described, and word was passed round that Sue Bridehead had not come in at closing-time . . .

At nine o'clock the names were called, Sue's being pronounced three times sonorously by Miss Traceley without eliciting an answer.

At a quarter past nine the seventy stood up to sing the evening hymn, and then knelt down to prayers. After prayers they went into supper, and every girl's thought was, Where is Sue Bridehead? Some of the students, who had seen Jude from the window, felt that they would not mind risking her punishment for the pleasure of being kissed by such a kindly faced young man. Hardly one among them believed in the cousinship.

Half an hour later they all lay in their cubicles, their tender feminine faces upturned to the flaring gas-jets which at intervals stretched down the long dormitories, every face bearing the legend The Weaker upon it, as the penalty of the sex wherein they were moulded, which by no possible exertion of their willing hearts and abilities could be made strong while the inexorable laws of nature remain what they are. They formed a pretty, suggestive, pathetic sight, of whose pathos and beauty they were themselves unconscious, and would not discover till, amid the storms and strains of after-years, with their injustice, loneliness, child-bearing, and bereavement, their minds would revert to this experience as to something which had been allowed to slip past them insufficiently regarded.

Thomas Hardy, from *Jude the Obscure*, 1895

## To Teach the Young Idea

'Cannot you tell me of some way in which a woman may earn money?'

'A woman? What rate of woman? Do you mean yourself? That question is easily answered. A woman from the uneducated classes can get a subsistence by washing and cooking, by milking cows and going to service, and, in some parts of the kingdom, by working in a cottonmill, or burnishing plate, as you have no doubt seen for yourself at Birmingham. But, for an educated woman, a woman with the powers which God gave her, religiously improved, with a reason which lays life open before her, an understanding which surveys science as its appropriate task, and a conscience which would make every species of responsibility safe, – for such a woman there is in all England no chance of subsistence but by teaching – that almost ineffectual teaching, which can never countervail the education of circumstances, and for which not one in a thousand is fit – or by being a superior Miss Nares – the feminine gender of the tailor and the hatter.'

'The tutor, the tailor, and the hatter. Is this all?'

'All; except that there are departments of art and literature from which it is impossible to shut women out. These are not, however, to be regarded as resources for bread. Besides the number who succeed in art and literature being necessarily extremely small, it seems pretty certain that no great achievements, in the domains of art and imagination, can be looked for from either men or women who labour there to supply their lower wants, or for any other reason than the pure love of their work. While they toil in any one of the arts of expression, if they are not engrossed by some loftier meaning, the highest which they will end with expressing will be, the need of bread.'

Harriet Martineau, from Deerbrook, 1839

Women long for an education to teach them *to teach*, to teach them the laws of the human mind and how to apply them – and knowing how imperfect, in the present state of the world, such an education must be, they long for experience, not patch-work experience, but experience followed up and systematized, to enable them to know what they are about and *where* they are 'casting their bread', and whether it is '*bread*' or a stone.

Florence Nightingale, from Cassandra, 1852

There lived in the Northern Parts of *England*, a Gentlewoman who undertook the Education of young Ladies; and this Trust she endeavour'd faithfully to discharge, by instructing those committed to her Care in Reading, Writing, Working, and in all proper Forms of Behaviour. And tho' her principal Aim was to improve their Minds in all useful Knowledge; to render them obedient to their Superiors, and gentle, kind, and affectionate to each other; yet did she not omit teaching them an exact Neatness in their Persons and Dress, and a perfect Gentility in their whole Carriage.

This Gentlewoman, whose Name was *Teachum*, was the Widow of a Clergyman, with whom she had lived nine Years in all the Harmony and Concord which forms the only satisfactory Happiness in the married State. Two little Girls (the youngest of which was born before the second Year of their Marriage was expired) took up a great Part of their Thoughts; and it was their mutual Design to spare no Pains or Trouble in their Education.

Mr *Teachum* was a very sensible Man, and took great Delight in improving his Wife; as she also placed her chief Pleasure in receiving his Instructions. One of his constant Subjects of Discourse to her was concerning the Education of Children: So that, when in his last illness his Physicians pronounced him beyond the Power of their Art to relieve, he expressed great Satisfaction in the Thought of leaving his Children to the Care of so prudent a Mother.

Mrs *Teachum* tho' exceedingly afflicted by such a Loss, yet thought it her Duty to call forth all her Resolutions to conquer her Grief, in order to apply herself to the Care of these her dear Husband's Children. But her Misfortunates were not here to end: For within a Twelvemonth after the Death of her Husband, she was deprived of both her Children by a violent Fever that then raged in the Country; and about the same time, by the unforeseen Breaking of a Banker, in whose Hands almost all her Fortune was just then placed, she was bereft of the Means of her future Support.

The Christian Fortitude with which (thro' her Husband's Instructions) she had armed her Mind, had not left it in the Power of any outward Accident to bereave her of her Understanding, or to make her incapable of doing what was proper on all Occasions. Therefore, by the Advice of all her Friends, she undertook what she was so well qualified for; namely, the Education of Children. But as she was moderate in her Desires, and did not seek to raise a great Fortune, she was resolved to take no more Scholars than she could have an Eye to herself, without the Help of other Teachers; and, instead of making Interest to fill her School, it was looked upon as a great Favour when she would take any Girl: And as her Number was fixed to Nine, which she on no Account would be prevailed on to increase, great Application was made when any Scholar went away, to have her Place supplied; and happy were they who could get a Promise for the next Vacancy.

Mrs *Teachum* was about Forty Years old, tall and genteel in her Person, tho' somewhat inclined to Fat. She had a lively and commanding Eye, insomuch that she naturally created an Awe in all her little Scholars; except when she condescended to smile, and talk familiarly to them; and then she had something perfectly kind and tender in her Manner. Her Temper was so extremely calm and good, that tho' she never omitted reprehending, and that pretty severely, any Girl that was guilty of the smallest Fault proceeding from an evil Disposition; yet for no Cause whatsoever was she provoked to be in a Passion: But she kept up such a Dignity and Authority by her steady Behaviour, that the Girls greatly feared to incur her Displeasure by disobeying her Commands; and were equally pleased with her Approbation, when they had done anything worthy her Commendation.

At the Time of the ensuing History, the School (being full) consisted of the Nine following young ladies:

Miss *Jenny Peace*,

| | |
|---|---|
| Miss *Sukey Jennett*, | Miss *Nanny Spruce*, |
| Miss *Dolly Friendly*, | Miss *Betty Ford*, |

Miss *Lucy Sly*,     Miss *Henny Fret*,

Miss *Patty Lockit*,    Miss *Polly Suckling*.

The eldest of these was but fourteen Years old, and none of the rest had yet attained their twelfth Year.

     Sarah Fielding, from *The Governess or Little Female Academy*, 1749

How delightful it would be to be a governess! To go out into the world; to enter upon a new life; to act for myself; to exercise my unused faculties; to try my unknown powers; to earn my own maintenance, and something to comfort and help my father, mother, and sister, besides exonerating them from the provision of my food and clothing; to show papa what his little Agnes could do; to convince mama and Mary that I was not quite the helpless, thoughtless being they supposed. And then, how charming to be intrusted with the care and education of children! Whatever others said, I felt I was fully competent to the task: the clear remembrance of my own thoughts and feelings in early childhood would be a surer guide than the instructions of the most mature adviser. I had but to turn from my little pupils to myself at their age, and I should know, at once, how to win their confidence and affections; how to waken the contrition of the erring; how to embolden the timid, and console the afflicted; how to make Virtue practicable, Instruction desirable, and Religion lovely and comprehensible.

– Delightful task!

To teach the young idea how to shoot!'. . .

By these means I hoped, in time, both to benefit the children, and to gain the approbation of their parents; and also to convince my friends at home that I was not so wanting in skill and prudence as they supposed. I knew the difficulties I had to contend with were great; but I knew, (at least, I believed,) unremitting patience and perseverance could overcome them, and night and morning I implored Divine assistance to this end. But either the children were so incorrigible, the parents so unreasonable, or myself so mistaken in my views, or so unable to carry them out, that my best intentions and most strenuous efforts seemed productive of no better result, than sport to the children, dissatisfaction to their parents, and torment to myself.

The task of instruction was as arduous for the body as the mind. I had to run after my pupils, to catch them, to carry, or drag them to the table, and often forcibly to hold them there, till the lesson was done. Tom, I frequently put into a corner, seating myself before him in a chair, with the book which contained the little task that must be said or read, before he was released, in my hand. He was not strong enough to push both me and the chair away; so he would stand twisting his body and face into the most grotesque and singular contortions – laughable, no doubt, to an unconcerned spectator, but not to me – and uttering loud yells and doleful outcries, intended to represent weeping, but wholly without the accompaniment of tears. I knew this was done solely for the purpose of annoying me; and, therefore, however I might inwardly tremble with impatience and irritation, I manfully strove to suppress all visible signs of molestation, and affected to sit, with calm indifference, waiting till it should please him to cease this pastime, and prepare for a run in the garden, by casting his eye on the book, and reading or repeating the few words he was required to say.

Sometimes he would determine to do his writing badly; and I had to hold his hand to prevent him from purposely blotting or disfiguring the paper. Frequently I threatened that, if he did not do better, he should have another line: then he would stubbornly refuse to write this line; and I, to save my word, had finally to resort to the expedient of holding his fingers upon the pen, and forcibly drawing his hand up and down till, in spite of his resistance, the line was in some sort completed.

Yet Tom was by no means the most unmanageable of my pupils; sometimes, to my great joy, he would have the sense to see that his wisest policy was to finish his tasks, and go out and amuse himself till I and his sisters came to join him, which, frequently, was not at all, for Mary Ann seldom followed his example in this particular. She apparently preferred rolling on the floor to any other amusement. Down she would drop like a leaden weight; and when I, with great difficulty, had succeeded in rooting her thence, I had still to hold her up with one arm, while, with the other, I held the book from which she was to read or spell her lesson. As the dead weight of the big girl of six became too heavy for one arm to bear, I transferred it to the other; or, if both were weary of the burden, I carried her into a corner, and told her she might come out when she should find the use of her feet, and stand up; but she generally preferred lying there like a log till dinner or tea time, when, as I could not deprive her of her meals, she must be liberated, and would come crawling out with a grin of triumph on her round, red face.

Often she would stubbornly refuse to pronounce some particular word in her lesson; and I now regret the lost labour I have had in striving to conquer her obstinacy. If I had passed it over as a matter of no consequence, it would have been better for both parties than vainly striving to overcome it, as I did; but I thought it my absolute duty to crush this vicious tendency in the bud; and so it was, if I could have done it: and, had my powers been less limited, I might have enforced obedience; but as it was, it was but a trial of strength between her and me, in which she generally came off victorious; and every victory served to encourage and strengthen her for a future contest.

In vain I argued, coaxed, entreated, threatened, scolded; in vain I kept her in from play, or, if obliged to take her out, refused to play with her, or to speak kindly, or have anything to do with her; in vain I tried to set before her the advantages of doing as she was bid, and being loved, and kindly treated in consequence, and the disadvantages of persisting in her absurd perversity. Sometimes, when she asked me to do something for her, I would answer –

'Yes, I will, Mary Ann, if you will only say that word. Come! you'd better say it at once, and have no more trouble about it.'

'No.'

'Then, of course, I can do nothing for you!'

With me, at her age, or under, neglect and disgrace were the most dreadful of punishments; but on her they made no impression.

Sometimes, exasperated to the utmost pitch, I would shake her violently by the shoulders, or pull her long hair, or put her in the corner, – for which she punished me with loud, shrill, piercing screams, that went through my head like a knife. She knew I hated this, and when she had shrieked her utmost, would look into my face with an air of vindictive satisfaction, exclaiming –

'*Now* then! *that*'s for you!'

And then shriek again and again, till I was forced to stop my ears. Often these dreadful cries would bring Mrs Bloomfield up to inquire what was the matter?

'Mary Ann is a naughty girl, ma'am.'

'But what are these shocking screams?'

'She is screaming in a passion.'

'I never heard such a dreadful noise! You might be killing her. Why is she not out with her brother?'

'I cannot get her to finish her lessons.'

'But Mary Ann must be a *good* girl, and finish her lessons.'

This was blandly spoken to the child. 'And I hope I shall *never* hear such terrible cries again!'

And fixing her cold, stony eyes upon me with a look that could not be mistaken, she would shut the door, and walk away.

Anne Brontë, from Agnes Grey, 1847

# Writing Women

### *The Author to Her Book*

Thou ill-form'd offspring of my feeble brain,
Who after birth didst by my side remain,
Till snatched from thence by friends, less wise than true,
Who thee abroad, expos'd to public view,
Made thee in rags, halting to th' press to trudge,
Where errors were not lessened (all may judge);
At thy return my blushing was not small,
My rambling brat (in print) should mother call;
I cast thee by as one unfit for light,
Thy visage was so irksome in my sight;
Yet being mine own, at length affection would
Thy blemishes amend, if so I could.
I wash'd thy face, but more defects I saw,
And rubbing off a spot, still made a flaw.
I stretched thy joints to make thee even feet,
Yet still thou run'st more hobbling than is meet;
In better dress to trim thee was my mind,
But nought save home-spun cloth i'th'house I find;
In this array, 'mongst vulgars mayst thou roam;
In critics' hands beware thou dost not come;
And take thy way where yet thou art not known.
If for thy Father asked, say thou hadst none:
And for thy Mother, she alas is poor,
Which caus'd her thus to send thee out of door.

Anne Bradstreet, 1612–72

I worked on, on.

Through all the bristling fence of nights and days
Which hedges time in from the eternities,
I struggled, – never stopped to note the stakes
Which hurt me in my course. The midnight oil
Would stink sometimes; there came some vulgar needs:
I had to live that therefore I might work,
And, being but poor, I was constrained, for life,
To work with one hand for the booksellers
While working with the other for myself

And art: you swim with feet as well as hands,
Or make small way. I apprehended this, –
In England no one lives by verse that lives;
And, apprehending, I resolved by prose
To make a space to sphere my living verse.
I wrote for cyclopædias, magazines,
And weekly papers, holding up my name
To keep it from the mud. I learnt the use
Of the editorial 'we' in a review
As courtly ladies the fine trick of trains,
And swept it grandly through the open doors
As if one could not pass through doors at all
Save so encumbered. I wrote tales beside,
Carved many an article on cherry-stones
To suit light readers, – something in the lines
Revealing, it was said, the mallet-hand,
But that, I'll never vouch for: what you do
For bread will taste of common grain, not grapes,
Although you have a vineyard in Champagne;
Much less in Nephelococcygia
As mine was, peradventure.
                                    Having bread
For just so many days, just breathing-room
For body and verse, I stood up straight and worked
My veritable work. And as the soul
Which grows within a child makes the child grow, –
Or as the fiery sap, the touch from God,
Careering through a tree, dilates the bark
And roughs with scale and knob, before it strikes
The summer foliage out in a green flame –
So life, in deepening with me, deepened all
The course I took, the work I did. Indeed
The academic law convinced of sin;
The critics cried out on the falling off,
Regretting the first manner. But I felt
My heart's life throbbing in my verse to show
It lived, it also – certes incomplete,
Disordered with all Adam in the blood,
But even its very tumours, warts and wens
Still organized by and implying life.

    Elizabeth Barrett Browning, from *Aurora Leigh*, 1857

One deep and steady conviction, obtained from my own experience and observation, largely qualified any apprehensions I might have, and was earnestly impressed by me upon my remonstrating friends; that enormous loss of strength, energy and time is occasioned by the way in which people go to work in literature, as if its labours were in all respects different from any other kind of toil. I am confident that intellectual industry and intellectual punctuality are as practicable as industry and punctuality in any other direction. I have seen vast misery of conscience and temper arise from the irresolution and delay caused by waiting for congenial moods, favourable circumstances, and so forth. I can speak, after long experience, without any doubt on this matter. I have suffered, like other writers, from indolence, irresolution, distaste to my work, absence of 'inspiration', and all that: but I have also found that sitting down, however, reluctantly, with the pen in my hand, I have never worked for one quarter of an hour without finding myself in full train; so that all the quarter hours, arguings, doubtings, and hesitation as to whether I should work or not which I gave way to in my inexperience, I now regard as so much waste, not only of time but, far worse, of energy. To the best of my belief, I never but once in my life left my work because I could not do it: and that single occasion was on the opening day of an illness. When once experience had taught me that I could work when I chose, and within a quarter of an hour of my determining to do so, I was relieved, in a great measure, from those embarrassments and depressions which I see afflicting many an author who waits for a mood instead of summoning it, and is the sport, instead of the master, of his own impressions and ideas. As far as the grosser physical influences are concerned, an author has his lot pretty much in his own hands, because it is in his power to shape his habits in accordance with the laws of nature: and an author who does not do this has no business with the lofty vocation. I am very far indeed from desiring to set up my own practices as an example for others; and I do not pretend that they are wholly rational, or the best possible; but, as the facts are clear, – that I have, without particular advantages of health and strength, done an unusual amount of work without fatal, perhaps without injurious consequences, and without the need of pernicious stimulants and peculiar habits, – it may be as well to explain what my methods were, that others may test them experimentally, if they choose.

Harriet Martineau, from *Autobiography*, 1877

I have been tempted to begin writing by George Eliot's life – with that curious kind of self-compassion which one cannot get clear of. I wonder if I am a little envious of her? . . . When people comment upon the number of books I have written, and I say that I am so far from being proud of the fact that

I should like at least half of them forgotten, they stare – and yet it is quite true; and even here I could no more go solemnly into them, and tell why I had done this or that, than I could fly. They are my work, which I like in the doing, which is my natural way of occupying myself, though they are never so good as I meant them to be. And when I have said that, I have said all that is in me to say.

I don't quite know why I should put this all down. I suppose because George Eliot's life has, as I said above, stirred me up to an involuntary confession. How I have been handicapped in life! Should I have done better if I had been kept, like her, in a mental greenhouse and taken care of? This is one of the things it is perfectly impossible to tell. In all likelihood our minds and our circumstances are so arranged that, after all, the possible way is the way that is best; yet it is a little hard sometimes not to feel with Browning's Andrea, that the men who have no wives, who have given themselves up to their art, have had an almost unfair advantage over us who have been given perhaps more than one Lucrezia to take care of. And to feel with him that perhaps in the after-life four square walls in the New Jerusalem may be given for another trial! . . . I used to be intensely impressed in the Laurence Oliphants with that curious freedom from human ties which I have never known; and that they felt it possible to make up their minds to do what was best without any sort of *arrière pensée*, without having to consider whether they could or not. Curious freedom! I have never known what it was. I have always had to think of other people, and to plan everything – for my own pleasure, it is true, very often, but always in subjection to the necessity which bound me to them. On the whole, I have had a great deal of my own way, and have insisted upon getting what I wished, but only at the cost of infinite labour, and of carrying a whole little world with me whenever I moved. I have not been able to rest, to please myself, to take the pleasures that have come in my way, but have always been forced to go on without a pause. When my poor brother's family fell upon my hands, and especially when there was question of Frank's education, I remember that I said to myself, having then perhaps a little stirring of ambition, that I must make up my mind to think no more of that, and that to bring up the boys for the service of God was better than to write a fine novel, supposing even that it was in me to do so. Alas! the work has been done; the education is over; my good Frank, my steady, good boy, is dead. It seemed rather a fine thing to make that resolution (though in reality I had no choice); but now I think that if I had taken the other way, which seemed the less noble, it might have been better for all of us. I might have done better work. I should in all probability have earned nearly as much for half the production had I done less; and I might have had the satisfaction of knowing that there was something laid up for them and for my old age; while they might have learned habits of work which now seem beyond recall. Who can tell? I did with much labour what I thought the best, and there is only a *might have been* on the other side . . .

Let me be done with this – I wonder if I will ever have time to put a few autobiographical bits down before I die. I am in very little danger of having my life written, and that is all the better in this point of view – for what could be said of me? George Eliot and George Sand make me half inclined to cry over my poor little unappreciated self – 'Many love me (*i.e.*, in a sort of way), but by none am I enough beloved.' These two bigger women did things which I have never felt the least temptation to do – but how very much more enjoyment they seem to have got out of their life, how much more praise and homage and honour! I would not buy their fame with these disadvantages, but I do feel very small, very obscure, beside them, rather a failure all round, never securing any strong affection, and throughout my life, though I have had all the usual experiences of woman, never impressing anybody, – what a droll little complaint! – why should I? I acknowledge frankly that there is nothing in me – a fat, little, commonplace woman, rather tongue-tied – to impress any one; and yet there is a sort of whimsical injury in it which makes me sorry for myself.

from *The Autobiography of Mrs M. O. W. Oliphant*, 1899

*Monday 25 October* (first day of winter time) [1920]
Why is life so tragic; so like a little strip of pavement over an abyss. I look down; I feel giddy; I wonder how I am ever to walk to the end. But why do I feel this? Now that I say it I don't feel it. The fire burns; we are going to hear the Beggars Opera. Only it lies about me; I can't keep my eyes shut. It's a feeling of impotence: of cutting no ice. Here I sit at Richmond, & like a lantern stood in the middle of a field my light goes up in darkness. Melancholy diminishes as I write. Why then don't I write it down oftener? Well, one's vanity forbids. I want to appear a success even to myself. Yet I don't get to the bottom of it. Its having no children, living away from friends, failing to write well, spending too much on food, growing old – I think too much of whys & wherefores; too much of myself. I don't like time to flap round me. Well then, work. Yes, but I so soon tire of work – can't read more than a little, an hour's writing is enough for me. Out here no one comes in to waste time pleasantly. If they do, I'm cross. The labour of going to London is too great. Nessa's children grow up, & I cant have them in to tea, or go to the Zoo. Pocket money doesn't allow of much. Yet I'm persuaded that these are trivial things: its life itself, I think sometimes, for us in our generation so tragic – no newspaper placard without its shriek of agony from some one.

McSwiney this afternoon & violence in Ireland;* or it'll be the strike. Unhappiness is everywhere; just beyond the door; or stupidity which is worse. Still I don't pluck the nettle out of me. To write Jacob's Room again will revive my fibres, I feel. Evelyn is done: but I don't like what I write now. And with it all how happy I am – if it weren't for my feeling that its a strip of pavement over an abyss.

from *The Diary of Virginia Woolf*

### Roles

Emily Bronte's cleaning the car:
water sloshes over her old trainers
as she scrubs frail blood-shapes from the windscreen
and swirls the hose-jet across the roof.
When it's done she'll go to the supermarket;
then, if she has to, face her desk.

I'm striding on the moor in my hard shoes,
a shawl over my worsted bodice,
the hem of my skirt scooping dew from the grass
as I pant up towards the breathless heights.
I'll sit on a rock I know and write a poem.
It may not come out as I intend.

Fleur Adcock, from *Time Zones*, 1991

### Business Girls

I am the hostess of the Ferry Inn,
a house beyond reproach:
a moon, in a dress of white,
welcoming the man that comes with coin.

What I desire is to bring delight,
to be for all my guests a flawless world,

---

* Alderman Terence Joseph McSwiney, Lord Mayor of Cork, 1920, MP for mid-Cork since December 1918, died in the early hours of 25 October in Brixton Prison after being on hunger strike since 16 August. McSwiney had been sentenced by court martial to two years imprisonment for holding a Sinn Fein Court in Cork City Hall.

to sing among them at their usual talk
as I pour out the mead.

Gwerfyl Mechain, fifteenth century,
tr. from the Welsh by Gillian Spraggs, 1994

### A Song on the South Sea, 1720

Ombre and basset laid aside,
  New games employ the fair;
And brokers all those hours divide
  Which lovers used to share.

The court, the park, the foreign song
  And harlequin's grimace
Forlorn; amidst the city throng
  Behold each blooming face.

With Jews and Gentiles undismayed
  Young tender virgins mix;
Of whiskers nor of beards afraid,
  Nor all the cozening tricks.

Bright jewels, polished once to deck
  The fair one's rising breast,
Or sparkle round her ivory neck,
  Lie pawned in iron chest.

The gayer passions of the mind
  How avarice controls!
Even love does now no longer find
  A place in female souls.

  Anne Finch, Countess of Winchilsea

Many a long hour did I wait in his great hall, while scores passed in and out; many of them looking curiously at me. The flunkeys, noble creatures! marvelled exceedingly at the yellow woman whom no excuses could get rid of, nor impertinence dismay, and showed me very clearly that they resented my persisting in remaining there in mute appeal from their sovereign will. At last I gave that up, after a message from Mrs H that the full complement of nurses had been secured, and that my offer could not be entertained. Once again I tried, and had an interview this time with one of Miss Nightingale's companions. She gave me the same reply, and I read in her face the fact, that had there been a vacancy, I should not have been chosen to fill it.

As a last resort, I applied to the managers of the Crimean Fund to know whether they would give me a passage to the camp – once there I would trust to something turning up. But this failed also, and one cold evening I stood in the twilight, which was fast deepening into wintry night, and looked back upon the ruins of my last castle in the air. The disappointment seemed a cruel one. I was so conscious of the unselfishness of the motives which induced me to leave England – so certain of the service I could render among the sick soldiery, and yet I found it so difficult to convince others of these facts. Doubts and suspicions arose in my heart for the first and last time, thank Heaven. Was it possible that American prejudices against colour had some root here? Did these ladies shrink from accepting my aid because my blood flowed beneath a somewhat duskier skin than theirs? Tears streamed down my foolish cheeks, as I stood in the fast thinning streets; tears of grief that any should doubt my motives – that Heaven should deny me the opportunity that I sought. Then I stood still, and looking upward through and through the dark clouds that shadowed London, prayed aloud for help. I dare say that I was a strange sight to the few passers-by, who hastened homeward through the gloom and mist of that wintry night. I dare say those who read these pages will wonder at me as much as they who saw me did; but you must all remember that I am one of an impulsive people, and find it hard to put that restraint upon my feelings which to you is so easy and natural.

The morrow, however, brought fresh hope. A good night's rest had served to strengthen my determination. Let what might happen, to the Crimea I would go. If in no other way, then would I upon my own responsibility and at my own cost. There were those there who had known me in Jamaica, who had been under my care; doctors who would vouch for my skill and willingness to aid them, and a general who had more than once helped me, and would do so still. Why not trust to their welcome and kindness, and start at once? If the authorities had allowed me, I would willingly have given them my services as a nurse; but as they declined them, should I not open an hotel for invalids in the Crimea in my own way? I had no more idea of what the Crimea was than the home authorities themselves perhaps, but having once made up my mind, it was not long before cards were printed and speeding across the Mediterranean to my friends before Sebastopol. Here is one of them:

BRITISH HOTEL.
MRS MARY SEACOLE
(*Late of Kingston, Jamaica*),

Respectfully announces to her former kind friends, and to the
Officers of the Army and Navy generally,
That she has taken her passage in the screw-steamer 'Hollander', to start
from London on the 25th of January, intending on her arrival at Balaclava
to establish a mess-table and comfortable quarters for sick and convalescent
officers.

This bold programme would reach the Crimea in the end of January, at a
time when any officers would have considered a stall in an English stable
luxurious quarters compared to those he possessed, and had nearly forgotten
the comforts of a mess-table. It must have read to them rather like a mockery,
and yet, as the reader will see, I succeeded in redeeming my pledge.

While this new scheme was maturing, I again met Mr Day in England. He
was bound to Balaclava upon some shipping business, and we came to the
understanding that (if it were found desirable) we should together open a
store as well as an hotel in the neighbourhood of the camp. So was originated
the well-known firm of Seacole and Day (I am sorry to say, the camp wits
dubbed it Day and Martin), which, for so many months, did business upon
the now deserted high road from the then busy harbour of Balaclava to the
front of the British army before Sebastopol. These new arrangements were
not allowed to interfere in any way with the main object of my journey. A
great portion of my limited capital was, with the kind aid of a medical friend,
invested in medicines which I had reason to believe would be useful; with the
remainder I purchased those home comforts which I thought would be most
difficult to obtain away from England . . .

So cheered at the outset, I watched without a pang the shores of England
sink behind the smooth sea, and turned my gaze hopefully to the as yet
landless horizon, beyond which lay that little peninsula to which the eyes and
hearts of all England were so earnestly directed.

So cheerily! the good ship ploughed its way eastward ho! for Turkey.

Mary Seacole, from *The Wonderful Adventures of Mrs Seacole in Many Lands*, 1857

[8 March, 1885]
I spend my time now in alternate days of work and rest. The physical part of my
work absorbs so much energy that I have little left for thought and feeling. Work
is the best narcotic, providing the patient is strong enough to take it. All is chaos
at present. Long trudges through Whitechapel after applicants and references,
and tenants tumbling in anyhow. A drift population of all classes and races; a
constantly decomposing mass of human beings; few arising out of it, but many
dropping down dead, pressed out of existence by the struggle. A certain weird

romance with neither beginning nor end; visiting amongst these people in their dingy homes. They seem light-hearted enough, in spite of misery and disease. More often feel envy than pity. Shall in the future, when other workers are found, and when once I am fairly started in the practical work, undertake less of the management, and use the work more as an opportunity for observation. Mean some day to master, as far as my power goes, what is theoretically thought out in social questions. Earnestly hope I shall never get conceited again, or look upon my work as more than the means for remaining contented and free from pain. Relief to be alone ... Society constantly increasing: have none of that terrible nightmare feeling about it of last year. But work brings Society into its proper place as a rest and relaxation, instead of an effort and an excitement. Trust I shall never make social capital out of my work. That with me is a danger, as I enjoy retailing my experiences, independently of any effect I may produce, and the 'vanity motive' comes in to strengthen desire. Perhaps the past year of suffering will decrease my egotism, and instead of cold observation and analysis, all done with the egotistical purpose of increasing knowledge, there will be the interest which comes from feeling, and from the desire humbly to serve those around me.

Beatrice Webb, from My Apprenticeship, 1926

## Business Girls

From the geyser ventilators
  Autumn winds are blowing down
On a thousand business women
  Having baths in Camden Town.

Waste pipes chuckle into runnels,
  Steam's escaping here and there,
Morning trains through Camden cutting
  Shake the Crescent and the Square.

Early nip of changeful autumn,
  Dahlias glimpsed through garden doors,
At the back precarious bathrooms
  Jutting out from upper floors;

And behind their frail partitions
  Business women lie and soak,
Seeing through the draughty skylight
  Flying clouds and railway smoke.

Rest you there, poor unbelov'd ones,
Lap your loneliness in heat.
All too soon the tiny breakfast,
Trolley-bus and windy street!
John Betjeman, 1954

I don't think you can ever eliminate the economic factor motivating women to prostitution. Even a call girl could never make as much in a straight job as she could at prostitution. All prostitutes are in it for the money. With most uptown call girls, the choice is not between starvation and life, but it is a choice between $5,000 and $25,000 or between $10,000 and $50,000. That's a pretty big choice: a pretty big difference. You can say that they're in this business because of the difference of $40,000 a year. A businessman would say so. Businessmen do things because of the difference of $40,000 a year. Call girls do go into capitalism and think like capitalists. But you can't say, even of the call girl, that she has so many other ways to earn an adequate living. Even with an undergraduate degree, chances are that she couldn't do better than earn $5,000 or $6,000 a year, outside of prostitution. Because it's very *hard* for women to earn an adequate living and so we do not have much economic choice – even the call girl. And the minority woman on the street – the poor woman – she has no choice at all.

For white women you usually can't say that there's no choice but prostitution. There is. But the choice itself is a choice between working for somebody else and going into business for yourself. Going into business for yourself and hoping to make a lot of money. There's that choice. Prostitution on those terms is a kind of laissez-faire capitalism. But it's also slavery, psychologically. And it's also feudalism, where the protection of a pimp is offered in return for services. Unless you're starving so bad you literally have no choice – as some women do – the choice is between a lower-middle income and a really good one. A junkie has very little choice. For the junkie the only choice is getting off junk, a tough thing to do. Then too, a junkie off junk wouldn't be a junkie anymore. Prostitution is a kind of addiction too. It's an addiction to money. I felt that.

The worst part about prostitution is that you're obliged not to sell sex only, but your humanity. That's the worst part of it: that what you're selling is your human dignity. Not really so much in bed, but in accepting the agreement – in becoming a bought person. When I really felt like a whore was when I had to talk to them, fucking up to them really while only talking. That's why I don't like to go out to dinner and why I don't like to spend the night. Because when they talk about 'niggers', you've just got to go 'uh-huh, uh-huh' and agree with them. That's what I really couldn't stand. It was that kind of thing. That's when I really felt I was kissing their ass – *more* than when I was literally kissing their ass. That's when I really felt that I was a whore. That's the most humiliating thing – having to agree with them all the time because you're bought.

That's why it's not as easy as just saying 'prostitution is selling a service'. That's why it's selling your soul and not selling a service. In business people sell their souls too, and that's why business destroys people – how would you feel about selling encyclopedias to poor people? But there's a special indignity in prostitution, as if sex were dirty and men can only enjoy it with someone *low*. It involves a type of contempt, a kind of disdain, and a kind of triumph over another human being. Guys who can't get it up with their wives can do it with whores. They have to pay for it. For some of them, *paying* for it is very important.

But a lot of them didn't make me feel degraded. Most of them didn't. If they had, I wouldn't have stayed. Some of them did – for example, the southerners. They were awful. And there's something about some men – the way they fuck – they lean on you and poke you with their bones. I'm sure they're not conscious of it. I found that so much more with southerners. They hurt me. And they've got to use all the *words* – all the words they can't say to their wives, covering you with the language of their shame. And their anger. That was another thing I didn't like either. When you're doing prostitution – if only in order to cope – you've got to have tremendous defences. You've just gotta turn off, somehow. Drugs or will power, you've got to cut yourself off.

I think that the conviction that females are dirty, that their genitals are dirty, really sticks to us. I think that's why I don't like men to go down on me. Because I think I'm dirty. I just don't like it because I think I must be dirty – and I think they're not. Maybe they clean themselves. A lot comes from this belief in our dirt – like I was douching all the time. Some of them like you to be dirty. One guy said to me, 'I would like it if you didn't douche for a week.' They want to go down on you and, another thing, they want you to come. That was another thing that I didn't like. Here I go, thinking about all the things I don't like. And now I'm really getting into it. I know I didn't like it and I don't want to get into it again. One of the worst things about it was the faking. You have to fake orgasm. They expect it because that proves their masculinity. That's one of the worst things about it. That's really being a whore, being so dishonest. I don't know how they believe it – johns. Some of the ones I've had were even bachelors – good-looking guys with a lot of money, eligible young men. Very good-looking with a lot of money, didn't want to marry, wanted to go to whores. They had a tremendous fear of getting involved because that's giving something.

J's account, from *The Prostitution Papers*,
ed. Kate Millett, 1975

'Well, now,' said Wimsey, 'why do people kill people?'

He was sitting in Miss Katharine Climpson's private office. The establishment was ostensibly a typing bureau, and indeed there were three efficient female typists who did very excellent work for authors and men of science from time to time. Apparently the business was a large and flourishing one, for work frequently had to be refused on the ground that the staff was working at full pressure. But on other floors of the building there were other activities. All the employees were women – mostly elderly, but a few still young and attractive – and if the private register in the steel safe had been consulted, it would have been seen that all these women were of the class unkindly known as 'superfluous'. There were spinsters with small fixed incomes, or no incomes at all; widows without family; women deserted by peripatetic husbands and living on a restricted alimony, who, previous to their engagement by Miss Climpson, had had no resources but bridge and boarding-house gossip. There were retired and disappointed school-teachers; out-of-work actresses; courageous people who had failed with hat-shops and tea-parlours; and even a few Bright Young Things, for whom the cocktail party and the nightclub had grown boring. These women seemed to spend most of their time in answering advertisements. Unmarried gentlemen who desired to meet ladies possessed of competences with a view to matrimony; sprightly sexagenarians, who wanted housekeepers for remote country districts; ingenious gentlemen with financial schemes, on the look-out for capital; literary gentlemen, anxious for female collaborators; plausible gentlemen about to engage talent for productions in the provinces; benevolent gentlemen, who could tell people how to make money in their spare time – gentlemen such as these were very liable to receive applications from members of Miss Climpson's staff. It may have been coincidence that these gentlemen so very often had the misfortune to appear shortly afterwards before the magistrate on charges of fraud, blackmail, or attempted procuration, but it is a fact that Miss Climpson's office boasted a private telephone-line to Scotland Yard, and that few of her ladies were quite so unprotected as they appeared. It is also a fact that the money which paid for the rent and upkeep of the premises might, by zealous enquirers, have been traced to Lord Peter Wimsey's banking account. His lordship was somewhat reticent about this venture of his, but occasionally, when closeted with Chief Inspector Parker or other intimate friends, referred to it as 'My Cattery'.

Dorothy L. Sayers, from *Strong Poison*, 1930

### Action

I can lay down that history
I can lay down my glasses
I can lay down the imaginary lists
of what to forget and what must be
done. I can shake the sun
out of my eyes and lay everything down
on the hot sand, and cross
the whispering threshold and walk
right into the clear sea, and float there,
my long hair floating, and fishes
vanishing all around me. Deep water.
Little by little one comes to know
the limits and depths of power.

Denise Levertov, from *Overland to the Islands*, 1958

God give me work till my life shall end
and life till my work is done.

Inscription on the grave of Winifred Holtby, 1898–1935

GIRLS AND BOYS
AND OTHER LIFE FORMS

*The Spindle: Lament for Baucis**

Though she was just an unmarried girl of nineteen years,
her three hundred lines of verse are equal to Homer.
Whether she stood twirling her spindle in fear of her mother,
or else working at her loom, she applied herself continually
to the service of the Muses.

from an anonymous Greek epigram on Erinna

GIRLS: Torty-tortoise, what are you doing in the middle of the ring?
TORTOISE: (*scuttling from side to side*) I am weaving wool and Milesian weft.
GIRLS: And what was your son doing when he was lost?
TORTOISE: From the white horses into the sea he SPRANG! (*On the last word
the Tortoise jumps up to chase the other girls; the first one to be caught becomes
the new Tortoise.*)

Girl's game recorded by Julius Pollux of Naucratis, second century AD

. . . into the wave
[you sprang] from the white horses with crazy bounds.
'Aiai!' I screamed. [Then it was my turn to be] tortoise,
and leaping up, [I raced] through the pen in the great courtyard.
Unlucky Baucis! this is why . . . I mourn for you,
and in my heart . . . these traces still lie warm.
Now, they are only embers, those things [we used to share]:
of dolls . . . in our chambers . . . brides . . . towards dawn
[my/your] mother . . . woolworkers . . . about the cloth shot with purple

Ah! [in those days] the bogey-woman [so] frightened [us two] little ones:
. . . on her head she had [huge] ears,
and she roamed around on four feet;
she would change her appearance [from one thing to another].
But when the time came that [you went to your marriage] bed,
you forget all the things which while you were still a child
. . . you had heard from your mother, dear Baucis:
. . . Aphrodite [put] forgetfulness [in your heart].
So, crying out for you . . . the rest I set aside.
For my feet [are] not [so] profane [as to leave] the house,

---

* Erinna's friend who died suddenly, immediately after her marriage, and for whom Erinna also
wrote two surviving epitaphs.

nor [is it fit that I should] set eyes on your [corpse],
nor lament with my flowing hair uncovered . . .
the regard I feel for you crimsons my [cheeks] and tears them.

. . . always in the past . . . nineteen . . . Erinna . . . dear
[girls] . . . looking at a spindle . . . know that to you . . .
spinning round . . . for this reason my regard . . . unmarried
girls . . . perceiving . . . and flowing hair . . .

Grey-headed women, gentle in speech, who are the flower of old age among
mortals

. . . you dear . . . O Baucis! . . . weeping . . . a flame . . . hearing
howling . . . O Hymen! . . . O Hymen! . . . Aiai! unlucky
Baucis! . . .

From here to Hades an echo swims vainly across;
silence among the dead; the darkness flows over my eyes.

> Erinna of Telos, fourth century BC,
> tr. Gillian Spraggs (Ellipses indicate a missing word or words; words in square
> brackets are doubtful or conjectural.)

## Songs of Innocence

Work or play are all one to him, his games are his work; he knows no difference.
He brings to everything the cheerfulness of interest, the charm of freedom,
and he shows the bent of his own mind and the extent of his knowledge. Is
there anything better worth seeing, anything more touching or more delightful,
than a pretty child, with merry, cheerful glance, easy contented manner, open
smiling countenance, playing at the most important things, or working at the
lightest amusements?

> Jean-Jacques Rousseau, *Emile*, 1762,
> tr. Barbara Foxley, 1911

### The Chimney Sweeper

When my mother died I was very young,
And my father sold me while yet my tongue
Could scarcely cry *'weep 'weep, 'weep 'weep!*
So your chimneys I sweep, and in soot I sleep.

There's little Tom Dacre, who cried when his head,
That curled like a lamb's back, was shaved; so I said,
'Hush Tom, never mind it, for when your head's bare,
You know that the soot cannot spoil your white hair.'

And so he was quiet, and that very night,
As Tom was asleeping he had such a sight –
That thousands of sweepers, Dick, Joe, Ned, and Jack,
Were all of them locked up in coffins of black;

And by came an angel, who had a bright key,
And he opened the coffins and set them all free;
Then down a green plain leaping, laughing they run,
And wash in a river and shine in the sun.

Then naked and white, all their bags left behind,
They rise upon clouds and sport in the wind.
And the angel told Tom, if he'd be a good boy,
He'd have God for his father and never want joy.

And so Tom awoke, and we rose in the dark,
And got with our bags and our brushes to work.
Though the morning was cold, Tom was happy and warm;
So if all do their duty, they need not fear harm.

William Blake, *Songs of Innocence*, 1789

Behold the Child among his new-born blisses,
A six years' darling of a pigmy size!
See, where 'mid work of his own hand he lies,
Fretted by sallies from his mother's kisses,
With light upon him from his father's eyes!
See, at his feet, some little plan or chart,
Some fragment from his dream of human life,
Shaped by himself with newly-learned art;
    A wedding or a festival,
    A mourning or a funeral;
        And this hath now his heart,
    And unto this he frames his song:
        Then will he fit his tongue
To dialogues of business, love, or strife;
        But it will not be long
        Ere this be thrown aside,

And with new joy and pride
The little Actor cons another part;
Filling from time to time his 'humorous stage'
With all the Persons, down to palsied Age,
That Life brings with her in her equipage;
    As if his whole vocation
    Were endless imitation.

Thou, whose whole exterior semblance doth belie
    Thy Soul's immensity;
Thou best Philosopher, who yet dost keep
Thy heritage, thou Eye among the blind,
That, deaf and silent, read'st the eternal deep,
Haunted for ever by the eternal mind, –
    Mighty Prophet! Seer blest!
    On whom those truths do rest,
Which we are toiling all our lives to find,
In darkness lost, the darkness of the grave;
Thou, over whom thy Immortality
Broods like the Day, a Master o'er a Slave,
A presence which is not to be put by;
    To whom the grave
Is but a lonely bed without the sense or sight
    Of day or the warm light,
A place of thought where we in waiting lie;
Thou little Child, yet glorious in the might
Of heaven-born freedom on thy being's height,
Why with such earnest pains dost thou provoke
The years to bring the inevitable yoke,
Thus blindly with thy blessedness at strife?
Full soon thy soul shall have her earthly freight,
And custom lie upon thee with a weight,
Heavy as frost, and deep almost as life!
        William Wordsworth, from 'Intimations of Immortality from
            Recollections of Early Childhood', 1807

FIRST TWIN: (*who has flown to a high branch*) See, it comes, the Wendy!
    (*They all see it now*)
    How white it is!
*A dot of light is pursuing the bird malignantly.*

TOOTLES: That is Tinker Bell. Tink is trying to hurt the Wendy. (*He makes a cup of his hands and calls.*) Hullo, Tink!
*A response comes down in the fairy language.*
She says Peter wants us to shoot the Wendy.
NIBS: Let us do what Peter wishes.
SLIGHTLY: Ay, shoot it; quick, bows and arrows.
TOOTLES: (*first with his bow*) Out of the way, Tink; I'll shoot it. (*His bolt goes home.*)
*Wendy, who has been fluttering among the treetops in her white nightgown, falls straight to earth. No one could be more proud than Tootles.*
I have shot the Wendy; Peter will be so pleased.
*From some tree on which Tink is roosting comes the tinkle we can now translate, 'You silly ass'. Tootles falters.*
Why do you say that?
*The Others feel he may have blundered, and draw away from Tootles.*
SLIGHTLY: (*examining the fallen one more minutely*) This is no bird; I think it must be a lady.
NIBS: (*who would have preferred it to be a bird*) And Tootles has killed her.
CURLY: Now I see, Peter was bringing her to us.
*They wonder for what object.*
SECOND TWIN: To take care of us?
*Undoubtedly for some diverting purpose.*
OMNES: (*though every one of them had wanted to have a shot at her*) Oh, Tootles!
TOOTLES: (*gulping*) I did it. When ladies used to come to me in dreams I said 'Pretty Mother', but when she really came I shot her! (*He perceives the necessity of a solitary life for him.*) Friends, goodbye.
SEVERAL: (*not very enthusiastically*) Don't go.
TOOTLES: I must; I am so afraid of Peter.
*He has gone but a step toward oblivion when he is stopped by a crowing as of some victorious cock.*
OMNES: Peter!
*They make a paling of themselves in front of Wendy as Peter skims round the treetops and reaches earth.*
PETER: Greetings, boys! (*Their silence chafes him.*) I am back; why do you not cheer? Great news, boys, I have brought at last a mother for us all.
SLIGHTLY: (*vaguely*) Ay, ay.
PETER: She flew this way; have you not seen her?
SECOND TWIN: (*as Peter evidently thinks her important*) Oh mournful day!
TOOTLES: (*making a break in the paling*) Peter, I will show her to you.
THE OTHERS: (*closing the gap*) No, no.
TOOTLES: (*majestically*) Stand back, all, and let Peter see.

The paling dissolves, and Peter sees Wendy prone on the ground.

J. M. Barrie, from *Peter Pan*, 1904

## The Young Idea

The duetie which we owe them doth straitly commaund us to see them well brought up. For what be young *maidens* in respect of our sex? Are they not the seminary of our succession? the naturall frye, from whence we are to chuse our naturall, next and most necessarie freindes? The very selfe same creatures, which were made for our comfort, the onely good to garnish our alonenesse, the nearest companions in our weale or wo? the peculiar and priviest partakers in all our fortunes? borne for us to life, bound to us till death? And can we in conscience but carefully thinke of them, which are so many wayes linked unto us? Is it either nothing, or but some small thing, to have our childrens mothers well furnished in minde, well strengthened in bodie? which desire by them to maintaine our succession? or is it not their good to be so well garnished, which good being defeated in them by our indiligence, of whom they are to have it, doth it not charge us with breache of duetie, bycause they have it not? They are committed and commended unto us, as pupilles unto tutours, as bodies unto heades, nay as bodies unto soules: so that if we tender not their education duetifully, they maye urge that against us, if at any time either by their owne right, or by our default, they winne the upper roome and make us stand bare head, or be bolder with us to.

They that write of the use of our bodies, do greatly blame such parents, as suffer not their children to use the left hand, as well as the right, bycause thereby they weaken their strength and the use of their limmes: and can we be without blame, who seeke not to strengthen that, which was once taken from us, and yet taryeth with us, as a part of us still: knowing it to be the weaker? Or is there any better meane to strengthen their minde, then that knowledge of God, of religion, of civil, of domesticall dueties, which we have by our traine, and ought not to denie them being comprised in bookes, and is to be compassed in youth?

Richard Mulcaster, from 'The Education of Girls', *Positions*, 1581

Few are the modes of earning a subsistence, and those very humiliating. Perhaps to be an humble companion to some rich old cousin, or what is still worse, to live with strangers, who are so intolerably tyrannical, that none of their own relations can bear to live with them, though they should even expect a fortune in reversion. It is impossible to enumerate the many hours of anguish such a person must spend. Above the servants, yet considered by them as a spy, and ever reminded of her inferiority when in conversation with the superiors. If she cannot condescend to mean flattery, she has not a chance of being a favourite; and should any of the visitors take notice of her, and she for a moment forget her subordinate state, she is sure to be reminded of it.

Painfully sensible of unkindness, she is alive to every thing, and many sarcasms reach her, which were perhaps directed another way. She is alone, shut out from equality and confidence, and the concealed anxiety impairs her constitution; for she must wear a cheerful face, or be dismissed. The being dependant on the caprice of a fellow creature, though certainly very necessary in this state of discipline, is yet a very bitter corrective, which we would fain shrink from.

A teacher at a school is only a kind of upper servant, who has more work than the menial ones.

A governess to young ladies is equally disagreeable. It is ten to one if they meet with a reasonable mother; and if she is not so, she will be continually finding fault to prove she is not ignorant, and be displeased if her pupils do not improve, but angry if the proper methods are taken to make them do so. The children treat them with disrespect, and often with insolence. In the mean time life glides away, and the spirits with it; 'and when youth and genial years are flown', they have nothing to subsist on; or, perhaps, on some extraordinary occasion, some small allowance may be made for them, which is thought a great charity.

The few trades which are left, are now gradually falling into the hands of the men, and certainly they are not very respectable.

It is hard for a person who has a relish for polished society, to herd with the vulgar, or to condescend to mix with her former equals when she is considered in a different light. What unwelcome heart-breaking knowledge is then poured in on her! I mean a view of the selfishness and depravity of the world; for every other acquirement is a source of pleasure, though they may occasion temporary inconveniences. How cutting is the contempt she meets with! – A young mind looks round for love and friendship; but love and friendship fly from poverty: expect them not if you are poor! The mind must then sink into meanness, and accommodate itself to its new state, or dare to be unhappy. Yet I think no reflecting person would give up the experience and improvement they have gained, to have avoided the misfortunes; on the contrary, they are thankfully ranked amongst the choicest blessings of life, when we are not under their immediate pressure.

How earnestly does a mind full of sensibility look for disinterested friendship, and long to meet with good unalloyed. When fortune smiles they hug the dear delusion; but dream not that it is one. The painted cloud disappears suddenly, the scene is changed, and what an aching void is left in the heart! a void which only religion can fill up – and how few seek this internal comfort!

A woman, who has beauty without sentiment, is in great danger of being seduced; and if she has any, cannot guard herself from painful mortifications. It is very disagreeable to keep up a continual reserve with men she has been formerly familiar with; yet, if she places confidence, it is ten to one but she is deceived. Few men seriously think of marrying an inferior; and if they have honour enough not to take advantage of the artless tenderness of a woman who loves, and thinks not of the difference of rank, they do not undeceive her until she has anticipated happiness, which, contrasted with her dependant situation, appears delightful. The disappointment is severe; and the heart receives a wound which does not easily admit of a compleat cure, as the good that is missed is not valued according to its real worth: for fancy drew the picture, and grief delights to create food to feed on.

If what I have written should be read by parents, who are now going on in thoughtless extravagance, and anxious only that their daughters may be *genteelly educated*, let them consider to what sorrows they expose them; for I have not over-coloured the picture.

Though I warn parents to guard against leaving their daughters to encounter so much misery; yet if a young woman falls into it, she ought not to be discontented. Good must ultimately arise from every thing, to those who look beyond this infancy of their being; and here the comfort of a good conscience is our only stable support. The main business of our lives is to learn to be virtuous; and He who is training us up for immortal bliss, knows best what trials will contribute to make us so; and our resignation and improvement will render us respectable to ourselves, and to that Being, whose approbation is of more value than life itself. It is true, tribulation produces anguish, and we would fain avoid the bitter cup, though convinced its effects would be the most salutary. The Almighty is then the kind parent, who chastens and educates, and indulges us not when it would tend to our hurt. He is compassion itself, and never wounds but to heal, when the ends of correction are answered.

Mary Wollstonecraft, from *Thoughts on the Education of Daughters*, 1787

The lower-fourth form, in which Tom found himself at the beginning of the next half-year, was the largest form in the lower school, and numbered upwards of forty boys. Young gentlemen of all ages from nine to fifteen were to be found there, who expended such part of their energies as was devoted to Latin and Greek upon a book of Livy, the 'Bucolics' of Virgil and the 'Hecuba' of Euripides, which were ground out in small daily portions. The driving of this unlucky lower-fourth must have been grievous work to the unfortunate master, for it was the most unhappily constituted of any in the school.

Here stuck the great stupid boys, who, for the life of them, could never master the accidence; the objects alternately of mirth and terror to the youngsters, who were daily taking them up and laughing at them in lesson, and getting kicked by them for so doing in play-hours. There were no less than three unhappy fellows in tail coats, with incipient down on their chins, whom the Doctor and the master of the form were always endeavouring to hoist into the Upper school, but whose parsing and construing resisted the most well-meant shoves. Then came the mass of the form, boys of eleven and twelve, the most mischievous and reckless age of British youth, of whom East and Tom Brown were fair specimens. As full of tricks as monkeys, and of excuses as Irishwomen, making fun of their master, one another, and their lessons, Argus himself would have been puzzled to keep an eye on them; and as for making them steady or serious for half an hour together, it was simply hopeless. The remainder of the form consisted of young prodigies of nine and ten, who were going up the school at the rate of a form a half-year, all boys' hands and wits being against them in their progress. It would have been one man's work to see that the precocious youngsters had fair play; and as the master had a good deal besides to do, they hadn't, and were for ever being shoved down three or four places, their verses stolen, their books inked, their jackets whitened, and their lives otherwise made a burden to them . . .

[In] the monthly examinations . . . the Doctor came round to examine their form, for one long, awful hour, in the work which they had done in the preceding month. The second monthly examination came round soon after Tom's fall, and it was with anything but lively anticipations that he and the other lower-fourth boys came in to prayers on the morning of the examination day.

Prayers and calling-over seemed twice as short as usual, and before they could get construes of a tithe of the hard passages marked in the margin of their books, they were all seated round, and the Doctor was standing in the middle, talking in whispers to the master. Tom couldn't hear a word which passed, and never lifted his eyes from his book; but he knew by a sort of magnetic instinct that the Doctor's under-lip was coming out, and his eye beginning to burn, and his gown getting gathered up more and more tightly in his left hand. The suspense was agonizing, and Tom knew that he was sure on such occasions to make an example of the School-house boys. 'If he would only begin,' thought Tom, 'I shouldn't mind.'

At last the whispering ceased, and the name which was called out was not Brown. He looked up for a moment, but the Doctor's face was too awful; Tom wouldn't have met his eye for all he was worth, and buried himself in his book again.

The boy who was called up first was a clever, merry School-house boy, one of their set: he was some connection of the Doctor's, and a great favourite, and ran in and out of his house as he liked, and so was selected for the first victim.

'Triste lupus stabulis,' began the luckless youngster, and stammered through some eight or ten lines.

'There, that will do,' said the Doctor; 'now construe.'

On common occasions, the boy could have construed the passage well enough probably, but now his head was gone.

'Triste lupus, the sorrowful wolf,' he began.

A shudder ran through the whole form, and the Doctor's wrath fairly boiled over; he made three steps up to the construer, and gave him a good box on the ear. The blow was not a hard one, but the boy was so taken by surprise that he started back; the form caught the back of his knees and over he went on to the floor behind. There was a dead silence over the whole school; never before and never again while Tom was at school did the Doctor strike a boy in lesson. The provocation must have been great. However, the victim had saved his form for that occasion, for the Doctor turned to the top bench, and put on the best boys for the rest of the hour; and though, at the end of the lesson, he gave them all such a rating as they did not forget, this terrible field-day passed over without any severe visitations in the shape of punishments or floggings. Forty young scapegraces expressed their thanks to the 'sorrowful wolf' in their different ways before the second lesson.

Thomas Hughes, from *Tom Brown's School-Days*, 1859

Only the Almighty can make a New Woman. Put broadly, up to the age of puberty, the girl, all other things being equal, beats the boy; with puberty the damsel throws away every month a vast amount of fluid power in the order of Nature. Let us call this *pelvic power*. Assuming the girl to be the superior to the boy up to the pelvic power stage, – which, indeed, anyone can observe for himself, in his own sphere, – but once arrived at the stage of pelvic power, and the damsel is left behind in her lessons by her brother in the natural order of things, or else the girl's brain saps the pelvis of its power, when she will also lose in the race with the boy, because he will be physically well, while she, with disordered pelvic life, must necessarily be in ill-health more or less. The whole thing is a mere question of quantity of energy ... The New Woman is only possible in a novel, not in Nature ... I have very many times watched the careers of exceedingly studious girls who spent the great mass of their power in mental work, and in every case the pelvic power decreased in even pace with the expenditure of mental power. Not one exception to this have I ever seen, and all the lady students of the higher grades whom it has been my duty to professionally advise were suffering in regard to their pelvic lives and power.

James Compton Burnett, *Delicate, Backward, Puny and Stunted Children*, 1895

Maggie found the Latin Grammar quite soothing after her mathematical mortification; for she delighted in new words, and quickly found that there was an English Key at the end, which would make her very wise about Latin, at slight expense. She presently made up her mind to skip the rules in the Syntax – the examples became so absorbing. These mysterious sentences, snatched from an unknown context, – like strange horns of beasts, and leaves of unknown plants, brought from some far-off region, – gave boundless scope to her imagination, and were all the more fascinating because they were in a peculiar tongue of their own, which she could learn to interpret. It was really very interesting – the Latin Grammar that Tom had said no girls could learn: and she was proud because she found it interesting. The most fragmentary examples were her favourites. *Mors omnibus est communis* would have been jejune, only she liked to know the Latin; but the fortunate gentleman whom every one congratulated because he had a son 'endowed with *such* a disposition' afforded her a great deal of pleasant conjecture, and she was quite lost in the 'thick grove penetrable by no star', when Tom called out, 'Now, then, Magsie, give us the Grammar!' . . .

Maggie obeyed, and took the open book.
'Where do you begin, Tom?'

'O, I begin at "*Appellativa arborum*", because I say all over again what I've been learning this week.'

Tom sailed along pretty well for three lines; and Maggie was beginning to forget her office of prompter in speculating as to what *mas* could mean, which came twice over, when he stuck fast at *Sunt etiam volucrum*.

'Don't tell me, Maggie; *Sunt etiam volucrum* . . . *Sunt etiam volucrum* . . . *ut ostrca, cetus . . .*'

'No,' said Maggie, opening her mouth and shaking her head.

'*Sunt etiam volucrum*,' said Tom, very slowly, as if the next words might be expected to come sooner when he gave them this strong hint that they were waited for.

'C, e, u,' said Maggie, getting impatient.

'O, I know – hold your tongue,' said Tom. '*Ceu passer, hirundo: Ferarum*

*... ferarum ...*' Tom took his pencil and made several hard dots with it on his book-cover ... '*ferarum ...*'

'O dear, O dear, Tom,' said Maggie, 'what a time you are! *Ut ...*'

'*Ut, ostrea...*'

'No, no,' said Maggie, '*ut, tigris ...*'

'O yes, now I can do,' said Tom; 'it was *tigris, vulpes*, I'd forgotten: *ut tigris, vulpes; et Piscium.*'

With some further stammering and repetition, Tom got through the next few lines.

'Now, then,' he said, 'the next is what I've just learnt for to-morrow. Give me hold of the book a minute.'

After some whispered gabbling, assisted by the beating of his fist on the table, Tom returned the book.

'*Mascula nomina in a*,' he began.

'No, Tom,' said Maggie, 'that doesn't come next. It's *Nomen non creskens genīttivo ...*'

'*Creskens genittivo*,' exclaimed Tom, with a derisive laugh, for Tom had learned this omitted passage for his yesterday's lesson, and a young gentleman does not require an intimate or extensive acquaintance with Latin before he can feel the pitiable absurdity of false quantity. '*Creskens genittivo!* What a little silly you are, Maggie!'

'Well, you needn't laugh, Tom, for you didn't remember it at all. I'm sure it's spelt so; how was I to know?'

'Phee-e-e-h ! I told you girls couldn't learn Latin. It's *Nomen non crescens genitivo.*' ...

Nevertheless it was a very happy fortnight to Maggie, this visit to Tom. She was allowed to be in the study while he had his lessons, and in her various readings got very deep into the examples in the Latin Grammar. The astronomer who hated women generally, caused her so much puzzling speculation that she one day asked Mr Stelling if all astronomers hated women, or whether it was only this particular astronomer. But, forestalling his answer, she said,

'I suppose it's all astronomers: because, you know, they live up in high towers, and if the women came there, they might talk and hinder them from looking at the stars.'

Mr Stelling liked her prattle immensely, and they were on the best terms. She told Tom she should like to go to school to Mr Stelling, as he did, and learn just the same things. She knew she could do Euclid, for she had looked into it again, and she saw what A B C meant: they were the names of the lines.

138

'I'm sure you couldn't do it, now,' said Tom; 'and I'll just ask Mr Stelling if you could.'

'I don't mind,' said the little conceited minx. 'I'll ask him myself.'

'Mr Stelling,' she said, that same evening when they were in the drawing-room, 'couldn't I do Euclid, and all Tom's lessons, if you were to teach me instead of him?'

'No; you couldn't,' said Tom, indignantly. 'Girls can't do Euclid: can they, sir?'

'They can pick up a little of everything, I daresay,' said Mr Stelling. 'They've a great deal of superficial cleverness; but they couldn't go far into anything. They're quick and shallow.'

Tom, delighted with this verdict, telegraphed his triumph by wagging his head at Maggie behind Mr Stelling's chair. As for Maggie, she had hardly ever been so mortified. She had been so proud to be called 'quick' all her little life, and now it appeared that this quickness was the brand of inferiority. It would have been better to be slow, like Tom.

'Ha, ha! Miss Maggie!' said Tom, when they were alone; 'you see it's not such a fine thing to be quick. You'll never go far into anything, you know.'

George Eliot, from The Mill on the Floss, 1860

A mood of final emancipation came to me the next morning. I leant against a long wall underneath a window, when suddenly a voice began to thunder from inside. 'Very important. Causal conjunctions. We went very deeply into this last week. Read it out.' 'Causal conjunctions,' quavered a choir of young voices. 'Quippe, qui, and quoniam take the indicative.' 'Quippe, qui, and quoniam,' bellowed the usher, interrupting them, 'take the indicative.' The rasping voice sounded like the cry of a wild animal, as if one had passed on the top of a bus by the Zoo, but the uncouth language blended perfectly with the summer scene outside. 'Take this down – take it down, will you,' the roar continued. 'Conjectus est in carcerem – he was thrown into prison – quod patrem occidisset – on the grounds that he had killed his father – qui eo tempore – who at that time was flying into Italy – in Italiam refugiebat. RE-FU-GI-BAT,' he thundered, and the pedagogic rhythms floated out into the sun and along the dusty hedgerows. 'Conjectus est in carcerem,' mumbled the scribbling pupils; 'quippe, qui, and quoniam,' they chanted; 'causal conjunctions', till the words were lost above the Isle of Purbeck, a drone above the drone of bees.

Cyril Connolly, from The Condemned Playground, 1929

# The Rising Generation

The rising Australian generation is represented by a thin, lanky youth of about fifteen. He is milking. The cow-yard is next the house, and is mostly ankle-deep in slush. The boy drives a dusty, discouraged-looking cow into the bail, and pins her head there; then he gets tackle on to her right hindleg, hauls it back, and makes it fast to the fence. There are eleven cows, but not one of them can be milked out of the bail – chiefly because their teats are sore. The selector does not know what makes the teats sore, but he has an unquestioning faith in a certain ointment, recommended to him by a man who knows less about cows than he does himself, which he causes to be applied at irregular intervals – leaving the mode of application to the discretion of his son. Meanwhile the teats remain sore.

Having made the cow fast, the youngster cautiously takes hold of the least sore teat, yanks it suddenly, and dodges the cow's hock. When he gets enough milk to dip his dirty hands in, he moistens the teats, and things go on more smoothly. Now and then he relieves the monotony of his occupation by squirting at the eye of a calf which is dozing in the adjacent pen. Other times he milks into his mouth. Every time the cow kicks, a burr or a grass-seed or a bit of something else falls into the milk, and the boy drowns these things with a well-directed stream – on the principle that what's out of sight is out of mind.

Sometimes the boy sticks his head into the cow's side, hangs on by a teat, and dozes, while the bucket, mechanically gripped between his knees, sinks lower and lower till it rests on the ground. Likely as not he'll doze on until his mother's shrill voice startles him with an inquiry as to whether he intends to get that milking done to-day; other times he is roused by the plunging of the cow, or knocked over by a calf which has broken through a defective panel in the pen. In the latter case the youth gets tackle on to the calf, detaches its head from the teat with the heel of his boot, and makes it fast somewhere. Sometimes the cow breaks or loosens the leg-rope and gets her leg into the bucket and then the youth clings desperately to the pail and hopes she'll get her hoof out again without spilling the milk. Sometimes she does, more often she doesn't – it depends on the strength of the boy and the pail and on the strategy of the former. Anyway, the boy will lam the cow down with a jagged yard shovel, let her out, and bail up another.

When he considers that he has finished milking he lets the cows out with their calves and carries the milk down to the dairy, where he has a heated argument with his mother, who – judging from the quantity of milk – has reason to believe that he has slummed some of the milkers. This he indignantly denies, telling her she knows very well the cows are going dry.

Henry Lawson, from 'A Day on a Selection', *While the Billy Boils*, 1896

There was no girl over twelve or thirteen living permanently at home. Some were sent out to their first place at eleven. The way they were pushed out into the world at that tender age might have seemed heartless to a casual observer. As soon as a little girl approached school-leaving age, her mother would say, 'About time you was earnin' your own livin', me gal,' or, to a neighbour, 'I shan't be sorry when our young So-and-So gets her knees under somebody else's table. Five slices for breakfast this mornin', if you please!' From that time onward the child was made to feel herself one too many in the overcrowded home; while her brothers, when they left school and began to bring home a few shillings weekly, were treated with a new consideration and made much of. The parents did not want the boys to leave home. Later on, if they wished to strike out for themselves, they might even meet opposition, for their money, though barely sufficient to keep them in food, made a little more in the family purse, and every shilling was precious. The girls, while at home, could earn nothing . . .

After the girls left school at ten or eleven, they were usually kept at home for a year to help with the younger children, then places were found for them locally in the households of tradesmen, schoolmasters, stud grooms, or farm bailiffs. Employment in a public house was looked upon with horror by the hamlet mothers, and farm-house servants were a class apart. 'Once a farm-house servant, always a farm-house servant' they used to say, and they were more ambitious for their daughters.

The first places were called 'petty places' and looked upon as stepping-stones to better things. It was considered unwise to allow a girl to remain in her petty place more than a year; but a year she must stay whether she liked it or not, for that was the custom. The food in such places was good and abundant, and in a year a girl of thirteen would grow tall and strong enough for the desired 'gentlemen's service', her wages would buy her a few clothes, and she would be learning.

The employers were usually very kind to these small maids. In some houses they were treated as one of the family; in others they were put into caps and aprons and ate in the kitchen, often with one or two of the younger children of the house to keep them company. The wages were small, often only a shilling a week; but the remuneration did not end with the money payment. Material, already cut out and placed, was given them to make their underwear, and the Christmas gift of a best frock or a winter coat was common. Caps and

aprons and morning print dresses, if worn, were provided by the employer.
'She shan't want for anything while she is with me' was a promise frequently
made by a shopkeeper's wife when engaging a girl, and many were even better
than their word in that respect. They worked with the girls themselves and
trained them; then as they said, just as they were becoming useful they left
to 'better themselves'.

The mothers' attitude towards these mistresses of small households was
peculiar. If one of them had formerly been in service herself, her situation
was avoided, for 'a good servant makes a bad missis' they said. In any case
they considered it a favour to allow their small untrained daughters to 'oblige'
(it was always spoke of as 'obliging') in a small household. They were jealous
of their children's rights, and ready to rush in and cause an upset if anything
happened of which they did not approve; and they did not like it if the small
maid became fond of her employer or her family, or wished to remain in her
petty place after her year was up. One girl who had been sent out at eleven
as maid to an elderly couple and had insisted upon remaining there through
her teens, was always spoken of by her mother as 'our poor Em'. 'When I
sees t'other girls and how they keeps on improvin' an' think of our poor Em
wastin' her life in a petty place, I could sit down an' howl like a dog, that I
could,' she would say, long after Em had been adopted as a daughter by the
people to whom she had become attached.

Of course there were queer places and a few definitely bad places; but
these were the exception and soon became known and avoided. Laura once
accompanied a schoolfellow to interview a mistress who was said to require a
maid . . .

It was late afternoon when, coming out of a deep, narrow lane with a stream
trickling down the middle, they saw before them a grey-stone mansion with
twisted chimney-stacks and a sundial standing in long grass before the front
door. Martha and Laura were appalled at the size of the house. Gentry must
live there. Which door should they go to and what should they say?

In a paved yard a man was brushing down a horse, hissing so loudly as he
did so that he did not hear their first timid inquiry. When it was repeated
he raised his head and smiled. 'Ho! Ho!' he said. 'Yes, yes, it's Missis at the
house there you'll be wanting, I'll warrant.'

'Please does she want a maid?'

'I dare say she do. She generally do. But where's the maid? Goin' to roll
yourselves up into one, all three of ye? You go on round by that harness-room
and across the lawn by the big pear trees and you'll find the back door. Go
on; don't be afraid. She's not agoin' to eat ye.'

In response to their timid knock, the door was opened by a youngish
woman. She was like no one Laura had ever seen. Very slight – she would

have been called 'scraggy' in the hamlet – with a dead white face, dark, arched brows, and black hair brushed straight back from her forehead, and with all this black and whiteness set off by a little scarlet jacket that, when Laura described it to her mother later, was identified as a garibaldi. She seemed glad to see the children, though she looked doubtful when she heard their errand and saw Martha's size.

'So you want a place?' she asked as she conducted them into a kitchen as large as a church and not unlike one with its stone-paved floor and central pillar. Yes, she wanted a maid, and she thought Martha might do. How old was she? Twelve? And what could she do? Anything she was told? Well, that was right. It was not a hard place, for, although there were sixteen rooms, only three or four of them were in use. Could she get up at six without being called? There would be the kitchen range to light and the flues to be swept once a week, and the dining-room to be swept and dusted and the fire lighted before breakfast. She herself would be down in time to cook breakfast. No cooking was required, beyond preparing vegetables. After breakfast Martha would help her with the beds, turning out the rooms, paring the potatoes and so on; and after dinner there was plenty to do – washing up, cleaning knives and boots and polishing silver. And so she went on, mapping out Martha's day, until at nine o'clock she would be free to go to bed, after placing hot water in her mistress's bedroom.

Laura could see that Martha was bewildered. She stood, twisting her scarf, curtseying, and saying 'Yes, mum' to every thing.

'Then, as wages, I can offer you two pounds ten a year. It is not a great wage, but you are very small, and you'll have an easy place and a comfortable home. How do you like your kitchen?'

Martha's gaze wandered round the huge place, and once more she said, 'Yes, mum.'

'You'll find it nice and cosy here, eating your meals by the fire. You won't feel lonely, will you?'

This time Martha said, 'No, mum.'

'Tell your mother I shall expect her to fit you out well. You will want caps and aprons. I like my maids to look neat. And tell her to let you bring plenty of changes, for we only wash once in six weeks. I have a woman in to do it all up,' and although Martha knew her mother had not a penny to spend on her outfit, and that she had been told the last thing before she left home that morning to ask her prospective employer to send her mother her first month's wages in advance to buy necessaries, once again she said, 'Yes, mum.'

Flora Thompson, from *Lark Rise to Candleford*, 1945

*Follower*

My father worked with a horse-plough,
His shoulders globed like a full sail strung
Between the shafts and the furrow.
The horses strained at his clicking tongue.

An expert. He would set the wing
And fit the bright steel-pointed sock.
The sod rolled over without breaking.
At the headrig, with a single pluck

Of reins, the sweating team turned round
And back into the land. His eye
Narrowed and angled at the ground,
Mapping the furrow exactly.

I stumbled in his hob-nailed wake,
Fell sometimes on the polished sod;
Sometimes he rode me on his back
Dipping and rising to his plod.

I wanted to grow up and plough,
To close one eye, stiffen my arm.
All I ever did was follow
In his broad shadow round the farm.

I was a nuisance, tripping, falling,
Yapping always. But today
It is my father who keeps stumbling
Behind me, and will not go away.

  Seamus Heaney, from *Death of a Naturalist*, 1966


# The Cry of the Children

I'm sure I don't know how to spell my name. We go at four in the morning,
and sometimes at half-past four. We begin to work as soon as we get down.
We get out after four, sometimes at five, in the evening. We work the whole
time except an hour for dinner, and sometimes we haven't time to eat. I hurry*
by myself, and have done so for long. I know the corves are very heavy they

---

* To hurry was to push carts ('corves') loaded with coal from the coalface to the shaft.

are the biggest corves anywhere about. The work is far too hard for me: the sweat runs off me all over sometimes. I am very tired at night. Sometimes when we get home at night we have not power to wash us, and then we go to bed. Sometimes we fall asleep in the chair. Father said last night it was both a shame and a disgrace for girls to work as we do, but there was nought else for us to do. I have tried to get winding to do, but could not. I begun to hurry when I was seven and I have been hurrying ever since. I have been 11 years in the pit. The girls are always tired. I was poorly twice this winter, it was with headache. I hurry for Robert Wiggins: he is not akin to me. I riddle for him. We all riddle for them except the littlest when there is two. We don't always get enough to eat and drink, but we get a good supper. I have known my father go at two in the morning to work when we worked at Twibell's, where there is a day-hole to the pit, and he didn't come out till four. I am quite sure that we work constantly 12 hours except on Saturdays. We wear trousers and our shifts in the pit, and great big shoes clinkered and nailed. The girls never work naked to the waist in our pit. The men won't insult us in the pit. The conduct of the girls in the pit is good enough sometimes, and sometimes bad enough. I never went to a day-school. I went a little to a Sunday school, but I soon gave it over. I thought it too bad to be confined both Sundays and week-days. I walk about and get the fresh air on Sundays. I have not learnt to read. I don't know my letters. I never learnt nought. I never go to church or chapel; there is no church or chapel at Gawber, there is none nearer than a mile. If I was married I would not go to the pits, but I know some married women that do. The men do not insult the girls with us, but I think they do in some.

Ann Eggley, *Parliamentary Papers*, 1842

Go out, children, from the mine and from the city,
     Sing out, children, as the little thrushes do;
Pluck your handfuls of the meadow-cowslips pretty,
     Laugh aloud, to feel your fingers let them through!
But they answer, 'Are your cowslips of the meadows
     Like our weeds anear the mine?
Leave us quiet in the dark of the coal-shadows,
     From your pleasures fair and fine!

'For oh,' say the children, 'we are weary,
     And we cannot run or leap;
If we cared for any meadows, it were merely
     To drop down in them and sleep.

145

Our knees tremble sorely in the stooping,
   We fall upon our faces, trying to go;
And, underneath our heavy eyelids drooping,
   The reddest flower would look as pale as snow.
For, all day, we drag our burden tiring
     Through the coal-dark, underground;
Or, all day, we drive the wheels of iron
     In the factories, round and round.

'For, all day, the wheels are droning, turning,
   Their wind comes in our faces,
Till our hearts turn, our heads with pulses burning,
   And the walls turn in their places:
Turns the sky in the high window blank and reeling,
   Turns the long light that drops adown the wall,
Turn the black flies that crawl along the ceiling,
   All are turning, all the day, and we with all.
And all day, the iron wheels are droning,
     And sometimes we could pray,
"Oh ye wheels," (breaking out in a mad moaning)
     "Stop! be silent for to-day!" '
       Elizabeth Barrett Browning, from 'The Cry of the Children', 1843

See, too, these emerge from the bowels of the earth! Infants of four and five years of age, many of them girls, pretty and still soft and timid; entrusted with the fulfilment of most responsible duties, and the nature of which entails on them the necessity of being the earliest to enter the mine and the latest to leave it. Their labour indeed is not severe, for that would be impossible, but it is passed in darkness and in solitude. They endure that punishment which philosophical philanthropy has invented for the direst criminals, and which those criminals deem more terrible than the death for which it is substituted. Hour after hour elapses, and all that reminds the infant trappers of the world they have quitted and that which they have joined, is the passage of the coal-wagons for which they open the air-doors of the galleries, and on keeping which doors constantly closed, except at this moment of passage, the safety of the mine and the lives of the persons employed in it entirely depend.

      Benjamin Disraeli, from *Sybil or The Two Nations*, 1845

'The chief manager [of the blacking business], James Lamert, the relative who had lived with us in Bayham-street, seeing how I was employed from day to day, and knowing what our domestic circumstances then were, proposed that I should go into the blacking warehouse, to be as useful as I could, at a salary, I think, of six shillings a week. I am not clear whether it was six or seven. I am inclined to believe, from my uncertainty on this head, that it was six at first, and seven afterwards. At any rate the offer was accepted very willingly by my father and mother, and on a Monday morning I went down to the blacking warehouse to begin my business life.

'It is wonderful to me how I could have been so easily cast away at such an age. It is wonderful to me, that, even after my descent into the poor little drudge I had been since we came to London, no one had compassion enough on me – a child of singular abilities, quick, eager, delicate, and soon hurt, bodily or mentally – to suggest that something might have been spared, as certainly it might have been, to place me at any common school. Our friends, I take it, were tired out. No one made any sign. My father and mother were quite satisfied. They could hardly have been more so, if I had been twenty years of age, distinguished at a grammar-school, and going to Cambridge.

'The blacking warehouse was the last house on the left-hand side of the way, at old Hungerford-stairs. It was a crazy, tumble-down old house, abutting of course on the river, and literally overrun with rats. Its wainscotted rooms and its rotten floors and staircase, and the old grey rats swarming down in the cellars, and the sound of their squeaking and scuffling coming up the stairs at all times, and the dirt and decay of the place, rise up visibly before me, as if I were there again. The counting-house was on the first floor, looking over the coal-barges and the river. There was a recess in it, in which I was to sit and work. My work was to cover the pots of paste-blacking; first with a piece of oil-paper, and then with a piece of blue paper; to tie them round with a string; and then to clip the paper close and neat, all round, until it looked as smart as a pot of ointment from an apothecary's shop. When a certain number of grosses of pots had attained this pitch of perfection, I was to paste on each a printed label; and then go on again with more pots. Two or three other boys were kept at similar duty downstairs on similar wages. One of them came up, in a ragged apron and a paper cap, on the first Monday morning, to show me the trick of using the string and tying the knot. His name was Bob Fagin; and I took the liberty of using his name, long afterwards, in *Oliver Twist*.

'Our relative had kindly arranged to teach me something in the dinner-hour; from twelve to one, I think it was; every day. But an arrangement so incompatible with counting-house business soon died away, from no fault of his or mine; and for the same reason, my small work-table, and my grosses of pots, my papers, string, scissors, paste-pot, and labels, by little and little, vanished out of the recess in the counting-house and kept company with the other small work-tables, grosses of pots, papers, string, scissors, and paste-pots, downstairs. It was not long, before Bob Fagin and I, and another boy whose name was Paul Green, but who was currently believed to have been christened Poll (a belief which I transferred, long afterwards again, to Mr Sweedlepipe, in *Martin Chuzzlewit*), worked generally, side by side. Bob Fagin was an orphan, and lived with his brother-in-law, a waterman. Poll Green's father had the additional distinction of being a fireman, and was employed at Drury-lane theatre; where another relation of Poll's, I think his little sister, did imps in the pantomimes.

'No words can express the secret agony of my soul as I sunk into this companionship; compared these everyday associates with those of my happier childhood; and felt my early hopes of growing up to be a learned and distin-guished man, crushed in my breast. The deep remembrance of the sense I had of being utterly neglected and hopeless; of the shame I felt in my position; of the misery it was to my young heart to believe that, day by day, what I had learned, and thought, and delighted in, and raised my fancy and my emulation up by, was passing away from me, never to be brought back any more; cannot be written. My whole nature was so penetrated with the grief and humiliation of such considerations, that even now, famous and caressed and happy, I often forget in my dreams that I have a dear wife and children; even that I am a man; and wander desolately back to that time of my life.'

J. Forster, from *The Life of Charles Dickens*, 1874

A very general industry is the carding of hooks and eyes, and the advantage of it is that the tiniest mite can here render assistance. Mother and her little girls sew the eyes on to the cards, and then baby passes the hooks into these eyes. Mother and the girls then sew down the hooks and the card is complete. There are four dozen hooks and eyes on each card, and gross and gross of cards go to a pack. Shall we calculate the number of stitches which a pack demands? No, we have no time for mental arithmetic, but we can guess the total fairly accurately by the cotton we consume. One has to supply one's own cotton and the speed with which it is used up cannot fail to impress us . . .

Back of Richard Street I found a woman and a little girl, who were both as white of face as is the paper upon which I trace their painful records, who were dying of starvation in the hook-and-eye trade. 'Starting,' she said, 'the two of us early on Saturday morning and working hard all day Saturday, and beginning again on Monday morning and on till dinner-time, we earned 1*s* 6*d*. You get 10*d* for a pack, and you find your own cotton and needles. Me and my little girl – she is the only one of my five children who can help as yet – worked yesterday from 4.30 p.m. till past 11, and we earned 4*d* between us.' None of these people had eaten anything all that day. There was only a little tea and sugar in the house. The babies were crying . . .

There was deep pathos in all these scenes, but the spectacle which, when I think back upon these heavy hours, will always haunt me with greatest sorrow is one I saw in a kitchen, in a house off Jennens Row, in a courtyard under the lee of a common lodging. Here, late one evening, I found three little children, busy at work at a table on which were heaped up piles of cards, and a vast mass of tangled hooks and eyes. The eldest girl was eleven, the next was nine, and a little boy of five completed the companionship. They were all working as fast as their little fingers could work. The girls sewed, the baby hooked. They were too busy to raise their eyes from their tasks – the clear eyes of youth under the flare of the lamp! Here were the energy, the interest, which in our youth we all bring to our several tasks in the happy ignorance of the weight and stress of the years and years of drudgery to come.

I looked at these bright eyes, these quick and flexible fingers, and I thought of the old woman of ninety whom I had seen in the morning in Unit Street. I remembered her eyes which had the glaze of approaching dissolution upon them; I remembered the knotted, labour-gnarled hands. Her eyes had been bright once. She, too, had brought interest and energy to the miserable tasks in which her life began. Years had followed years, decade had added itself to decade. There had been no change brought by chance or time.

The drudgery is eternal. There is no hope of relief. One treads, firmly at first, and then with faltering steps, the millround of one's allotted task, until the end, which is the nameless grave. And it was because I read in the clear eyes of those children the ignorance of this cruel but indisputable postulate of the lives of the very poor, that their very brightness, their cheerfulness filled me with more poignant sorrow than any I had felt till then. *Quous Tandem*. How long? How long? All your life and till the grave.

Robert Sherard, from *The Child-Slaves of Britain*, 1905

The next morning, at half-past five, Darius began his career in earnest. He was 'mould-runner' to a 'muffin-maker', a muffin being not a comestible but a small plate, fashioned by its maker on a mould. The business of Darius was to run as hard as he could with the mould, and a newly created plate adhering thereto, into the drying-stove. This 'stove' was a room lined with shelves, and having a red-hot stove and stove-pipe in the middle. As no man of seven could reach the upper shelves, a pair of steps was provided for Darius, and up these he had to scamper. Each mould with its plate had to be leaned carefully against the wall, and if the soft clay of a new-born plate was damaged, Darius was knocked down. The atmosphere outside the stove was chill, but owing to the heat of the stove, Darius was obliged to work half naked. His sweat ran down his cheeks, and down his chest, and down his back, making white channels, and lastly it soaked his hair.

When there were no moulds to be sprinted into the drying-stove, and no moulds to be carried less rapidly out, Darius was engaged in clay-wedging. That is to say, he took a piece of raw clay weighing more than himself, cut it in two with a wire, raised one half above his head and crashed it down with all his force upon the other half, and he repeated the process until the clay was thoroughly soft and even in texture. At a later period it was discovered that hydraulic machinery could perform this operation more easily and more effectually than the brawny arms of a man of seven. At eight o'clock in the evening Darius was told that he had done enough for that day, and that he must arrive at five sharp the next morning to light the fire, before his master the muffin-maker began to work. When he inquired how he was to light the fire his master kicked him jovially on the thigh and suggested that he should ask another mould-runner. His master was not a bad man at heart, it was said, but on Tuesdays, after Sunday and Saint Monday, masters were apt to be capricious.

Darius reached home at a quarter to nine, having eaten nothing but bread all day. Somehow he had lapsed into the child again. His mother took him on her knee, and wrapped her sacking apron round his ragged clothes, and cried over him and cried into his supper of porridge, and undressed him and put him to bed. But he could not sleep easily because he was afraid of being late the next morning . . .

By six o'clock on Saturday night Darius had earned a shilling for his week's work. But he could only possess himself of the shilling by going to a magnificent public-house with his master the muffin-maker. This was the first time that he had ever been inside a public-house. The place was crowded with men, women, and children eating the most lovely hot rolls and drinking beer, in an atmosphere exquisitely warm. And behind a high counter a stout jolly man was counting piles and piles and piles of silver. Darius's master, in company with other boys' masters, gave this stout man four sovereigns to change, and it was an hour before he changed them. Meanwhile Darius was instructed that he must eat a roll like the rest, together with cheese. Never had he tasted anything so luscious. He had a match with his mentor, as to which of them could spin out his roll the longer, honestly chewing all the time; and he won. Someone gave him half a glass of beer. At half-past seven he received his shilling, which consisted of a sixpenny-piece and four pennies;

and, leaving the gay public-house, pushed his way through a crowd of tearful women with babies in their arms at the doors, and went home.

Arnold Bennett, from *Clayhanger*, 1910

# In the Fields

We trudged on, over wide stubbles, with innumerable weeds; over wide fallows, in which the deserted ploughs stood frozen fast; then over clover and grass, burnt black with frost; then over a field of turnips, where we passed a large fold of hurdles, within which some hundred sheep stood, with their heads turned from the cutting blast. All was dreary, idle, silent; no sound or sign of human beings. One wondered where the people lived, who cultivated so vast a tract of civilized, over-peopled, nineteenth-century England. As we came up to the fold, two little boys hailed us from the inside – two little wretches with blue noses and white cheeks, scarecrows of rags and patches, their feet peeping through bursten shoes twice too big for them, who seemed to have shared between them a ragged pair of worsted gloves, and cowered among the sheep, under the shelter of a hurdle, crying and inarticulate with cold.

'What's the matter, boys?'

'Turmits is froze, and us can't turn the handle of the cutter. Do ye gie us a turn, please?'

We scrambled over the hurdles, and gave the miserable little creatures the benefit of ten minutes' labour. They seemed too small for such exertion: their little hands were purple with chilblains, and they were so sorefooted they could scarcely limp. I was surprised to find them at least three years older than their size and looks denoted, and still more surprised, too, to find that their salary for all this bitter exposure to the elements – such as I believe I could not have endured two days running – was the vast sum of one shilling a week, Sundays included. 'They didn't never go to school, nor to church neither, except just now and then, sometimes – they had to mind the shep.'

I went on, sickened with the contrast between the highly-bred, over-fed, fat, thick-woolled animals, with their troughs of turnips and malt-dust, and their racks of rich clover-hay, and their little pent-house of rock-salt, having nothing to do but to eat and sleep, and eat again, and the little half-starved shivering animals who were their slaves. Man the master of the brutes? Bah! As society is now, the brutes are the masters – the horse, the sheep, the bullock, is the master, the labourer is their slave. 'Oh! but the brutes are eaten!' Well; the horses at least are not eaten – they live, like landlords, till they die. And those who are eaten, are certainly not eaten by their human servants. The sheep they fat, another kills, to parody Shelley; and, after all, is not the labourer, as well as the sheep, eaten by you, my dear Society? – devoured body and soul, not the less really because you are longer about the meal, there being an old prejudice against cannibalism, and also against murder – except after the Riot Act has been read.

Charles Kingsley, from *Alton Locke, Tailor and Poet, 1850*

On the day that I was eight years of age, I left school, and began to work fourteen hours a day in the fields, with from forty to fifty other children of whom, even at that early age, I was the eldest. We were followed all day long by an old man carrying a long whip in his hand which he did not forget to use. A great many of the children were only five years of age. You will think that I am exaggerating, but I am *not*, it is as true as the Gospel. Thirty-five years ago is the time I speak of, and the place, Croyland in Lincolnshire, nine miles from Peterborough. I could even now name several of the children who began at the age of five to work in the gangs, and also the name of the ganger.

We always left the town, summer and winter, the moment the old Abbey clock struck six. Anyone who has read *Hereward the Wake*, by Charles Kingsley, will have read a good description of this Abbey. We had to walk a very long way to our work, never much less than two miles each way, and very often five miles each way. The large farms all lay a good distance from the town, and it was on those farms that we worked. In the winter, by the time we reached our work, it was light enough to begin, and of course we worked until it was dark and then had our long walk home. I never remember to have reached home sooner than six and more often seven, even in winter. In the summer, we did not leave the fields in the evening until the clock had struck six, and then of course we must walk home, and this walk was no easy task for us children who had worked hard all day on the ploughed fields.

In all the four years I worked in the fields, I never worked one hour under cover of a barn, and only once did we have a meal in a house. And I shall never forget that one meal or the woman who gave us it. It was a most terrible day. The cold east wind (I suppose it was an east wind, for surely no wind ever blew colder), the sleet and snow which came every now and then in showers seemed almost to cut us to pieces. We were working upon a large farm that lay half-way between Croyland and Peterborough. Had the snow and sleet come continuously we should have been allowed to come home, but because it only came at intervals, of course we had to stay. I have been out in all sorts of weather but never remember a colder day. Well, the morning passed along somehow. The ganger did his best for us by letting us have a run in our turns, but that did not help us very much because we were too numbed with the cold to be able to run much. Dinner-time came, and we were preparing to sit down under a hedge and eat our cold dinner and drink our cold tea, when we saw the shepherd's wife coming towards us, and she said to our ganger, 'Bring these children into my house and let them eat their dinner there.' We went into that very small two-roomed cottage, and when we got into the largest room there was not standing room for us all, but this woman's heart was large, even if her house was small, and so she put her few chairs and table out into the garden, and then we all sat down in a ring upon the floor. She then placed in our midst a very large saucepan of hot boiled potatoes, and bade us help ourselves. Truly, although I have attended scores of grand parties and banquets since that time, not one of them has seemed half as good to me as that meal did. I well remember that woman. She was one of the plainest women I ever knew; in fact she was what the world would call quite ugly, and yet I can't think of her even now without thinking of that verse in one of our hymns, where it says,

'No, Earth has angels though their forms are moulded
But of such clay as fashions all below,
Though harps are wanting, and bright pinions folded,
We know them by the love-light on their brow.'

Had I time I could write how our gang of children, one winter's night, had to wade for half a mile through the flood. These floods occur nearly every winter, when the Wash overflows her banks. In harvest-time we left home at four o'clock in the morning, and stayed in the fields until it was dark, about nine o'clock. As a rule the gangs were disbanded during the harvest, each child going to work with its own friends, and when the corn was cut, the whole families would go gleaning the corn left in the fields, this being, of course, the gleaners' own property. A great many families gleaned sufficient to keep them in bread for the whole of the winter.

For four years, summer and winter, I worked in these gangs – no holidays of any sort, with the exception of very wet days and Sundays – and at the end of that time it felt like Heaven to me when I was taken to the town of Leeds, and put to work in the factory. Talk about White Slaves, the Fen district at that time was the place to look for them.

> Mrs Barrow, 'A Childhood in the Fens about 1850–60',
> from *Life As We Have Known It*, ed. Margaret Llewellyn Davies, 1931

When the sun was dropping low, Ántonia came up the big south draw with her team. How much older she had grown in eight months! She had come to us a child, and now she was a tall, strong young girl, although her fifteenth birthday had just slipped by. I ran out and met her as she brought her horses up to the windmill to water them. She wore the boots her father had so thoughtfully taken off before he shot himself, and his old fur cap. Her outgrown cotton dress switched about her calves, over the boot-tops. She kept her sleeves rolled up all day, and her arms and throat were burned as brown as a sailor's. Her neck came up strongly out of her shoulders, like the bole of a tree out of the turf. One sees that draught-horse neck among the peasant women in all old countries.

She greeted me gaily, and began at once to tell me how much ploughing she had done that day. Ambrosch, she said, was on the north quarter, breaking sod with the oxen.

'Jim, you ask Jake how much he ploughed to-day. I don't want that Jake get more done in one day than me. I want we have very much corn this fall.'

While the horses drew in the water, and nosed each other, and then drank again, Ántonia sat down on the windmill step and rested her head on her hand.

'You see the big prairie fire from your place last night? I hope your grandpa ain't lose no stacks?'

'No, we didn't. I came to ask you something, Tony. Grandmother wants to know if you can't go to the term of school that begins next week over at the sod school-house. She says there's a good teacher, and you'd learn a lot.'

Ántonia stood up, lifting and dropping her shoulders as if they were stiff. 'I ain't got time to learn. I can work like mans now. My mother can't say no more how Ambrosch do all and nobody to help him. I can work as much as him. School is all right for little boys. I help make this land one good farm.'

She clucked to her team and started for the barn. I walked beside her, feeling vexed. Was she going to grow up boastful like her mother, I wondered? Before we reached the stable, I felt something tense in her silence, and glancing up I saw that she was crying. She turned her face from me and looked off at the red streak of dying light, over the dark prairie.

I climbed up into the loft and threw down the hay for her, while she unharnessed her team. We walked slowly back toward the house. Ambrosch had come in from the north quarter, and was watering his oxen at the tank.

Ántonia took my hand. 'Sometime you will tell me all those nice things you learn at the school, won't you, Jimmy?' she asked with a sudden rush of feeling in her voice. 'My father, he went much to school. He know a great deal; how to make the fine cloth like what you not got here. He play horn and violin, and he read so many books that the priests in Bohemie come to talk to him. You won't forget my father, Jim?'

'No,' I said, 'I will never forget him.'

Mrs Shimerda asked me to stay for supper. After Ambrosch and Ántonia had washed the field dust from their hands and faces at the wash-basin by the kitchen door, we sat down at the oilcloth-covered table. Mrs Shimerda ladled meal mush out of an iron pot and poured milk on it. After the mush we had fresh bread and sorghum molasses, and coffee with the cake that had been kept warm in the feathers. Ántonia and Ambrosch were talking in Bohemian; disputing about which of them had done more ploughing that day. Mrs Shimerda egged them on, chuckling while she gobbled her food.

Presently Ambrosch said sullenly in English: 'You take them ox to-morrow and try the sod plough. Then you not be so smart.'

His sister laughed. 'Don't be mad. I know it's awful hard work for break sod. I milk the cow for you to-morrow if you want' . . .

I began to wish I had not stayed for supper. Everything was disagreeable to me. Ántonia ate so noisily now, like a man, and she yawned often at the table and kept stretching her arms over her head, as if they ached. Grandmother had said, 'Heavy field work'll spoil that girl. She'll lose all her nice ways and get rough ones.' She had lost them already.

After supper I rode home through the sad, soft spring twilight. Since winter I had seen very little of Ántonia. She was out in the fields from sunup until sundown. If I rode over to see her where she was ploughing, she stopped at the end of a row to chat for a moment then gripped her plough-handles, clucked to her team, and waded on down the furrow, making me feel that she was now grown up and had no time for me. On Sundays she helped her mother make garden or sewed all day. Grandfather was pleased with Ántonia. When we complained of her, he only smiled and said, 'She will help some fellow get ahead in the world.'

Nowadays Tony could talk of nothing but the prices of things, or how much she could lift and endure. She was too proud of her strength. I knew, too, that Ambrosch put upon her some chores a girl ought not to do, and that the farm-hands around the country joked in a nasty way about it. Whenever I saw her come up the furrow, shouting to her beasts, sunburned, sweaty, her dress open at the neck, and her throat and chest dust-plastered, I used to think of the tone in which poor Mr Shimerda, who could say so little, yet managed to say so much when he exclaimed, 'My Án-tonia!'

Willa Cather, from *My Ántonia*, 1918


# Shepherds and Guards

We lay like lizards in the long grass round the stones of the foremost cairn upon the hill-top and saw the garrison parade. Three hundred and ninety-nine infantry, little toy men, ran about when the bugle sounded, and formed up in stiff lines below the black building till there was more bugling: then they scattered, and after a few minutes the smoke of cooking fires went up. A herd of sheep and goats in charge of a little ragged boy issued out towards us. Before he reached the foot of the hills there came a loud whistling down the valley from the north, and a tiny, picture-book train rolled slowly into view across the hollow sounding bridge and halted just outside the station, panting out white puffs of steam.

The shepherd lad held on steadily, driving his goats with shrill cries up our hill for the better pasture on the western side. We sent two Juheina down behind a ridge beyond sight of the enemy, and they ran from each side and caught him. The lad was of the outcast Heteym, pariahs of the desert, whose poor children were commonly sent on hire as shepherds to the tribes about them. This one cried continually, and made efforts to escape as often as he saw his goats straying uncared-for about the hill. In the end the men lost patience and tied him up roughly, when he screamed for terror that they would kill him. Fauzan had great ado to make him quiet, and then questioned him about his Turkish masters. But all his thoughts were for the flock: his eyes followed them miserably while the tears made edged and crooked tracks down his dirty face.

Shepherds were a class apart. For the ordinary Arab the hearth was a university, about which their world passed and where they heard the best talk, the news of their tribe, its poems, histories, love tales, lawsuits and bargainings. By such constant sharing in the hearth councils they grew masters of expression, dialecticians, orators, able to sit with dignity in any gathering and never at a loss for moving words. The shepherds missed the whole of this. From infancy they followed their calling, which took them in all seasons and weathers, day and night, into the hills and condemned them to loneliness and brute company. In the wilderness, among the dry bones of nature, they grew up natural, knowing nothing of man and his affairs; hardly sane in ordinary talk; but very wise in plants, wild animals and the habits of their own goats and sheep, whose milk was their chief sustenance. With manhood they became sullen, while a few turned dangerously savage, more animal than man, haunting the flocks, and finding the satisfaction of their adult appetites in them, to the exclusion of more licit affections.

For hours after the shepherd had been suppressed only the sun moved in our view. As it climbed we shifted our cloaks to filter its harshness, and basked in luxurious warmth. The restful hill-top gave me back something of the sense-interests which I had lost since I had been ill. I was able to note once more the typical hill scenery, with its hard stone crests, its sides of bare rock, and lower slopes of loose sliding screes, packed, as the base was approached, solidly with a thin dry soil. The stone itself was glistening, yellow, sunburned stuff; metallic in ring, and brittle; splitting red or green or brown as the case might be. From every soft place sprouted thorn-bushes; and there was frequent grass, usually growing from one root in a dozen stout blades, knee-high and straw-coloured: the heads were empty ears between many-feathered arrows of silvery down. With these, and with a shorter grass, whose bottle-brush heads of pearly grey reached only to the ankle, the hill-sides were furred white and bowed themselves lowly towards us with each puff of the casual wind . . .

At dusk we climbed down again with the goat-herd prisoner, and what we could gather of his flock. Our main body would come this night, so that Fauzan and I wandered out across the darkling plain till we found a pleasant gun-position in some low ridges not two thousand yards from the station. On our return, very tired, fires were burning among the trees. Shakir had just arrived, and his men and ours were roasting goat-flesh contentedly. The shepherd was tied up behind my sleeping place, because he had gone frantic when his charges were unlawfully slaughtered. He refused to taste the supper; and we only forced bread and rice into him by the threat of dire punishment if he insulted our hospitality. They tried to convince him that we should take the station next day and kill his masters; but he would not be comforted, and afterwards, for fear lest he escape, had to be lashed to his tree again.

T. E. Lawrence, from *Seven Pillars of Wisdom*, 1926

I was not forced to join the Red Guards. I was keen to do so. In spite of what was happening around me, my aversion and fear had no clear object, and it never occurred to me to question the Cultural Revolution or the Red Guards explicitly. They were Mao's creations, and Mao was beyond contemplation.

Like many Chinese, I was incapable of rational thinking in those days. We were so cowed and contorted by fear and indoctrination that to deviate from the path laid down by Mao would have been inconceivable. Besides, we had been overwhelmed by deceptive rhetoric, disinformation, and hypocrisy, which made it virtually impossible to see through the situation and to form an intelligent judgement.

Back at school, I heard that there had been many complaints from 'reds' demanding to know why they had not been admitted to the Red Guards. That was why it was important to be there on National Day, as there was going to be a big enrolment, incorporating all the rest of the 'reds'. So, at the very time the Cultural Revolution had brought disaster on my family, I became a Red Guard.

I was thrilled by my red armband with its gold characters. It was the fashion of the day for Red Guards to wear old army uniforms with leather belts, like the one Mao was seen wearing at the beginning of the Cultural Revolution. I was keen to follow the fashion, so as soon as I was enrolled I rushed home, and from the bottom of an old trunk I dug out a pale-grey Lenin jacket which had been my mother's uniform in the early 1950s. It was a little too big, so I got my grandmother to take it in. With a leather belt from a pair of my father's trousers my costume was complete. But out on the streets I felt very uncomfortable. I found my image too aggressive. Still, I kept the outfit on.

Soon after this my grandmother went to Peking. I had to stay in the school, having just joined the Red Guards. Because of what had happened at home, the school frightened and startled me all the time. When I saw the 'blacks' and 'greys' having to clean the toilets and the grounds, their heads bowed, a creeping dread came over me, as though I were one of them. When the Red Guards went off at night on house raids, my legs went weak, as if they were heading for my family. When I noticed pupils whispering near me, my heart started to palpitate frantically: were they saying that I had become a 'black', or that my father had been arrested?

But I found a refuge: the Red Guard reception office . . .

One hot night two rather coarse middle-aged women turned up at the reception office, which was boisterous as usual. They introduced themselves as the director and deputy director of a residents' committee near the school. They talked in a very mysterious and grave manner, as though they were on some grand mission. I had always disliked this kind of affectation, so I turned my back. But soon I could tell that an explosive piece of information had been delivered. The people who had been hanging around started shouting, 'Get a truck! Get a truck! Let's all go there!' Before I knew what was happening, I was swept out of the room by the crowd and into a truck. As Mao had ordered the workers to support the Red Guards, trucks and drivers were permanently at our service. In the truck, I was squeezed next to one of the women. She was retelling her story, her eyes full of eagerness to ingratiate herself with us. She said that a woman in her neighbourhood was the wife of a Kuomintang officer who had fled to Taiwan, and that she had hidden a portrait of Chiang Kai-shek in her apartment.

I did not like the woman, especially her toadying smile. And I resented her for making me go on my first house raid. Soon the truck stopped in front of a narrow alley. We all got out and followed the two women down the cobbled path. It was pitch-dark, the only light coming from the crevices between the planks of wood that formed the walls of the houses. I staggered and slipped, trying to fall behind. The apartment of the accused woman consisted of two rooms, and was so small that it could not hold our truckful of people. I was only too happy to stay outside. But before long someone shouted that space had been made for those outside to come in and 'receive an education in class struggle'.

As soon as I was pressed into the room with the others, my nostrils were filled with the stench of faeces, urine, and unwashed bodies. The room had been turned upside down. Then I saw the accused woman. She was perhaps in her forties, kneeling in the middle of the room, partly naked. The room was lit by a bare fifteen-watt bulb. In its shadows, the kneeling figure on the floor looked grotesque. Her hair was in a mess, and part of it seemed to be matted with blood. Her eyes were bulging out in desperation as she shrieked: 'Red Guard masters! I do not have a portrait of Chiang Kai-shek! I swear I do not!' She was banging her head on the floor so hard there were loud thuds and blood oozed from her forehead. The flesh on her back was covered with cuts and bloodstains. When she lifted her bottom in a kowtow, murky patches were visible and the smell of excrement filled the air. I was so frightened that I quickly averted my eyes. Then I saw her tormentor, a seventeen-year-old boy named Chian, whom up to now I had rather liked. He was lounging in a chair with a leather belt in his hand, playing with its brass buckle. 'Tell the truth, or I'll hit you again,' he said languidly.

Chian's father was an army officer in Tibet. Most officers sent to Tibet left their families in Chengdu, the nearest big city in China proper, because Tibet was considered an uninhabitable and barbaric place. Previously I had been rather attracted by Chian's languorous manner, which had given an impression of gentleness. Now I murmured, trying to control the quaking in my voice, 'Didn't Chairman Mao teach us to use verbal struggle [*wen-dou*] rather than violent struggle [*wu-dou*]? Maybe we shouldn't . . . ?'

My feeble protest was echoed by several voices in the room. But Chian cast us a disgusted sideways glance and said emphatically: 'Draw a line between yourselves and the class enemy. Chairman Mao says, "Mercy to the enemy is cruelty to the people!" If you are afraid of blood, don't be Red Guards!' His face was twisted into ugliness by fanaticism. The rest of us fell silent. Although it was impossible to feel anything but revulsion at what he was doing, we could not argue with him. We had been taught to be ruthless to class enemies. Failure to do so would make us class enemies ourselves. I turned and walked quickly into the garden at the back. It was crammed with Red Guards with shovels. From inside the house the sound of lashes started again, accompanied by screams that made my hair stand on end. The yelling must have been unbearable for the others too, because many swiftly straightened up from their digging: 'There is nothing here. Let's go! Let's go!' As we passed through the room, I caught sight of Chian standing casually over his victim. Outside the door, I saw the woman informer with the ingratiating eyes. Now there was a cringing and frightened look there. She opened her mouth as if to say something, but no words came out. As I glanced at her face, it dawned on me that there was no portrait of Chiang Kai-shek. She had denounced the poor woman out of vindictiveness. The Red Guards were being used to settle old scores. I climbed back into the truck full of disgust and rage.

Jung Chang, from *Wild Swans: Three Daughters of China*, 1991

## Prodigious Stock

– *Tristram*, said he, shall be made to conjugate every word in the dictionary, backwards and forwards the same way; – every word, *Yorick*, by this means, you see, is converted into a thesis or an hypothesis; – every thesis and hypothesis have an offspring of propositions; – and each proposition has its own consequences and conclusions; every one of which leads the mind on again, into fresh tracks of enquiries and doubtings. – The force of this engine, added my father, is incredible in opening a child's head. – 'Tis enough, brother *Shandy*, cried my uncle *Toby*, to burst it into a thousand splinters. –

I presume, said *Yorick*, smiling – it must be owing to this, – (for let logicians say what they will, it is not to be accounted for sufficiently from the bare use of the ten predicaments) – That the famous *Vincent Quirino*, amongst the many other astonishing feats of his childhood, of which the Cardinal *Bembo* has given the world so exact a story, – should be able to paste up in the public schools at *Rome*, so early as in the eighth year of his age, no less than four thousand five hundred and fifty different theses, upon the most abstruse points of the most abstruse theology; – and to defend and maintain them in such sort, as to cramp and dumbfound his opponents. – What is that, cried my father, to what is told us of *Alphonsus Tostatus*, who, almost in his nurse's arms, learned all the sciences and liberal arts without being taught anyone of them? – What shall we say of the great *Piereskius*? – That's the very man, cried my uncle *Toby*, I once told you of, brother *Shandy*, who walked a matter of five hundred miles, reckoning from *Paris* to *Shevling*, and from *Shevling* back again, merely to see *Stevinus*'s flying chariot. – He was a very great man! added my uncle *Toby* (meaning *Stevinus*) – He was so, brother *Toby*, said my father (meaning *Piereskius*) – and multiplied his ideas so fast, and increased his knowledge to such a prodigious stock, that, if we may give credit to an anecdote concerning him, which we cannot withhold here, without shaking the authority of all anecdotes whatever – at seven years of age, his father committed entirely to his care the education of his younger brother, a boy of five years old, – with the sole management of all his concerns. – Was the father as wise as the son? quoth my uncle *Toby*: – I should think not, said

*Yorick*: – But what are these, continued my father – (breaking out in a kind of enthusiasm) – what are these, to those prodigies of childhood in *Grotius, Scioppius, Heinsius, Politian, Pascal, Joseph Scaliger, Ferdinand de Cordoué*, and others – some of which left off their substantial forms at nine years old, or sooner, and went on reasoning without them; – others went through their classics at seven; – wrote tragedies at eight; – *Ferdinand de Cordoué* was so wise at nine, – 'twas thought the Devil was in him; – and at *Venice* gave such proofs of his knowledge and goodness, that the monks imagined he was *Antichrist*, or nothing. – Others were master of fourteen languages at ten, – finished the course of their rhetoric, poetry, logic, and ethics, at eleven, – put forth their commentaries upon *Servius* and *Martianus Capella* at twelve, – and at thirteen received their degrees in philosophy, laws, and divinity: – But you forget the great *Lipsius*, quoth *Yorick*, who composed a work the day he was born: – They should have wiped it up, said my uncle *Toby*, and said no more about it.

Laurence Sterne, from *The Life and Opinions of Tristram Shandy,* 1759

## Peter Goole
### Who Ruined His Father and Mother
### By Extravagance

#### Part 1

Young Peter Goole, a child of nine
Gave little reason to complain.
Though an imaginative youth
He very often told the truth,
And never tried to black the eyes
Of Comrades of superior size.
He did his lessons (more or less)
Without extravagant distress,
And showed sufficient intellect,
But failed in one severe defect;
It seems he wholly lacked a sense
Of limiting the day's expense,
And money ran between his hands
Like water through the Ocean Sands.
Such conduct could not but affect
His parent's fortune, which was wrecked
Like many and many another one
By folly in a spendthrift son:

By that most tragical mischance,
An Only Child's Extravagance.

There came a day when Mr Goole
– The Father of this little fool –
With nothing in the bank at all
Was up against it, like a wall.
He wrang his hands, exclaiming, 'If
I only had a bit of Stiff
How different would be my life!'
Whereat his true and noble wife
Replied, to comfort him, 'Alas!
I said that this would come to pass!
Nothing can keep us off the rocks
But Peter's little Money Box.'
The Father, therefore (and his wife),
They prised it open with a knife –
But nothing could be found therein
Save two bone buttons and a pin.

### Part II

They had to sell the house and grounds
For less than twenty thousand pounds,
And so retired, with broken hearts,
To vegetate in foreign parts,
And ended their declining years
At Blidah – which is near Algiers.
There, in the course of time, they died,
And there lie buried side by side.
While when we turn to Peter, he
The cause of this catastrophe,
There fell upon him such a fate
As makes me shudder to relate.
Just in its fifth and final year,
His University Career
Was blasted by the new and dread
Necessity of earning bread.
He was compelled to join a firm
Of Brokers – in the summer term!

And even now, at twenty-five,
He has to WORK to keep alive!

Yes! All day long from 10 till 4!
For half the year or even more;
With but an hour or two to spend
At luncheon with a city friend.

Hilaire Belloc, from *New Cautionary Tales*, 1930


William's family long remembered the silence and peace that marked the next few afternoons. During them, William, outstretched upon the floor of the summer-house, wrote his play with liberal application of ink over his person and clothes and the surrounding woodwork. William was not of that class of authors who neglect the needs of the body. After every few words he took a deep draught from a bottle of Orange Ale that stood on his right and a bite from an ink-coated apple on his left. He had laid in a store of apples and sweets and chocolates under the seat of the summer-house for his term of authorship. Every now and then he raised a hand to his frowning brow in thought, leaving upon it yet another imprint of his ink-sodden fingers.

'Where is he?' said his father in a hushed wonder at the unwonted peace.

'He's in the summer-house writing a play,' said his wife.

'I hope it's a nice long one,' said her husband.

Richmal Crompton, from 'What Delayed the Great Man', *William Again*, 1923


Then the panto season was over and we were on the road again. Fifteen years old, now. Five foot, six inches. Little brown bobs, though Nora often talked wistfully about going blonde. She felt the future lay with blondes. Should we? Shouldn't we? One thing was certain – she couldn't do it unilaterally. On our own, you wouldn't look at us twice. But, put us together . . .

We were hardened old troupers, by now. We had our printed cards: 'Dora and Leonora, 49 Bard Road, London s.w.2.' You always had to travel on a Sunday, when the trains went slow out of respect for the Sabbath and some-times stopped dead in the middle of a field as if taken short. We feared no bedbugs, nor cockroaches, fleas could not daunt our spirits. We learned to despise the 'Wood' family, that is, the empty seats. We lived off the Scotch eggs the landladies put out for late supper, after the show. Grandma went spare when she heard about the Scotch eggs. 'It's only sausage meat,' I said. 'They wrap some sausage meat round the hard-boiled egg. You know what they make sausage meat out of, sawdust and the bits of old elastic.' Grandma wasn't having any. 'Cannibals!' she said.

But now we knew the world didn't end when Grandma disapproved. Greatly daring, knowing what she'd say, egged on by the other girls, we finally invested in some little bits of rabbit fur to snuggle into when the wind blew chill. 'Dead bunny,' said Grandma when she saw. As we grew up, cracks appeared between us. She loved us but she often disapproved.

We were just slips of girls but we soon knew our way around. We had our little handbags with the little gilt powder compacts and the puffs; when in doubt, we powdered our noses, to give us time to think up repartee. A rat once ate my powder puff in the dressing room at the Nottingham Theatre Royal. We kept our make-up in the standard two-tier tin – rouge, Leichner, that solid mascara you sliced off into a tiny tin frying pan and melted over a candle. Then you put it on with a matchstick, quick, quick, quick, before it got hard.

Grandma kept the programmes, every show we ever were in, right from that first *Babes in the Wood* up to the ones from ENSA. She made up big scrapbooks. After she went, there they were, stored away in a trunk in the loft – the whole of our lives. We felt bad when we saw those scrapbooks, we remembered how we'd teased her, we'd brought home sausage rolls and croco-dile handbags, but she'd kept on snipping out the cuttings, pasting them in. Piles of scrapbooks, the cuttings turned by time to the colour of the freckles on the back of an old lady's hand. Her hand. My hand, as it is now. When you touch the old newsprint, it turns into brown dust, like the dust of bones.

Angela Carter, from Wise Children, 1991

# WORKING TOGETHER

## Not Ashamed

And the Lord God took the man, and put him into the garden of Eden to dress it and to keep it . . .

And the Lord God said, It is not good that the man should be alone; I will make a help meet for him . . .

And the Lord God caused a deep sleep to fall upon Adam and he slept; and he took one of his ribs, and closed up the flesh instead thereof:

And the rib, which the Lord God had taken from the man, made he a woman, and brought her unto the man.

And Adam said, This is now bone of my bones, and flesh of my flesh: she shall be called Woman because she was taken out of Man.

Therefore shall a man leave his father and mother, and shall cleave unto his wife: and they shall be one flesh.

And they were both naked, the man and his wife, and they were not ashamed.

Genesis 2:15, 18, 21–25

I conclude then, my friend, that none of the occupations which comprehend the ordering of a state belong to woman as woman, nor yet to man as man; but natural gifts are to be found here and there, in both sexes alike; and, so far as her nature is concerned, the woman is admissable to all pursuits as well as the man; though in all of them the woman is weaker than the man.

Precisely so.

Shall we then hold, I imagine, that one woman may have talents for medicine, and another be without them; and that one may be musical, and another unmusical?

Undoubtedly.

And shall we not also say, that one woman may have qualifications for gymnastic exercises, and for war, and another be unwarlike, and without a taste for gymnastics?

I think we shall.

Again, may there not be a love of knowledge in one, and a distaste for it in another? and may not one be spirited, and another spiritless?

True again.

If that be so, there are some women who are fit, and others who are unfit, for the office of guardians. For were not those the qualities that we selected, in the case of the men, as marking their fitness for that office?

Yes, they were.

Then as far as the guardianship of a state is concerned, there is no difference between the natures of the man and of the woman, but only various degrees of weakness and strength.

Apparently there is none.

Then we shall have to select duly qualified women also, to share in the life and official labours of the duly qualified men; since we find that they are competent to the work, and of kindred nature with the men.

Just so.

And must we not assign the same pursuit to the same natures?

We must.

Then we are now brought round by a circuit to our former position, and we admit that it is no violation of nature to assign music and gymnastic to the wives of our guardians.

Precisely so.

Then our intended legislation was not impracticable, or visionary, since the proposed law was in accordance with nature: rather it is in the existing usage, contravening this of ours, that to all appearance contravenes nature.

So it appears.

Our inquiry was, whether the proposed arrangement would be practicable, and whether it was the most desirable one, was it not?

It was.

Are we quite agreed that it is practicable?

Yes.

Then the next point to be settled, that it is also the most desirable arrangement?

Yes, obviously.

Very well; if the question is how to render a woman fit for the office of guardian, we shall not have one education for men, and another for women, especially as the nature to be wrought upon is the same in both cases.

No, the education will be the same.

> Plato, 427–348 BC, from *The Republic*, Book V,
> tr. J. L. Davies and D. J. Vaughan, 1898


## Double-Fold Toil

Tillers of the earth have few idle months;
In the fifth month their toil is double-fold.

A south wind visits the fields at night;
Suddenly the ridges are covered with yellow corn.

Wives and daughters shoulder baskets of rice,
Youths and boys carry flasks of wine,
In a long train, to feed the workers in the field –
The strong reapers toiling on the southern hill,
Whose feet are burned by the hot earth they tread,
Whose backs are scorched by the flames of the shining sky.
Tired they toil, caring nothing for the heat,
Grudging the shortness of the long summer day.
A poor woman with a young child at her side
Follows behind, to glean the unwanted grain.
In her right hand she holds the fallen ears,
On her left arm a broken basket hangs.
Listening to what they said as they worked together
I heard something that made me very sad:
They lost in grain-tax the whole of their own crop;
What they glean here is all they will have to eat.

And I to-day – in virtue of what desert
Have I never once tended field or tree?
My government-pay is three hundred 'stones';
At the year's end I have still grain in hand.
Thinking of this, secretly I grew ashamed
And all day the thought lingered in my head.

Po Chu-i, AD 806,
tr. Arthur Waley, 1946

## Clearing the Fields

We clear the grasses and trees,
We plough and carve the land,
Two thousand men and women scrabbling weeds
Along the low wet lands, along the dyke walls.
The masters, the eldest sons,
The labourers, the hired servants,
They mark out the fields, they ply their colters,
Overflowing food baskets are brought to them,
They gaze on their fair wives
And press close to them.

They have sharp plowshares,
They set to work on the south acres,
They sow the many kinds of grain.
Each seed holds a moist germ;
Splendidly, splendidly the young grain shoots forth,
Sleekly, sleekly the young plants rise,
Tenderly, tenderly comes the young grain.
Thousands of weeders scrabbling among the weeds!
Host upon host of reapers!
Close-huddled stooks arranged in due order!
Myriads, many hundred thousands and millions of grains!
From them come wine and sweet liquor,
Offering to the ancestors, the male and the female,
In fulfilment of sacrifices.
So glory shall come to the land.
They will have a sharp smell of pepper,
They will give comfort to the aged.
It is not only here that it is so,
It is not only now that it is so:
But in most ancient times ever and ever.

> Anon., from the Chou Dynasty, 1112–249 BC,
> tr. Robert Payne, 1947

Levin looked more attentively at Vanka Parmenich and his wife. They were loading their cart not far from him. Vanka stood on the cart, receiving, arranging, and stamping down the huge bales of hay which his pretty young wife deftly handed up to him, at first in armfuls and then on the pitch-fork. The young woman worked easily, cheerfully, and with skill. The fork could not at once penetrate the close-packed hay. She would start by loosening it with the prongs, stick the fork in, then with a rapid, supple movement, leaning the whole weight of her body behind the fork, at once with a bend of her back under the red belt she drew herself up, and, arching her full bosom under the white smock, with an adroit turn of the fork she pitched the hay high on to the cart. Vanka, obviously anxious to spare her every minute of unnecessary exertion, made haste to catch the hay in his widespread arms, and smoothed it evenly in the cart. When she had raked together what was left of the hay, the young wife shook off the bits that had fallen on her neck and, straightening the red kerchief that had slipped forward over her white, unsunburned forehead, crawled under the cart to fasten the load. Vanka was telling her how to tie the cord to the cross-piece and burst into a roar of laughter at something she said. Strong, young, freshly awakened love showed in both their faces.

The load was fastened. Vanka jumped down and took the quiet, well-fed horse by the bridle. His wife flung her rake on to the cart and, with a bold step, swinging her arms, went over to the other women, who had gathered into a circle to sing. Vanka reached the road and took his place in the line of loaded carts. The women, carrying their rakes over their shoulders, gay in their bright colours, fell in behind the carts, their voices ringing merrily. One of the women with a wild, untrained voice started a song and sang it as far as the refrain, when half a hundred powerful voices, some gruff, others soft, took it up from the beginning again.

The singing women were drawing nearer Levin and he felt as if a thunder-cloud of merriment were swooping down upon him. The cloud swooped down and enveloped him; and the haycock on which he was lying, the other haycocks, the carts, the whole meadow and the distant fields all seemed to advance and vibrate and throb to the rhythm of this madly merry song with its shouting and whistling and clapping. Levin felt envious of this health and mirthful-ness, and longed to take part in his expression of joy at being alive. But he could do nothing except lie and look on and listen. When the peasants and their song had disappeared out of sight and hearing, a weary feeling of despondency at his own isolation, his physical inactivity, his alienation from this world, came over him.

Some of the very peasants who had most disputed with him over the hay – whom he had been hard on or who had tried to cheat him – those very peasants had nodded happily to him, evidently not feeling and unable to feel any rancour against him, any regret, any recollection even of having intended to cheat him. All that had been swallowed up in the sea of cheerful common toil. God gave the day, God gave the strength for it. And the day and the strength were consecrated to labour, and that labour was its own reward. For whom the labour? What would be its fruits? These were idle considerations beside the point.

Levin had often admired this life, had often envied the men who lived it; but to-day for the first time, especially under the influence of what he had seen of the relations between Vanka Parmenich and his young wife, the idea came into his mind that it was in his power to exchange the onerous, idle, artificial, and selfish existence he was leading for that busy, honourable, delight-ful life of common toil.

The old man who had been sitting beside him had gone home long ago: the peasants had all dispersed. Those who lived near had ridden home, while those from a distance had gathered into a group for supper and to spend the night in the meadow. Levin, unnoticed by them, still lay on the haycock, looking round, listening, and thinking. The peasants who had remained for the night in the meadow scarcely slept all the short summer night. At first Levin heard merry chatter and general laughter over supper, then singing again and more laughter. The whole long day of toil had left upon them no trace of anything but gaiety.

Before dawn all grew quiet. Only the sounds of night were heard – the incessant croaking of frogs in the marsh and the horses snorting in the mist rising over the meadow before the morning. Rousing himself, Levin got up from the haycock and, looking at the stars, he saw that the night was over.

'Well, then, what am I going to do? How am I to set about it?' he said to himself, trying to put into words all he had been thinking and feeling in that brief night. All the thoughts and feelings he had passed through fell into three separate trains of thought. The first was the renunciation of his old life, of his utterly useless education. The idea of this renunciation gave him satisfaction, and was easy and simple. Another series of thoughts and mental images related to the life he longed to live now. The simplicity, the integrity, the sanity of this life he felt clearly, and he was convinced he would find in it the content, the peace, and the dignity, of the lack of which he was so painfully conscious. But the third line of thought brought him to the question of how to effect this transition from the old life to the new. And here nothing was clear. 'Take a wife? Have work and the necessity to work? Leave Pokrovskoe? Buy land? Join a peasant community? Marry a peasant girl? How am I to set about it? he asked himself again, and could find no answer. 'I haven't slept all night, though, and can't think it out now,' he said to himself. 'I'll work it out later. One thing is certain: this night has decided my fate. All my old dreams of family life were nonsense, not the real thing,' he told himself. 'It's all ever so much simpler and better' . . .

'How beautiful!' he thought, looking up at some fleecy white clouds poised in the middle of the sky right above his head, like a strange mother-of-pearl shell. 'How lovely everything is in this lovely night! And when did that shell have time to form? I was looking at the sky a moment ago and only two white streaks were to be seen. Yes, and my views of life changed in the same imperceptible way!'

He left the meadow and walked along the highway towards the village. A slight breeze was blowing up and it became grey and overcast with the moment of gloom that usually precedes daybreak and the final victory of light over darkness.

Leo Tolstoy, from *Anna Karenina*, 1877,

tr. Rosemary Edmunds, 1954

So we left the boat moored there, and went up on the slow slope of the hill; but I said to Dick on the way, being somewhat mystified: 'What was all that laughing about? what was the joke?'

'I can guess pretty well,' said Dick; 'some of them up there have got a piece of work which interests them, and they won't go to the haymaking, which doesn't matter at all, because there are plenty of people to do such easy-hard work as that; only, since haymaking is a regular festival, the neighbours find it amusing to jeer good-humouredly at them.'

'I see,' said I, 'much as if in Dickens's time some young people were so wrapped up in their work that they wouldn't keep Christmas.'

'Just so,' said Dick, 'only these people need not be young either.'

'But what did you mean by easy-hard work?' said I.

Quoth Dick: 'Did I say that? I mean work that tries the muscles and hardens them and sends you pleasantly weary to bed, but which isn't trying in other ways: doesn't harass you, in short. Such work is always pleasant if you don't overdo it. Only, mind you, good mowing requires some little skill. I'm a pretty good mower.' . . .

Walter and Clara were already talking to a tall man clad in his mason's blouse, who looked about forty, but was, I daresay, older, who had his mallet and chisel in hand; there were at work in the shed and on the scaffold about half a dozen men and two women, blouse-clad like the carles, while a very pretty woman who was not in the work but was dressed in an elegant suit of blue linen came sauntering up to us with her knitting in her hand. She welcomed us and said, smiling: 'So you are come up from the water to see the Obstinate Refusers: where are you going haymaking, neighbours?'

'O, right up above Oxford,' said Dick; 'it is rather a late country. But what share have you got with the Refusers, pretty neighbour?'

Said she, with a laugh: 'O, I am the lucky one who doesn't want to work; though sometimes I get it, for I serve as model to Mistress Philippa there when she wants one: she is our head carver; come and see her.'

She led us up to the door of the unfinished house, where a rather little woman was working with mallet and chisel on the wall near by. She seemed very intent on what she was doing, and did not turn round when we came up; but a taller woman, quite a girl she seemed, who was at working near by, had already knocked off, and was standing looking from Clara to Dick with delighted eyes. None of the others paid much heed to us.

The blue-clad girl laid her hand on the carver's shoulder and said: 'Now, Philippa, if you gobble up your work like that, you will soon have none to do; and what will become of you then?'

The carver turned round hurriedly and showed us the face of a woman of forty (or so she seemed), and said rather pettishly, but in a sweet voice:

'Don't talk nonsense, Kate, and don't interrupt me if you can help it.' She stopped short when she saw us, then went on with the kind smile of welcome which never failed us. 'Thank you for coming to see us, neighbours; but I am sure that you won't think me unkind if I go on with my work, especially when I tell you that I was ill and unable to do anything all through April and May; and this open air and the sun and the work together, and my feeling well again too, make a mere delight of every hour to me; and excuse me, I must go on.'

So we shook hands and turned our backs on the Obstinate Refusers, went down the slope to our boat, and before we had gone many steps heard the full tune of tinkling trowels mingle with the humming of the bees and the singing of the larks above the little plain of Basildon.

William Morris, from News From Nowhere, 1890

### Work and Wait

#### Husband

The sweet'ning fruit that fall shall bring
Is now a bud within its rind;
The nest the bird shall build in spring
Is now in moss and grass untwin'd;
The summer days will show us, hung
On boughs, the fruit and nest of young.
I waited on, through time and tide,
Till I could house you here, my bride.

#### Wife

If wedlock bonds in heaven are bound,
Then what's our lot will all come round.

#### Husband

My new-built house's brick-red side
A few years since was clay unfound;
My reeden roof, outslanting wide,
Was yet in seed unsprung from ground;
And now no house on Woodcombe land
Is put much better out of hand
Than this, that I, through time and tide,
Was bent to build for you to guide.

Wife

I'll try with heart, and hand, and head,
That you shall speed as you have sped.

Husband

A few years since my wheels, unmade,
Were living timber under bark;
And my new ploughshare's grey-blue blade
Was ore deep lying in the dark;
But now I have my gear, and now
Have bought two mares to haul or plough.
I waited on, in careful mood,
For stock to win our livelihood.

Wife

Aye 'work and wait's' the wisest way,
For 'work and wait' will win the day.

William Barnes, 1846

## Somebody Loves Us All

*Monday 9th June* [1800].   In the morning W. cut down the winter cherry tree. I sowed French Beans and weeded. A coronetted Landau went by, when we were sitting upon the sodded wall. The ladies (evidently Tourists) turned an eye of interest upon our little garden and cottage. We went to R. Newton's for pike-floats and went round to Mr Gell's Boat and on to the Lake to fish. We caught nothing – it was extremely cold. The Reeds and Bulrushes or Bullpipes of a tender soft green, making a plain whose surface moved with the wind. The reeds not yet tall. The lake clear to the Bottom, but saw no fish. In the evening I stuck peas, watered the garden and planted Brocoli. Did not walk for it was very cold. A poor Girl called to beg who had no work at home and was going in search of it to Kendal. She slept in Mr Benson's Lathe, and went off after Breakfast in the morning with 7*d* and a letter to the Mayor of Kendal.

*Thursday [31st July]*.   All the morning I was busy copying poems. Gathered peas, and in the afternoon Coleridge came, very hot, he brought the 2nd volume of the Anthology. The men went to bathe, and we afterwards sailed down to Loughrigg. Read poems on the water, and let the boat take its own long time upon Loughrigg and returned in the grey twilight. The moon just setting as we reached home.

*Friday 1st August.* In the morning I copied The Brothers. Coleridge and Wm went down to the lake. They returned and we all went together to Mary Point where we sate in the breeze and the shade, and read Wm's poems. Altered The Whirlblast etc. Mr Simpson came to tea and Mr B. Simpson afterwards. We drank tea in the orchard.

*Saturday Morning 2nd.* Wm and Coleridge went to Keswick. John went with them to Wytheburn and staid all day fishing and brought home 2 small pikes at night. I accompanied them to Lewthwaite's cottage and on my return papered Wm's room. I afterwards lay down till tea time and after tea worked at my shifts in the orchard. A grey evening. About 8 o'clock it gathered for rain and I had the scatterings of a shower, but afterwards the lake became of a glassy calmness and all was still. I sate till I could see no longer and then continued my work in the house.

*Sunday Morning 3rd.* I made pies and stuffed the pike – baked a loaf. Headache after dinner – I lay down. A letter from Wm rouzed me, desiring us to go to Keswick. After writing to Wm we walked as far as Mr Simpson's and ate black cherries. A Heavenly warm evening with scattered clouds upon the hills. There was a vernal greenness upon the grass from the rains of the morning and afternoon. Peas for dinner.

*Monday 4th.* Rain in the night. I tied up Scarlet beans, nailed the honey-suckles etc. etc. John was prepared to walk to Keswick all the morning. He seized a returned chaise and went after dinner. I pulled a large basket of peas and sent to Keswick by a returned chaise. A very cold evening. Assisted to spread out linen in the morning.

*Tuesday 5th.* Dried the linen in the morning, the air still cold. I pulled a bag full of peas for Mrs Simpson. Miss Simpson drank tea with me and supped on her return from Ambleside. A very fine evening. I sate on the wall making my shifts till I could see no longer. Walked half-way home with Miss Simpson.

*Wednesday 6th August.* A rainy morning. I ironed till dinner time – sewed till near dark – then pulled a basket of peas, and afterwards boiled and picked goose-berries. William came home from Keswick at 11 o'clock. A very fine night.

*Thursday Morning 7th August.* Packed up the mattrass, and went to Keswick. Boiled gooseberries – N.B. 2 lbs of sugar in the first panfull, 3 quarts in all good measure – 3 lbs in the 2nd 4 quarts – $2^1/_2$ lbs in the 3rd. A very fine day. William composing in the wood in the morning. In the evening we walked to Mary Point. A very fine sunset.

Dorothy Wordsworth, from *The Grasmere Journals*,
ed. Mary Moorman, 1970

## The Wife's Tale

When I had spread it all on linen cloth
Under the hedge, I called them over.
The hum and gulp of the thresher ran down
And the big belt slewed to a standstill, straw
Hanging undelivered in the jaws.
There was such quiet that I heard their boots
Crunching the stubble twenty yards away.

He lay down and said 'Give these fellows theirs,
I'm in no hurry,' plucking grass in handfuls
And tossing it in the air. 'That looks well.'
(He nodded at my white cloth on the grass.)
'I declare a woman could lay out a field
Though boys like us have little call for cloths.'
He winked, then watched me as I poured a cup
And buttered the thick slices that he likes.
'It's threshing better than I thought, and mind
It's good clean seed. Away over there and look.'
Always this inspection has to be made
Even when I don't know what to look for.

But I ran my hand in the half-filled bags
Hooked to the slots. It was hard as shot,
Innumerable and cool. The bags gaped
Where the chutes ran back to the stilled drum
And forks were stuck at angles in the ground
As javelins might mark lost battlefields.
I moved between them back across the stubble.

They lay in the ring of their own crusts and dregs
Smoking and saying nothing. 'There's good yield,
Isn't there?' – as proud as if he were the land itself –
'Enough for crushing and for sowing both.'
And that was it. I'd come and he had shown me
So I belonged no further to the work.
I gathered cups and folded up the cloth
And went. But they still kept their ease
Spread out, unbuttoned, grateful, under the trees.

Seamus Heaney, from *Door Into the Dark*, 1969

## *Filling Station*

Oh, but it is dirty!
– this little filling station,
oil-soaked, oil-permeated
to a disturbing, over-all
black translucency.
Be careful with that match!

Father wears a dirty,
oil-soaked monkey suit
that cuts him under the arms,
and several quick and saucy
and greasy sons assist him
(it's a family filling station),
all quite thoroughly dirty.

Do they live in the station?
It has a cement porch
behind the pumps, and on it
a set of crushed and grease-
impregnated wickerwork;
on the wicker sofa
a dirty dog, quite comfy.

Some comic books provide
the only note of color –
of certain color. They lie
upon a big dim doily
draping a taboret
(part of the set), beside
a big hirsute begonia.

Why the extraneous plant?
Why the taboret?
Why, oh why, the doily?
(Embroidered in daisy stitch
with marguerites, I think,
and heavy with gray crochet.)

Somebody embroidered the doily.
Somebody waters the plant,
or oils it, maybe. Somebody
arranges the rows of cans

so that they softly say:
ESSO – SO – SO – SO
to highly-strung automobiles.
Somebody loves us all.
Elizabeth Bishop, from *Collected Poems*, 1983

## A Coining of Money

I weel mind the welcoming I got from John Douce and his wife. It couldna be said he was unjustly a narrow man; but he was, maybe, a thought hard. His wife, however, was a handwaled woman, and had from the womb been ordained to bless the man she was made for.

We had some solid conversation anent what put it into my head to think of being an errand porter rather than a tradesman; and I replied that he might see I wasna of the right cut to be a prime tradesman, which was an admonishment no to try.

'Ay,' quo' the mistress, who had sat for some time before silent, 'guidman, he'll do weel, if that's his ain thought; for there's nothing helps on a man like a right knowledge of himself and what he's best fit for. The failures we meet with happen oftener from the man not knowing what he's fit for, than from want of ability. I aye doubt the thriving of those that itch for more than they seem to require' . . .

The next morning I rose betimes; and having covenanted with the carrier lad on the road, to shew me some of the town, we went hither and yon together till eight o'clock, in a very satisfactory manner . . . When I had learned myself well in the wynds and turns of Glasgow, I took my station aneath the pillars forenent the Tolbooth; but when I gaed home at breakfast time, a thought dowie because I had come no speed, Mrs Douce said it was not the right side of the street.

'One,' quoth she, 'should aye endeavour to begin the world on the right side of the causeway. It's no doubt a very creditable stance ye have taken; but it's no so good by a degree as the plainstones on the other side where the gentlemen congregate; – and, besides, ye must change that Kilmarnock bonnet. It gars you look of a country complexion. Do in Rome as they do in Rome; and mind never to make yourself kenspeckle unless it's in snodness; for maist folk, though they cannot tell why, have no broo of them that has onything out-o'-the-way about them.'

In consequence of this advice, I niffered after breakfast with another laddie for his hat with my bonnet and twopence, and took up my stance at a close mouth wester the Tontine, which was then bigging; the gentlemen, provost, and magistrates making then their houff at where the cross used to be, as I was told.

Good luck was in the change; for an Englisher soon after hired me to take a letter as far west as Madeira Court, and I made such nimble speed with the errand that he gave me a whole sixpence, the first white money I ever had received; in short, before the day was done, I had made a rough ninepence – that is, a bawbee over; and Mrs Douce, when I offered the half to John, would not let him touch it, saying that all I made the first day ought to be my own; for it was the luck arle of a fortune. It could not, therefore, but be said that I had a prospect in the very beginning.

The second day of my erranding, I mind weel, was not splendid; saving a tawlpenny job to the Broomie-law, for a scrimping shopkeeper, to a Greenock gabbart, with the bundle of a Highland tartan plaid, belonging to a nauby that was going Tobermory, I had but a scrimpit measure of luck. To be sure, towards the heel of the evening, a bailie, with a red north-west countenance, being vogie from his punchbowl and the funny stories of his cronies, hired me to go to Ruglen with a letter, on some 'lection ploy; for there was a great sough at that time of a Parlimenting, as it was called, which I have since learnt meant a general election. This achievement caused me to be in the gloaming before I got to John Douce's; and a weary wean I was, both with the length of the road and its sliddiness, caused by the forepart of the day being showery. Mrs Douce, seeing me so scomfished, took pains to hearten me, when I had rested myself, saying that there was no profit in running lang errands, and, therefore, I ought to eschew them.

'When ye're out o' the gait,' said she, 'far afield, like as to Ruglen, you may miss a shorter errand in the town, whereof the pay would be better, on a calculation; it would be hard, indeed, if the wage for twa hameart jobs were not as good as a runagate exploit to the country. Besides, there's a weariedness in a journey of one long continuance that's no to be coveted; one errand in the forenoon to sic like as Ruglen, does the best up for the remainder of the day.' . . .

But, although the erranding canno be said to be an ill ready-money business, when rightly followed out, it has its fasheries, as well as merchandizing; and I soon made an observe anent the same, which seems to shew what a wonderful regularity there is in all the works of Providence; and that was, that, counting by the days, it had a degree of uncertainty, proving it ought not to be trusted; but taking the earnings by the week together, it was more of a dependance; and, by the month, it was as good as a stated income, which you of the genteeler orders have no notion of. In short, before I was anything like half a year on the pavy of the Trongate, as I once heard a playactor man called the planestanes, the jingle of my peinor pig told, in sterling language, that erranding was an effectual calling, though, maybe, no just a coining of money; nor did I repent I had taken it up. As the winter, however, came on, with short days and long nights, I had my experience, that, like everything of a human nature, it had its blemish of onagreeables – particularly in the dark days of November, on which I discerned that, although the morning and the forepart of the day could not be objected to, the hinder end and the evening was always obstrapulous and showery, when porters, and erranders who are kind of 'prentices to them, are fain to howff and harbour in close mouths and other places, that, at times, would not be the waur of a souping, cuddling themselves with their hands in their bosoms or in their pouches.

Nevertheless, for all the wind and the sleet that we were exposed to, the first winter was won through, with an ettle; and when the fine, sunshiny spring mornings came round, there was mirth in my veins; and the skies, taking off their cloudy fause-faces, looked well pleased on the earth, new-washen with the growing showers.

John Galt, from 'A Rich Man', 1836

## The Workshop

In the end, hee opened his minde vnto her, and craued her good will. The maid (though shee took this motion kindly) said, shee would do nothing without consent of her parents. Whereupon a Letter was writ to her father, being a poore man dwelling at *Alesburie* in *Buckinghamshire*: who being joyfull of his daughters good fortune, speedily came to *Newberie*, where of her master he was friendly entertained: who after he had made him good cheare, shewed him all his seruants at worke, and euery office in his house.

> Within one roome being large and long,
> There stood two hundred Loomes full strong:
> Two hundred men the truth is so,
> Wrought in these Loomes all in a row.
> By euery one a pretty boy,
> Sate making quils with mickle joy;
> And in another place hard by,
> An hundred women merily,
> Were carding hard with joyfull cheere,
> Who singing sate with voices cleere.
> And in a chamber close beside,

Two hundred maidens did abide,
In petticoates of Stammell red,
And milke-white kerchers on their head:
Their smocke-sleeues like to winter snow,
That on the Westerne mountaines flow,
And each sleeue with a silken band,
Was featly tied at the hand.
These pretty maids did neuer lin,
But in that place all day did spin:
And spinning so with voices meet,
Like Nightingals they sung full sweet.
Then to another roome came they,
Where children were in poore aray:
And euery one sate picking wool,
The finest from the course to cull:
The number was seuen score and ten,
The children of poore silly men:
And these their labours to requite,
Had euery one a penny at night,
Beside their meat and drinke all day,
Which was to them a wondrous stay.
Within another place likewise,
Full fifty proper men he spies,
And these were Shearemen euery one,
Whose skill and cunning there was showne:
And hard by them there did remaine,
Full fourscore Rowers taking paine.
A Dye-house likewise had he then,
Wherein he kept full forty men:
And likewise in his fulling Mill,
Full twenty persons kept he still,
Each weeke ten good fat oxen he
Spent in his house for certaintie:
Beside good butter, cheese, and fish,
And many other wholesome dish.
He kept a Butcher all the yeere,
A Brewer eke for Ale and Beere:
A Baker for to bake his Bread,
Which stood his hushold in good stead.
Fiue Cookes within his kitchin great,
Were all the yeare to dresse his meat.

Sixe scullian boyes vnto their hands,
To make cleane dishes, pots, and pans,
Beside poore children that did stay,
To turne the broaches euery day.
The old man that did see this sight,
Was much amaz'd, as well he might:
This was a gallant Cloathier sure,
Whose fame for euer shall endure.

When the old man had seene this great household and family, then was he brought into the Ware-houses, some being fild with wool, some with flockes, some with woad and madder, and some with broadcloathes and kersies ready dyed and drest, beside a great number of others, some strecht on the Tenters, some hanging on poles, and a great many more lying wet in other places. Sir (quoth the old man) I wis che zee you bee bominable rich, and cham content you shall haue my daughter, and Gods blessing and mine light on you both.

But Father (quoth *Jacke* of *Newberie*) what will you bestow with her?

Marry heare you (quoth the old man) I vait cham but a poore man, but I thong God, cham of good exclamation among my neighbours, and they will as zoone take my vice for any thing as a richer mans: thicke I will bestow, you shall haue with a good will, because che heare very good condemnation of you in euery place, therefore chil giue you twenty Nobles and a weaning Calfe, and when I dye and my wife, you shall haue the reuelation of all my goods.

When *Jacke* heard his offer, he was straight content, making more reckoning of the womans modesty, than her Fathers money.

Thomas Deloney, from *The Pleasant Historie of Jacke of Newberie*, 1626

# Getting Up Steam

### Steam Loom Weaver

One morning in summer I did ramble,
In the pleasant month of June,
The birds did sing the lambkins play,
Two lovers walking in their bloom,
The lassie was a steam loom weaver,
The lad an engine driver keen,

All their discourse was about weaving.
And the getting up of steam.

She said my loom is out of fettle,
Can you right it yes or no,
You say you are an engine driver,
Which makes the steam so rapid flow;
My lams and jacks are out of order,
My laith in motion has not been,
So work away without delay,
And quickly muster up the steam.

I said fair maid you seem determined,
No longer for to idle be,
Your healds and laith I'll put in motion,
Then work you can without delay,
She said young man a pair of pickers,
A shuttle too I want you ween,
Without these three I cannot weave,
So useless would be the steam.

Dear lass these things I will provide,
But when to labour will you begin,
As soon my lad as things are ready
My loom shop you can enter in,
A shuttle true and pickers too,
This young man did provide amain.
And soon her loom was put in tune
So well it was supplied with steam.

Her loom worked well the shuttle flew,
His nickers play'd the tune nick-nack,
Her laith did move with rapid motion,
Her temples, healds, long-lambs and jacks,
Her cloth beam rolled the cloth up tight,
The yarn beam emptied soon its seam,
The young man cried your loom works, light
And quickly then off shot the steam.

She said young man another web,
Upon the beam let's get don't strike,
But work away while yet it's day,
This steam loom weaving well I like,

He said good lass I cannot stay,
But if a fresh warp you will beam
If ready when I come this way,
I'd strive for to get up the steam.

Anon., *c.* 1830, quoted in Martha Vicinus, *The Industrial Muse*, 1974

His words of encouragement were cut off by a long shout. She fought to inhale, and there was another, a prolonged hoot of astonishment.

'Ride it out, ride the wave . . .' he began to say. Again, his words were cut off. He had lost his place. Exhortations to rhythmic breathing were now inane. A gale had torn the instructions away from him. She held his forearm with both hands in a fierce grip. Her teeth were bared, the muscles and tendons of her neck were stretching to breaking point. He was lost. He could give her nothing more than his forearm.

He called out to her, 'Julie, Julie, I'm here with you.'

But she was alone. She was drawing breath and shouting again, this time wildly, as though in exhilaration, and when she had no more air in her lungs, it did not matter, the shout had to go on, and on. The contraction lifted her off her back and twisted her on to her side. The sheet was still gathered up to her waist and had knotted itself round her. He felt the bed frame tremble with her effort. There was a final click at the back of her throat and she was drawing breath again, tossing her head as she did so. When she looked at him, past him, her eyes were bright, wide with purpose. The brief despair had gone. She was back in control. He thought she was about to speak, but the grip on his arm was tightening again and she was away. Her lips shivered as they stretched tighter over the teeth and from deep in her chest came a strangled groan, a bottled-up, gurgling sound of colossal, straining effort. Then it tapered away, and she let her head fall back against the pillows.

She took deep breaths and spoke in a surprisingly normal voice. 'I need a cold drink, a glass of water.' He was about to stand when she restrained him. 'But I don't want you to go away. I think it might be coming.'

'No, no. The midwife isn't here yet.'

She smiled as if he had made a joke for her benefit. 'Tell me what you can see.'

He had to reach under her to get the sheet clear.

There was a shock, a jarring, a slowing down as he entered dream time. A quietness enveloped him. He had come before a presence, a revelation. He was staring down at the back of a protruding head. No other part of the body was visible. It faced down into the wet sheet. In its silence and complete stillness there was an accusation. Had you forgotten me? Did you not realize it was me all along? I am here. I am not alive. He was looking at the whorl of wet hair about the crown. There was no movement, no pulse, no breathing. It was not alive, it was a head on the block, and yet the demand was clear and pressing. This was my move. Now what is yours? Perhaps a second had passed since he had lifted back the sheet. He put out his hand. It was a blue-white marble sculpture he was touching, both inert and full of intent. It was cold, the wetness was cold, and beneath that there was a warmth, but too faint, the residual, borrowed warmth of Julie's body. That it was suddenly and obviously there, a person not from another town or from a different country, but from life itself, the simplicity of that, was communicating to him a clarity and precision of purpose. He heard himself say something reassuring to Julie, while he himself was comforted by a memory, brief and clear like a firework, of a sunlit country road, of wreckage and a head. His thoughts were resolving into simple, elementary shapes. This is really all we have got, this increase, this matter of life loving itself, everything we have has to come from this.

Julie was not yet ready to push. She was recovering her strength. He slid his hand round to the face, round the mouth and used his little finger to clear it of mucus. There was no breath. He moved his fingers down, below the lip of Julie's taut skin, to find the hidden shoulder. He could feel the cord there, thick and robust, a pulsing creature wound twice in a noose about the neck. He worked his forefinger round and pulled cautiously. The cord came easily, copiously, and as he lifted it clear of the head, Julie gave birth – he saw in an instant how active and generous the verb was – she summoned her will and her physical strength and gave. With a creaking, waxy sound the child slid into his hands. He saw only the long back, powerful and slippery, with grooved, muscular spine. The cord, still beating, hung across the shoulder and tangled round a foot. He was only the catcher, not the home, and his one thought was to return the child to its mother. As he was lifting it across they heard a snuffling sound and a single lucid cry. It lay face down with an ear towards its mother's heart. They drew the covers over it. Because the hot-water bottles were too heavy and hot, Stephen climbed into bed beside Julie and they kept the baby warm between them. The breathing was settling into a rhythm, and a warmer colour, a bloom of deep pink, was suffusing its skin.

It was only then that they began to exclaim and celebrate, and kiss and nuzzle the waxy head which smelled like a freshly baked bun. For minutes they were beyond forming sentences and could only make noises of triumph and wonder, and say each other's names aloud. Anchored by its cord, the baby lay with its head resting between its closed fists. It was a beautiful child. Its eyes were open, looking towards the mountain of Julie's breast. Beyond the bed was the window through which they could see the moon sinking into a gap in the pines. Directly above the moon was a planet. It was Mars, Julie said. It was a reminder of a harsh world. For now, however, they were immune, it was before the beginning of time, and they lay watching planet and moon descend through a sky that was turning blue.

They did not know how much later it was they heard the midwife's car stop outside the cottage. They heard the slam of its door and the tick of hard shoes on the brick path.

'Well?' Julie said. 'A girl or a boy?' And it was in acknowledgement of the world they were about to rejoin, and into which they hoped to take their love, that she reached down under the covers and felt.

Ian McEwan, from *The Child in Time*, 1987

# THE DIVISION OF LABOUR

The greatest improvement in the productive powers of labour, and the greater part of the skill, dexterity, and judgement with which it is anywhere directed, or applied, seem to have been the effects of the division of labour.

Adam Smith, from *The Wealth of Nations*, 1776

# A Proper Division

But after, when night was already receding from the mid-point of her course, and first repose had dispelled sleep from him, the same hour when some housewife, whose burden it is to endure life in dependence on her distaff and Minerva's slight aid, will awake the fire asleep in the ashes, and adding the night-hours to her working-time, set her maids a long task, and keep them at it by lamplight, to enable her to guard her marriage in purity and bring up her little sons; at this same hour, and with a will as active, the God whose Might is Fire arose from his soft bed to work at his forge. By Aeolian Lipara an island rises steeply on spray-steaming rocks in the sea near Sicily's flank, where an underground cavern and galleries leading from Etna, originally excavated by the smithying Cyclopes, roar thunderously; for in them strong blows are heard resounding on anvils and re-echoing their growl. Chalybean ingots hiss within chambers of rock and in the furnaces pants the fire. The island is Vulcan's home; and Vulcania is its name.

To this place at that hour the God whose Might is Fire came down from high Heaven. Cyclopes were working iron in a vast gallery; they were Thunderer, Lightener, and the bare-limbed Fire-Anvil. They had in hand a roughly shaped thunderbolt, of which a part was already shining-perfect but the rest remained unfinished; it was of the kind which the Father flings in great numbers down on the world from every quarter of the sky. They had fixed on to it three skeins of twisted rain, three belts of rain-charged cloud, and three of red fire and three of winged south wind. And now they were blending within their creation the flashes which bring the terror, the crashing, and the dread, with darting wrath wrapped in vindictive flames ... 'Away with all of it!' said Vulcan. 'Lay aside whatever you have begun, you Cyclopes of Etna, and give me your attention. We have arms to make for a man, a mortal warrior of high spirit. Now you need all your strength, your swift, grasping hands, and all your master-skill. Delay not an instant!' He said no more. All together the Cyclopes shared out their tasks fairly and went swiftly to work. Bronze and pure gold-ore flowed along the conduits, and wounding steel melted in a great furnace. They shaped out an immense shield fit for standing alone against all the missiles of Latium and they fixed all its seven layers fast together. Other Cyclopes, using bellows with a blast like the winds, drew in and discharged the air. Some tempered hissing bronze in a circular pool of water. The cavern rumbled under the anvils planted on its floor. With all their energy they raised arms rhythmically together and kept the mass of metal turning by the grip of their tongs.

Virgil, *Aeneid*, Book VIII, first century BC,
tr. W. Jackson Knight, 1956

To take an example, therefore, from a very trifling manufacture; but one in which the division of labour has been very often taken notice of, the trade of the pin-maker; a workman not educated to his business (which the division of labour has rendered a distinct trade), nor acquainted with the use of the machinery employed in it (to the invention of which the same division of labour has probably given occasion), could scarce, perhaps, with his utmost industry, make one pin in a day, and certainly could not make twenty. But in the way in which this business is now carried on, not only the whole work is a peculiar trade, but it is divided into a number of branches, of which the greater part are likewise peculiar trades. One man draws out the wire, another straights it, a third cuts it, a fourth points it, a fifth grinds it at the top for receiving the head; to make the head requires two or three distinct operations; to put it on is a peculiar business, to whiten the pins is another; it is even a trade by itself to put them into the paper; and the important business of making a pin is, in this manner, divided into about eighteen distinct operations, which, in some manufactories, are all performed by distinct hands, though in others the same man will sometimes perform two or three of them. I have seen a small manufactory of this kind where ten men only were employed, and where some of them consequently performed two or three distinct operations. But though they were very poor, and therefore but indifferently accommodated with the necessary machinery, they could, when they exerted themselves, make among them about twelve pounds of pins in a day. There are in a pound upwards of four thousand pins of a middling size. Those ten persons, therefore, could make among them upwards of forty-eight thousand pins in a day. Each person, therefore, making a tenth part of forty-eight thousand pins, might be considered as making four thousand eight hundred pins in a day. But if they had all wrought separately and independently, and without any of them having been educated to this peculiar business, they certainly could not each of them have made twenty, perhaps not one pin in a day; that is, certainly, not the two hundred and fortieth, perhaps not the four

thousand eight hundredth part of what they are at present capable of performing, in consequence of a proper division and combination of their different
operations.

Adam Smith, from *The Wealth of Nations*, 1770

When Izz Huett and Tess arrived at the scene of operations only a rustling
denoted that others had preceded them; to which, as the light increased, there
were presently added the silhouettes of two men on the summit. They were
busily 'unhaling' the rick, that is, stripping off the thatch before beginning to
throw down the sheaves; and while this was in progress Izz and Tess, with
the other women-workers, in their whitey-brown pinners, stood waiting and
shivering, Farmer Groby having insisted upon their being on the spot thus
early to get the job over if possible by the end of the day. Close under the
eaves of the stack, and as yet barely visible, was the red tyrant that the women
had come to serve – a timber-framed construction, with straps and wheels
appertaining – a threshing-machine which, whilst it was going, kept up a
despotic demand upon the endurance of their muscles and nerves.

A little way off there was another indistinct figure; this one black, with a
sustained hiss that spoke of strength very much in reserve. The long chimney
running up beside an ash-tree, and the warmth which radiated from the spot,
explained without the necessity of much daylight that here was the engine
which was to act as the *primum mobile* of this little world. By the engine stood
a dark motionless being, a sooty and grimy embodiment of tallness, in a sort
of trance, with a heap of coals by his side; it was the engineman. The isolation of his manner and colour lent him the appearance of a creature from
Tophet, who had strayed into the pellucid smokelessness of this region of
yellow grain and pale soil, with which he had nothing in common, to amaze
and to discompose its aborigines.

What he looked he felt. He was in the agricultural world, but not of it. He
served fire and smoke; these denizens of the fields served vegetation, weather,
frost, and sun. He travelled with his engine from farm to farm, from county
to country, for as yet the steam threshing-machine was itinerant in this part
of Wessex. He spoke in a strange northern accent; his thoughts being turned
inwards upon himself, his eye on his iron charge, hardly perceiving the scenes
around him, and caring for them not at all: holding only strictly necessary
intercourse with the natives, as if some ancient doom compelled him to wander
here against his will in the service of his Plutonic master. The long strap
which ran from the driving-wheel of his engine to the red thresher under the
rick was the sole tie-line between agriculture and him.

While they uncovered the sheaves he stood apathetic beside his portable

193

respository of force, round whose hot blackness the morning air quivered. He had nothing to do with preparatory labour. His fire was waiting incandescent, his steam was at high pressure, in a few seconds he could make the long strap move at an invisible velocity. Beyond its extent the environment might be corn, straw, or chaos; it was all the same to him. If any of the autochthonous idlers asked him what he called himself, he replied shortly, 'an engineer'.

The rick was unhaled by full daylight; the men then took their places, the women mounted, and the work began. Farmer Groby – or, as they called him, 'he' – had arrived ere this, and by his orders Tess was placed on the platform of the machine, close to the man who fed it, her business being to untie every sheaf of corn handed on to her by Izz Huett, who stood next, but on the rick; so that the feeder could seize it and spread it over the revolving drum, which whisked out every grain in one moment.

They were soon in full progress, after a preparatory hitch or two, which rejoiced the hearts of those who hated machinery. The work sped on till breakfast-time, when the thresher was stopped for half an hour; and on starting again after the meal the whole supplementary strength of the farm was thrown into the labour of constructing the straw-rick, which began to grow beside the stack of corn. A hasty lunch was eaten as they stood, without leaving their positions, and then another couple of hours brought them near to dinner-time; the inexorable wheels continuing to spin, and the penetrating hum of the thresher to thrill to the very marrow all who were near the revolving wire-cage.

Thomas Hardy, from *Tess of the d'Urbervilles*, 1891

## Symphony and Society

### Man Does, Woman Is

Studiously by lamplight I appraised
The palm of your hand, its heart-line
Identical with its head-line;
And you appraised the approving frown.

I spread my cards face-upwards on the table,
Not challenging you for yours.
Man does; but woman is –
Can a gamester argue with his luck?

Robert Graves, from *Man Does, Woman Is*, 1964

It is indisputable that women are, in general, as superior to men in a spontaneous expansion of sympathy and sociality, as they are inferior to men in understanding and reason. Their function in the economy of the family, and consequently of society, must therefore be to modify by the excitement of the social instinct the general direction necessarily originated by the cold and rough reason which is distinctive of Man. Apart from all consideration of material differences, and contemplating exclusively the noblest properties of our cerebral nature, we see that, of the two attributes which separate the human race from the brutes, the primary one indicates the necessary and invariable preponderance of the male sex, while the other points out the moderating function which is appropriate to Woman, even independently of material cares, which evidently constitute her most important special destination, but which are usually too exclusively insisted on, so as to disguise the direct social and personal vocation of the female sex.

Auguste Comte, from *Positive Philosophy*,
tr. Harriet Martineau, 1853

### The Meaningful Exchange

The man talks
the woman listens

The man is a teapot
with a dark green brew
of troubles.
He pours into the woman.
She carries his sorrows away
sloshing around in her belly.

The man swings off lighter.
Sympathy quickens him.
He watches women pass.
He whistles.

The woman lumbers away.
Inside his troubles are
snaking up through her throat.
Her body curls delicately
about them, worrying, nudging
them into some new meaningful shape
squatting now at the centre of her life.

How much lighter I feel,
the man says, ready
for business.
How heavy I feel, the woman
says: this must be love.

Marge Piercy, 1969

## The Kitchen Girl's Task

A demon took over Frank, chief
   at the café on the motorway:
arms akimbo, as midnight clicks, he
   summons one of the girls, says:

I want you to count the tealeaves
   we've used here today,
and I'll wait for the right answer.

The prince could not wait, he left her.
   Tears and the fumes of the bins
had sympathy from the clouds of morning.

The prince set out to find his enemies
   who would not wait for man or beast.
Regularly he wrote her letters,
   repeating her unchanging name.

One night, in a dream, she saw
   the little sodden leaves rise,
rank themselves in rows of ten.

She read his considerate lines:
   'How bright I remember your eyes
in all that dry glare.'

'Today we picked up the scent again.'
   'I've found true friends here!'
'We're having *Freedom*
   tattooed on our right wrists.'

Sometimes she put down cloth or knife
   to wander within the boundary.
She would not have heard Rumpelstiltskin
   if he had shouted in her ear.

Silence for her became a rule;
    she was ashamed – and Frank was there
ordering her to wipe the stoves
    and wash the floor as usual.

After a while it came to her
    that no two leaves were identical.
        Libby Houston, *At the Mercy*, 1981


## The Business of a Woman's Life

It is not my advice that you have asked as to the direction of your talents, but my opinion of them, and yet the opinion may be worth little, and the advice much. You evidently possess, and in no inconsiderable degree, what Words-worth calls the 'faculty of verse'. I am not depreciating it when I say that in these times it is not rare. Many volumes of poems are now published every year without attracting public attention, any one of which, if it had appeared half a century ago, would have obtained a high reputation for its author. Whoever, therefore, is ambitious of distinction in this way ought to be prepared for disappointment.

But it is not with a view to distinction that you should cultivate this talent, if you consult your own happiness. I, who have made literature my profession, and devoted my life to it, and have never for a moment repented of the deliberate choice, think myself, nevertheless, bound in duty to caution every young man who applies as an aspirant to me for encouragement and advice against taking so perilous a course. You will say that a woman has no need of such a caution; there can be no merit in it for her. In a certain sense this is true; but there is a danger of which I would, with all kindness and all earnestness, warn you. The day dreams in which you habitually indulge are likely to induce a distempered state of mind; and in proportion as all the ordinary uses of the world seem to you flat and unprofitable, you will be unfitted for them without becoming fitted for anything else. Literature cannot be the business of a woman's life, and it ought not to be. The more she is engaged in her proper duties, the less leisure will she have for it, even as an accomplishment and a recreation. To those duties you have not yet been called, and when you are you will be less eager for celebrity. You will not seek in imagination for excitement, of which the vicissitudes of this life, and the anxieties from which you must not hope to be exempted, be your state what it may, will bring with them but too much.

But do not suppose that I disparage the gift which you possess; nor that I would discourage you from exercising it. I only exhort you so to think of it, and so to use it, as to render it conducive to your own permanent good. Write poetry for its own sake, not in a spirit of emulation, and not with a view to celebrity; the less you aim at that the more likely you will be to deserve and finally to obtain it. So written, it is wholesome both for the heart and soul; it may be made in the surest means, next to religion, of soothing the mind and elevating it. You may embody in it your best thoughts and your wisest feelings, and in so doing discipline and strengthen them.

Farewell, madam. It is not because I have forgotten that I was once young myself that I write to you in this strain, but because I remember it. You will neither doubt my sincerity nor my goodwill; and however ill what has here been said may accord with your present views and temper, the longer you live the more reasonable it will appear to you. Though I may be but an ungracious adviser, you will allow me, therefore, to subscribe myself, with the best wishes for your happiness here and hereafter, your true friend.

Robert Southey, Letter to Charlotte Brontë, March 1837; from Elizabeth Gaskell, *The Life of Charlotte Brontë*, 1857

Ladies of Great Britain, we are clever, we are efficient, we are trustworthy, we are twice the women that our grandmothers were, but we have not enough devil in us. We are afraid of going back to first causes. We want to earn good wages. But we try to do it by being amenable and competent wage-slaves, and thus pleasing the capitalist. We never try to do it by fighting the capitalist and turning him out of the workshop. The other day Mr Ramsay MacDonald complained that women do not make good enough socialists for him. The whole trouble is that women make socialists which are just good enough for Mr Ramsay MacDonald. They accept as doles from the capitalist class what they should take as rights. Wherever one gets a gathering of women socialists, one gets a programme of such charity gifts from the State as free meals and school clinics for children: excellent things, but dangerous unless taken discontentedly as niggardly instalments of a long-due debt. They should watch such things critically lest their children grow up in servitude. A slave is more of a slave when he is well fed than when he is hungry.

It is strange that women who are independent and fearless in private life should not introduce their independence and fearlessness into their public life. This occurs to me especially in connection with elementary-school-teachers. The cheerfulness with which they have shouldered the responsibilities thrown on them by the free meals and medical examination of schoolchildren explains why the children love their school and their teachers.

Yet they submit to being paid salaries of from one-half to two-thirds the amount paid to men for similar work. They submit in spite of the fact that they could end the injustice in a week by a strike. What could the Government do if women teachers struck? There are no hungry teachers walking the streets, so degraded by poverty that – God forgive them and punish the capitalists – they will help to drag their fellows down to poverty, too, by blacklegging. The women teachers of England have their remedy in their own hands.

Yet not only do they not use it, but they consent to remain members of a quaint body called the National Union of Teachers, which, although it exacts an equal subscription from men and women alike, maintains this principle of unequal payment. The scale which it suggests for certified class-teachers is quite a humorous little effort. Apparently the male class-teacher is intended to get married at once, as his minimum salary is higher than the female's. True the difference is but £10, but the maintenance of a family can be the only excuse for any difference at all. His maximum salary is £200 against the female's £160. Puzzle: If the NUT thinks a class-teacher can keep a wife on the £10 surplus, how many children does it expect him to rear on the £40 surplus? Surely the birth-rate can't be going down!

I am no teacher, but I don't think much of that Union. I like to get value for my money, and a Union that takes my money and does not give me equal benefits with my fellow-unionist is no use to me. Decidedly the women members of the NUT ought to withdraw their support from their ungracious colleagues and form a union of their own.

But what is the explanation of the meekness which makes such impositions on women possible? It is perhaps nothing disgraceful to ourselves, nothing that need make us doubt our worthiness as citizens of the ideal State. Nietzsche says that a man who is aiming at Supermanhood passes through three phases: the camel, the lion and the child. At first the soul becomes mastered by the idea of duty and self-sacrifice. It desires to be a preserver of life. Thus far have women gone. They have no time to travel further, having left the home so recently. 'But when the camel is loaded, it goeth to the desert, and there it is transformed into a lion.' The soul finds that the life for which it has sacrificed itself is in its present state hardly worthy of preserving. It turns to rend and destroy life. To this stage have men come.

Let women make haste to become lions, and fearlessly attack the social system. So that together men and women may be transformed for the last time into the child, who, untroubled with the consciousness of material things, is concerned only with love and happiness.

Rebecca West, from 'Blacklegging and Timidity', *The Clarion*, 18 October 1912

## Ladies and Gentlemen

When Adam delved and Eve span,
Who was then the gentleman?

Anon.

1743

Man, to the Plough,
Wife, to the Cow,
Girl, to the Yarn,
Boy, to the Barn,
And your Rent will be netted.

1843

Man, Tally Ho
Miss, Piano,
Wife, Silk and Satin,
Boy, Greek and Latin,
And you'll all be Gazetted.

John Robey, 1843

Now E[lizabeth], here is another instance of the horrible injustice of this system of slavery. In my country or in yours, a man endowed with sufficient knowledge and capacity to be an engineer would, of course, be in the receipt of considerable wages; his wife would, together with himself, reap the advantages of his ability, and share the well-being his labor earned; he would be able to procure for her comfort in sickness or in health, and beyond the necessary household work, which the wives of most artisans are inured to, she would have no labor to encounter; in case of sickness even these would be alleviated by the assistance of some stout girl of all work or kindly neighbor, and the tidy parlor or snug bedroom would be her retreat if unequal to the daily duties of her own kitchen. Think of such a lot compared with that of the head engineer of Mr [Butler]'s plantation, whose sole wages are his coarse food and raiment and miserable hovel, and whose wife, covered with one filthy garment of ragged texture and dingy color, barefooted and bareheaded, is daily driven afield to labor with aching pain-racked joints, under the lash of a driver, or lies languishing on the earthen floor of the dismal plantation hospital in a condition of utter physical destitution and degradation such as the most miserable dwelling of the poorest inhabitant of your free Northern villages never beheld the like of. Think of the rows of tidy tiny houses in the long suburbs of Boston and Philadelphia, inhabited by artisans of just the same grade as this poor Ned, with their white doors and steps, their hydrants of inexhaustible fresh flowing water, the innumerable appliances for decent comfort of their cheerful rooms, the gay wardrobe of the wife, her cotton prints for daily use, her silk for Sunday churchgoing; the careful comfort of the children's clothing, the books and newspapers in the little parlor, the daily district school, the weekly parish church: imagine if you can – but you are happy that you cannot – the contrast between such an existence and that of the best mechanic on a Southern plantation.

> Frances Anne Kemble, from *Journal of a Residence on a Georgian Plantation in 1838–1839*, 1863

## Making Hay: Complaint and Answer

### *Margaret Has a Milking Pail*

Margaret has a milking pail,
    And she rises early;
Thomas has a threshing-flail
    And he's up betimes.
Sometimes crossing through the grass
    Where the dew lies pearly,
They say 'Good-morrow' as they pass
    By the leafy limes.

> Christina Rossetti, from *Sing-Song: A Nursery Rhyme Book*, 1872

When first the Lark sings Prologue to the Day,
We rise, admonish'd by his early Lay;
This new Employ with eager Haste to prove,
This new Employ, become so much our Love.
Alas! that human Joys should change so soon!
Our Morning Pleasure turns to Pain at Noon.
The Birds salute us, as to Work we go,
And with new Life our Bosoms seem to glow.
On our right Shoulder hangs the crooked Blade,
The Weapon destin'd to uncloath the Mead:

Our left supports the Whetstone, Scrip, and Beer;
This for our Scythes, and these ourselves to chear.
And now the Field, design'd to try our Might,
At length appears, and meets our longing Sight.
The Grass and Ground we view with careful Eyes,
To see which way the best Advantage lies;
And, Hero–like, each claims the foremost Place.
At first our Labour seems a sportive Race:
With rapid Force our sharpen'd Blades we drive,
Strain ev'ry Nerve, and Blow for Blow we give.
All strive to vanquish, tho' the Victor gains
No other Glory, but the greatest Pains.

    But when the scorching Sun is mounted high,
And no kind Barns with friendly Shade are nigh;
Our weary Scythes entangle in the Grass,
While Streams of Sweat run trickling down apace.
Our sportive Labour we too late lament;
And wish that Strength again, we vainly spent . . .
Supper and Sleep by Morn new Strength supply;
And out we set again, our Work to try;
But not so early quite, nor quite so fast,
As, to our Cost, we did the Morning past.

    Soon as the rising Sun has drank the Dew,
Another Scene is open to our View:
Our Master comes, and at his Heels a Throng
Of prattling Females, arm'd with Rake and Prong;
Prepar'd, while he is here, to make his Hay;
Or, if he turns his Back, prepar'd to play:
But here, or gone, sure of this Comfort still;
Here's Company, so they may chat their Fill.
Ah! were their Hands so active as their Tongues,
How nimbly then would move the Rankes and Prongs! . . .

Yet, spite of this, they bravely all go on;
Each scorns to be, or seem to be, outdone.
Meanwhile the changing Sky begins to lour,
And hollow Winds proclaim a sudden Show'r:
The tattling Crowd can scarce their Garments gain,
Before descends the thick impetuous Rain;
Their noisy Prattle all at once is done,
And to the Hedge they soon for Shelter run.

Thus I have seen, on a bright Summer's Day,
On some green Brake, a Flow of Sparrows play;
From Twig to Twig, from Bush to Bush they fly;
And with continu'd Chirping fill the Sky:
But, on a sudden, if a Storm appears,
Their chirping Noise no longer dins your Ears:
They fly for Shelter to the thickest Bush;
There silent sit, and All at once is hush.

> Stephen Duck, from *The Thresher's Labour*, 1736

For my own Part, I many a *Summer*'s Day
Have spent in throwing, turning, making Hay;
But ne'er could see, what you have lately found,
Our Wages paid for sitting on the Ground.
'Tis true, that when our Morning's Work is done,
And all our Grass expos'd unto the Sun,
While that his scorching Beams do on it shine,
As well as you, we have a Time to dine:
I hope, that since we freely toil and sweat
To earn our Bread, you'll give us Time to eat.
That over, soon we must get up again,
And nimbly turn our Hay upon the Plain;
Nay, rake and prow it in, the Case is clear;
Or how should Cocks in equal Rows appear? . . .

When Ev'ning does approach, we homeward hie,
And our domestic Toils incessant ply:
Against your coming Home prepare to get
Our Work all done, our House in order set;
*Bacon* and *Dumpling* in the Pot we boil,
Our Beds we make, our Swine we feed the while;
Then wait at Door to see you coming Home,
And set the Table out against you come:
Early next Morning we on you attend;
Our Children dress and feed, their Cloaths we mend;
And in the Field our daily Task renew,
Soon as the rising Sun has dry'd the Dew.

When Harvest comes, into the Field we go,
And help to reap the Wheat as well as you;
Or else we go the Ears of Corn to glean;

No Labour scorning, be it e'er so mean;
But in the Work we freely bear a Part,
And what we can, perform with all our Heart.
To get a Living we so willing are,
Our tender Babes into the Field we bear,
And wrap them in our Cloaths to keep them warm,
While round about we gather up the Corn;
And often unto them our Course do bend,
To keep them safe, that nothing them offend:
Our Children that are able, bear a Share
In gleaning Corn, such is our frugal Care.
When Night comes on, unto our Home we go,
Our Corn we carry, and our Infant too;
Weary, alas! but 'tis not worth our while
Once to complain, or *rest at ev'ry Stile*;
We must make haste, for when we Home are come,
Alas! we find our Work but just begun;
So many Things for our Attendance call,
Had we ten Hands, we could employ them all.
Our Children put to Bed, with greatest Care
We all Things for your coming Home prepare:
You sup, and go to Bed without delay,
And rest yourselves till the ensuing Day;

While we, alas! but little Sleep can have,
Because our froward Children cry and rave;
Yet, without fail, soon as Day-light doth spring,
We in the Field again our Work begin,
And there, with all our Strength, our Toil renew,
Till *Titan*'s golden Rays have dry'd the Dew;
The home we go unto our Children dear,
Dress, feed, and bring them to the Field with care.
Were this your Case, you justly might complain
That Day nor Night you are secure from Pain;
Those mighty Troubles which perplex your Mind,
(*Thistles* before, and *Females* come behind)
Would vanish soon, and quickly disappear,
Were you, like us, encumber'd thus with Care.
What you would have of us we do not know:
We oft' take up the Corn that you do mow;
We cut the Peas, and always ready are

In ev'ry Work to take our proper Share;
And from the Time that Harvest doth begin,
Until the Corn be cut and carry'd in,
Our Toil and Labour's daily so extreme
That we have hardly ever *Time to dream.*

Mary Collier, from *The Woman's Labour: An Epistle to Mr Stephen Duck in Answer to his late Poem, called The Thresher's Labour,* 1739

### A Scheme for Rural Employment

The women and children, who ought to provide a great part of the raiment, have nothing to do. The fields *must have men and boys*; but, where there are men and boys there will be *women* and *girls*; and, as the Lords of the Loom have now a set of *real slaves* by the means of whom they take away a great part of the employment of the country – *women* and *girls*, these must be kept by poor-rates in whatever degree they lose employment through the Lords of the Loom. One would think, that nothing can be much plainer than this; and yet you hear the *jolterheads* congratulating one another upon the increase of Manchester, and such places! My *straw affair* will certainly restore to the land some of the employment of its women and girls. It will be impossible for any of the '*rich ruffians*'; any of the horse-power or steam-power or air-power ruffians; any of these greedy, grinding ruffians, to draw together bands of men, women and children, and to make them slaves, in the working of *straw*. The raw material comes of *itself*, and the *hand*, and the *hand alone*, can convert it to use. I thought well of this before I took one single step in the way of supplanting the Leghorn bonnets. If I had not been *certain*, that no *rich ruffian*, no *white slave* holder, could ever arise out of it, assuredly one line upon the subject never would have been written by me. Better, a million times, that the money should go to Italy; better that it should go to enrich even the rivals and enemies of the country; than that it should enable these hard, these unfeeling men, to draw English people into crowds and make them slaves, and slaves too of the lowest and most degraded cast . . .

Mrs Mears, the farmer's wife, had made, of the crested dog's tail grass, a bonnet which she wears herself. I there saw girls platting the straw. They had made plat of several degrees of fineness; and, they sell it to some person or persons at Fareham, who, I suppose, make it into bonnets. Mrs Mears, who is a very intelligent and clever woman, has two girls at work, each of whom earns per week as much (within a shilling) as her father, who is a labouring man, earns per week. The father has at this time, only 7s. per week. These two girls (and not very stout girls) *earn six shillings a week each*: thus the income of this family is, from *seven shillings* a week, raised to *nineteen shillings a week*. I shall suppose that this may in some measure be owing to the generosity of ladies in the neighbourhood and to their desire to promote this domestic manufacture; but, if I suppose that these girls receive double compared to what they will receive for the same quantity of labour when the manufacture becomes more general, is it not a great thing to make the income of the family thirteen shillings a week instead of seven? Very little, indeed, could these poor things have done in the field during the last forty days. And, besides, how clean; how healthful; how every thing that one could wish, is this sort of employment! The farmer, who is also a very intelligent person, told me, that he should endeavour to introduce the manufacture as a thing to assist the obtaining of employment, in order to lessen the amount of the poor-rates. I think it very likely that this will be done in the parish of Durley. A most important matter it is, *to put paupers in the way of ceasing to be paupers.* I could not help admiring the zeal as well as the intelligence of the farmer's wife, who expressed her readiness to teach the girls and women of the parish in order to enable them to assist themselves. I shall hear, in all probability of their proceedings at Durley, and if I do, I shall make a point of communicating to the Public an account of those interesting proceedings. From the very first; from the first moment of my thinking about this straw affair, I regarded it as likely to assist in bettering the lot of the labouring people. If it has not this effect, I value it not. It is not worth the attention of any of us; but I am satisfied that this is the way in which it will work. I have the pleasure to know, that there is one labouring family, at any rate, *who are living well through my means.* It is I, who, without knowing them, without ever having seen them, without ever now knowing their names, have given the means of good living to a family who were before half-starved. This is indisputably my work; and when I reflect that there must necessarily be, now, some hundreds of families, and shortly, many thousands of families, in England, who are and will be, through my means, living well instead of being half-starved; I cannot but feel myself consoled . . . I have done more good than Bayley ever did in the whole course of his life, notwithstanding his pious Commentary on the Book of Common Prayer. I will allow nothing to be good, with regard to the labouring classes, unless it make an addition to their victuals, drink or clothing. As to their *minds,* that is much too sublime matter for me to think about. I know that they are in rags, and that they have not a bellyfull; and I know that the way to make them good, to make them honest, to make them dutiful, to make them kind to one another, is to enable them to live well; and I also know, that none of these things will ever be accomplished by Methodist sermons, and by those stupid, at once stupid and malignant things, and roguish things, called Religious Tracts.

William Cobbett, from Rural Rides, 1823

## A Befitting Trade

Give a man a trade befitting his sex, to a young man a trade befitting his age. Sedentary indoor employments, which make the body tender and effeminate, are neither pleasing nor suitable. No lad ever wanted to be a tailor. It takes some art to attract a man to this woman's work. The same hand cannot hold the needle and the sword. If I were king I would only allow needlework and dress-making to be done by women and cripples who are obliged to work at such trades. If eunuchs were required I think the Easterns were very foolish to make them on purpose. Why not take those provided by nature, that crowd of base persons without natural feeling? There would be enough and to spare. The weak, feeble, timid man is condemned by nature to a sedentary life, he is fit to live among women or in their fashion. Let him adopt one of their trades if he likes; and if there must be eunuchs let them take those men who dishonour their sex by adopting trades unworthy of it. Their choice proclaims a blunder on the part of nature; correct it one way or other, you will do not harm.

An unhealthy trade I forbid to my pupil, but not a difficult or dangerous one. He will exercise himself in strength and courage; such trades are for men not women, who claim no share in them. Are not men ashamed to poach upon the women's trades?

Women are not seen in shops in Italy, and to persons accustomed to the streets of England and France nothing could look gloomier. When I saw drapers selling ladies ribbons, pompons, net, and chenille, I thought these delicate ornaments very absurd in the coarse hands fit to blow the bellows and strike the anvil. I said to myself, 'In this country women should set up as steel-polishers and armourers.' Let each make and sell the weapons of his or her own sex; knowledge is acquired through use.

I know I have said too much for my agreeable contemporaries, but I sometimes let myself be carried away by my argument. If any one is ashamed to be seen wearing a leathern apron or handling a plane, I think him a mere slave of public opinion, ready to blush for what is right when people poke fun at it. But let us yield to parents' prejudices so long as they do not hurt the children. To honour trades we are not obliged to practise every one of them, so long as we do not think them beneath us. When the choice is ours and we are under no compulsion, why not choose the pleasanter, more attractive and more suitable trade. Metal work is useful, more useful, perhaps, than the rest, but unless for some special reason Emile shall not be a blacksmith, a locksmith nor an iron-worker. I do not want to see him a Cyclops at the forge. Neither would I have him a mason, still less a shoemaker. All trades must be carried on, but when the choice is ours, cleanliness should be taken into account; this is not a matter of class prejudice, our senses are our guides. In conclusion, I do not like those stupid trades in which the workmen mechanically perform the same action without pause and almost without mental effort. Weaving, stocking-knitting, stone-cutting; why employ intelligent men on such work? It is merely one machine employed on another.

All things considered, the trade I should choose for my pupil, among the trades he likes, is that of a carpenter. It is clean and useful; it may be carried on at home; it gives enough exercise; it calls for skill and industry, and while fashioning articles for everyday use, there is scope for elegance and taste. If your pupil's talents happened to take a scientific turn, I should not blame you if you gave him a trade in accordance with his tastes, for instance, he might learn to make mathematical instruments, glasses, telescopes, etc.

Jean-Jacques Rousseau, from *Emile*, 1762,

tr. Barbara Foxley, 1911

He relates how another working-man, being on tramp, came to St Helens, in Lancashire, and there looked up an old friend. He found him in a miserable, damp cellar, scarcely furnished; and when my poor friend went in, there sat poor Jack near the fire, and what did he, think you? why he sat and mended his wife's stockings with the bodkin; and as soon as he saw his old friend at the door-post, he tried to hide them. But Joe, that is my friend's name, had seen it, and said: 'Jack, what the devil art thou doing? Where is the missus? Why, is that thy work?' and poor Jack was ashamed, and said: 'No, I know this is not my work, but my poor missus is i' th' factory; she has to leave at half-past five and works till eight at night, and then she is so knocked up that she cannot do aught when she gets home, so I have to do everything for her what I can, for I have no work, nor had any for more nor three years, and I shall never have any more work while I live'; and then he wept a big tear. Jack again said: 'There is work enough for women folks and childer hereabouts, but none for men; thou mayest sooner find a hundred pounds on the road than work for men – but I should never have believed that either thou or any one else would have seen me mending my wife's stockings, for it is bad work. But she can hardly stand on her feet; I am afraid she will be laid up, and then I don't know what is to become of us, for it's a good bit that she has been the man in the house and I the woman; it is bad work, Joe'; and he cried bitterly, and said, 'It has not been always so.' 'No,' said Joe; 'but when thou hadn't no work, how hast thou not shifted?' 'I'll tell thee, Joe, as well as I can, but it was bad enough; thou knowest when I got married I had work plenty, and thou knows I was not lazy.' 'No, that thou wert not.' 'And we had a good furnished house, and Mary need not go to work. I could work for the two of us; but now the world is upside down. Mary has to work and I have to stop at home and mind the children, sweep and wash, bake and mend; and when the poor woman comes home at night, she is knocked up. Thou knows, Joe, it's hard for one that was used different.' 'Yes, boy, it is hard.' And then Jack began to cry again, and he wished he had never married, and that he had never been born; but he had never thought, when he wed Mary, that it would come to this. 'I have often cried over it,' said Jack. Now when Joe heard this, he told me that he had cursed and damned the factories, and the masters, and the Government, with all the curses that he had learned while he was in the factory from a child.

Can any one imagine a more insane state of things than that described in this letter? And yet this condition, which unsexes the man and takes from the woman all womanliness without being able to bestow upon the man true womanliness, or the woman true manliness – this condition which degrades, in the most shameful way, both sexes, and, through them, Humanity, is the last result of our much-praised civilization, the final achievement of all the effort and struggles of hundreds of generations to improve their own situation and that of their posterity. We must either despair of mankind, and its aims and efforts, when we see all our labour and toil result in such a mockery, or we must admit that human society has hitherto sought salvation in a false direction; we must admit that so total a reversal of the position of the sexes can have come to pass only because the sexes have been placed in a false position from the beginning. If the reign of the wife over the husband, as inevitably brought about by the factory system, is inhuman, the pristine rule of the husband over the wife must have been inhuman too. If the wife can now base her supremacy upon the fact that she supplies the greater part, nay, the whole of the common possession, the necessary inference is that this community of possession is no true and rational one, since one member of the family boasts offensively of contributing the greater share. If the family of our present society is being thus dissolved, this dissolution merely shows that, at bottom, the binding tie of this family was not family affection, but private interest lurking under the cloak of a pretended community of possessions.

Friedrich Engels, from *The Condition of the Working Classes in England*, 1844

Because of the outbreak of war I returned from Paris to Louvain where, while out walking with that celebrated physician and mathematician Gemma Frisius and looking for bones where the executed criminals are usually placed along the country roads – to the advantage of the students – I came upon a dried cadaver similar to that of the robber Galen mentions having seen. As I suspect the birds had freed that one of flesh, so they had cleansed this one, which had been partially burned and roasted over a fire of straw and then bound to a stake. Consequently the bones were entirely bare and held together only by the ligaments so that merely the origins and insertions of the muscles had been preserved . . . Observing the body to be dry and nowhere moist or rotten, I took advantage of this unexpected but welcome opportunity and, with the help of Gemma, I climbed the stake and pulled the femur away from the hipbone. Upon my tugging, the scapulae with the arms and hands also came away, although the fingers of one hand and both patellae as well as one foot were missing. After I had surreptitiously brought the legs and arms home in successive trips – leaving the head and trunk behind – I allowed myself to be shut out of the city in the evening so that I might obtain the thorax, which was held securely by a chain. So great was my desire to possess those bones that in the middle of the night, alone and in the midst of all those corpses, I climbed the stake with considerable effort, and did not hesitate to snatch away that which I so desired. When I had pulled down the bones I carried them some distance away and concealed them until the following day when I was able to fetch them home bit by bit through another gate of the city.

At first, however, I was unable to cut the ligaments because of their extraordinary hardness, and so I attempted to soften them in boiling water; finally and secretly I cooked all the bones to render them more suitable for my purpose. When they had been cleansed I constructed the skeleton that is preserved at Louvain in the home of my very dear old friend Gisbertus Carbo, companion in my boyhood studies and later distinguished as a student of medicine as well as of other branches of learning. With considerable effort I obtained the missing hand, foot, and two patellae from elsewhere and prepared this skeleton with such speed that I was able to convince everyone that I had brought it from Paris. Thus any suspicion of having made off with the bones was destroyed, although later the burgomaster was so favourably disposed towards the studies of the candidates in medicine that he was willing to grant whatever body was sought from him. He attained no little knowledge of anatomy and was in regular attendance whenever I conducted an anatomy there.

> Andreas Vesalius of Brussels, 1514–64,
> tr. C. D. O'Malley, 1964

There was something very fine in Lydgate's look just then, and any one might have been encouraged to bet on his achievement. In his dark eyes and on his mouth and brow there was that placidity which comes from the fulness of contemplative thought – the mind not searching, but beholding, and the glance seeming to be filled with what is behind it.

Presently Rosamond left the piano and seated herself on a chair close to the sofa and opposite her husband's face.

'Is that enough music for you, my lord?' she said, folding her hands before her and putting on a little air of meekness.

'Yes, dear, if you are tired,' said Lydgate, gently, turning his eyes and resting them on her, but not otherwise moving. Rosamond's presence at that moment was perhaps no more than a spoonful brought to the lake, and her woman's instinct in this matter was not dull.

'What is absorbing you?' she said, leaning forward and bringing her face nearer to his.

He moved his hands and placed them gently behind her shoulders.

'I am thinking of a great fellow, who was about as old as I am three hundred years ago, and had already begun a new era in anatomy.'

'I can't guess,' said Rosamond, shaking her head. 'We used to play at guessing historical characters at Mrs Lemon's, but not anatomists.'

'I'll tell you. His name was Vesalius. And the only way he could get to know anatomy as he did, was by going to snatch bodies at night, from graveyards and places of execution.'

'Oh!' said Rosamond, with a look of disgust on her pretty face, 'I am very glad you are not Vesalius. I should have thought he might find some less horrible way than that.'

'No, he couldn't,' said Lydgate, going on too earnestly to take much notice of her answer. 'He could only get a complete skeleton by snatching the whitened bones of a criminal from the gallows and burying them, and fetching them away by bits secretly, in the dead of night.'

'I hope he is not one of your great heroes,' said Rosamond, half-playfully, half-anxiously, 'else I shall have you getting up in the night to go to St Peter's churchyard. You know how angry you told me the people were about Mrs Goby. You have enemies enough already.'

'So had Vesalius, Rosy. No wonder the medical fogies in Middlemarch are jealous, when some of the greatest doctors living were fierce upon Vesalius because they had believed in Galen, and he showed that Galen was wrong. They called him a liar and a poisonous monster. But the facts of the human frame were on his side; and so he got the better of them.'

'And what happened to him afterwards?' said Rosamond, with some interest.

'Oh, he had a good deal of fighting to the last. And they did exasperate him enough at one time to make him burn a good deal of his work. Then he got ship-wrecked just as he was coming from Jerusalem to take a great chair at Padua. He died rather miserably.'

There was a moment's pause before Rosamond said, 'Do you know, Tertius, I often wish you had not been a medical man.'

'Nay, Rosy, don't say that,' said Lydgate, drawing her closer to him. 'That is like saying you wish you had married another man.'

'Not at all; you are clever enough for anything: you might easily have been something else. And your cousins at Quallingham all think that you have sunk below them in your choice of a profession.'

'The cousins at Quallingham may go to the devil!' said Lydgate, with scorn. 'It was like their impudence if they said anything of the sort to you.'

'Still,' said Rosamond, 'I do *not* think it is a nice profession, dear.' We know that she had much quiet perseverance in her opinion.

'It is the grandest profession in the world, Rosamond,' said Lydgate, gravely. 'And to say that you love me without loving the medical man in me, is like saying that you like eating a peach but don't like its flavour. Don't say it again, dear, it pains me.'

'Very well, Doctor Grave-face,' said Rosy, dimpling, 'I will declare in future that I dote on skeletons, and body-snatchers, and bits of things in phials, and quarrels with everybody, that end in your dying miserably.'

'No, no, not so bad as that,' said Lydgate, giving up remonstrance and petting her resignedly.

George Eliot, from *Middlemarch*, 1872


## Doctor

I am the doctor.
It is my joy to make people well.
It's convenenient, of course, if they sicken
in conventional ways. The mother like a caught moth
fluttering with bedpan by the bed.
The bigger kids fighting and teasing,
a husband in the cobwebs, a smell of stale dinner –
it has to be cooked and not eaten.

To this kind of fireside
I always bring hope and encouragement.
I approach through my smile and display
my incredible instruments. I refuse cups of tea
and wrapped barley sugar. Health? Yes,
yes, you can pick it alive from my lips.
'Little boy, little boy.'

His eyes open, gushing with confidence.
'Little boy, little boy.'
He gets well. He decides to grow up.

    Anne Stevenson, from *Enough of Green*, 1977


## Eve Separate and Alone

Now when as sacred light began to dawn
In Eden on the humid flowers, that breathed
Their morning incense, when all things that breathe,
From the earth's great altar send up silent praise
To the creator, and his nostrils fill
With grateful smell, forth came the human pair
And joined their vocal worship to the choir
Of creatures wanting voice, that done, partake
The season, prime for sweetest scents and airs:
Then commune how that day they best may ply
Their growing work: for much their work outgrew
The hands' dispatch of two, gardening so wide.
And Eve first to her husband thus began.
  Adam, well may we labour still to dress
This garden, still to tend plant, herb and flower,
Our pleasant task enjoined, but till more hands
Aid us, the work under our labour grows,
Luxurious by restraint; what we by day
Lop overgrown, or prune, or prop, or bind,
One night or two with wanton growth derides
Tending to wild. Thou therefore now advise
Or hear what to my mind first thoughts present,
Let us divide our labours, thou where choice
Leads thee, or where most needs, whether to wind
The woodbine round this arbour, or direct
The clasping ivy where to climb, while I
In yonder spring of roses intermixed
With myrtle, find what to redress till noon:
For while so near each other thus all day
Our task we choose, what wonder if so near
Looks intervene and smiles, or object new

Casual discourse draw on, which intermits
Our day's work brought to little, though begun
Early, and the hour of supper comes unearned . . .

 Thus saying, from her husband's hand her hand
Soft she withdrew, and like a wood-nymph light
Oread and dryad, or of Delia's train,
Betook her to the groves, but Delia's self
In gait surpassed and goddess-like deport,
Though not as she with bow and quiver armed,
But with such gardening tools as art yet rude,
Guiltless of fire had formed, or angels brought . . .

O much deceived, much failing, hapless Eve,
Of thy presumed return! Event perverse!
Thou never from that hour in Paradise
Found'st either sweet repast, or sound repose;
Such ambush hid among sweet flower and shades
Waited with hellish rancour imminent
To intercept thy way, or send thee back
Despoiled of innocence, of faith, of bliss.
For now, and since first break of dawn the fiend,
Mere serpent in acceptance, forth was come,
And on his quest, where likeliest he might find
The only two of mankind, but in them
The whole included race, his purposed prey.
In bower and field he sought, where any tuft
Of grove or garden-plot more pleasant lay,
Their tendance or plantation for delight,
By fountain or by shady rivulet
He sought them both, but wished his hap might find
Eve separate, he wished, but not with hope
Of what so seldom chanced, when to his wish,
Beyond his hope, Eve separate he spies,
Veiled in a cloud of fragrance, where she stood,
Half spied, so thick the roses bushing round
About her glowed, oft stooping to support
Each flower of slender stalk, whose head though gay
Carnation, purple, azure, or specked with gold,
Hung drooping unsustained, them she upstays
Gently with myrtle band, mindless the while,
Her self, though fairest unsupported flower,

From her best prop so far, and storm so nigh.
Nearer he drew, and many a walk traversed
Of stateliest covert, cedar, pine, or palm,
Then voluble and bold, now hid, now seen
Among thick-woven arborets and flowers
Embordered on each bank, the hand of Eve:
Spot more delicious than those gardens feigned
Or of revived Adonis, or renowned
Alcinous, host of old Laertes' son,
Or that, not mystic, where the sapient king
Held dalliance with his fair Egyptian spouse.
Much he the place admired, the person more.
As one who long in populous city pent,
Where houses thick and sewers annoy the air,
Forth issuing on a summer's morn to breathe
Among the pleasant villages and farms
Adjoined, from each thing met conceives delight,
The smell of grain, or tedded grass, or kine,
Or dairy, each rural sight, each rural sound;
If chance with nymph-like step fair virgin pass,
What pleasing seemed, for her now pleases more,
She most, and in her look sums all delight.
Such pleasure took the serpent to behold
This flowery plat, the sweet recess of Eve
Thus early, thus alone . . .

    John Milton, from *Paradise Lost*, Book IX, 1674


## Eve to Her Daughters

It was not I who began it.
Turned out into draughty caves,
hungry so often, having to work for our bread,
hearing the children whining,
I was nevertheless not unhappy.
Where Adam went I was fairly contented to go.
I adapted myself to the punishment: it was my life.

But Adam, you know . . . !
He kept on brooding over the insult,
over the trick They had played on us, over the scolding.

He had discovered a flaw in himself
and he had to make up for it.

Outside Eden the earth was imperfect,
the seasons changed, the game was fleet-footed,
he had to work for our living, and he didn't like it.
He even complained of my cooking
(it was hard to compete with Heaven).

So he set to work.
The earth must be made a new Eden
with central heating, domesticated animals,
mechanical harvesters, combustion engines,
escalators, refrigerators,
and modern means of communication
and multiplied opportunities for safe investment
and higher education for Abel and Cain
and the rest of the family.
You can see how his pride had been hurt.

In the process he had to unravel everything,
because he believed that mechanism
was the whole secret – he was always mechanical-minded.
He got to the very inside of the whole machine
exclaiming as he went, So this is how it works!
And now that I know how it works, why, I must have invented it.
As for God and the Other, they cannot be demonstrated,
and what cannot be demonstrated
doesn't exist.
You see, he had always been jealous.

Yes, he got to the centre
where nothing at all can be demonstrated.
And clearly he doesn't exist; but he refuses
to accept the conclusion.
You see, he was always an egotist.

It was warmer than this in the cave;
there was none of this fall-out.
I would suggest, for the sake of the children,
that it's time you took over.

But you are my daughters, you inherit my own faults of character,
you are submissive, following Adam

even beyond existence.
Faults of character have their own logic
and it always works out.
I observed this with Abel and Cain.

Perhaps the whole elaborate fable
right from the beginning
is meant to demonstrate this; perhaps it's the whole secret.
Perhaps nothing exists but our faults?
At least they can be demonstrated.

But it's useless to make
such a suggestion to Adam.
He has turned himself into God,
who is faultless, and doesn't exist.

Judith Wright, 1966

## An Ancient Gesture

I thought, as I wiped my eyes on the corner of my apron:
Penelope did this too.
And more than once: you can't keep weaving all day
And undoing it all through the night;
Your arms get tired, and the back of your neck gets tight;
And along towards morning, when you think it will never be light,
And your husband has been gone, and you don't know where, for years,
Suddenly you burst into tears;
There is simply nothing else to do.

And I thought, as I wiped my eyes on the corner of my apron:
This is an ancient gesture, authentic, antique,
In the very best tradition, classic, Greek;
Ulysses did this too.
But only as a gesture, – a gesture which implied
To the assembled throng that he was much too moved to speak.
He learned it from Penelope . . .
Penelope, who really cried.

Edna St Vincent Millay, 1954

## A Final Word

Yet, sister woman, though I cannot consent to find a Mozart or a Michael Angelo in your sex, cheerfully, and with the love that burns in the depths of admiration, I acknowledge that you can do one thing as well as the best of us men – a greater thing than even Milton is known to have done, or Michael Angelo: you can die grandly, and as goddesses would die, were goddesses mortal.

Thomas de Quincey, from *Joan of Arc*, 1874


Beauty is momentary in the mind –
The fitful tracing of a portal;
But in the flesh it is immortal.
The body dies; the body's beauty lives.
So evenings die, in their green going,
A wave, interminably flowing.
So gardens die, their meek breath scenting
The cowl of winter, done repenting.
So maidens die, to the auroral
Celebration of a maiden's choral.
Susanna's music touched the bawdy strings
Of those white elders; but, escaping,
Left only Death's ironic scraping.
Now, in its immortality, it plays
On the clear viol of her memory,
And makes a constant sacrament of praise.

Wallace Stevens, from 'Peter Quince at the Clavier', *Collected Poems*, 1954

ENGENDERING IDLENESS

# Of Idleness

As we see some idle-fallow grounds, if they be fat and fertile, to bring foorth store and sundrie roots of wilde and unprofitable weeds, and that to keepe them in ure we must subject and imploy them with certaine seeds for our use and service. And as wee see some women, though single and alone, often to bring foorth lumps of shapelesse flesh, whereas to produce a perfect and naturall generation, they must be manured with another kinde of seed: So is it of mindes, which except they be busied about some subject, that may bridle and keepe them under, they will here and there widely scatter themselves through the vaste field of imaginations . . .

It is not long since I retired my selfe unto mine owne house, with full purpose, as much as lay in me, not to trouble my selfe with any businesse, but solitarily and quietly to weare out the remainder of my well-nigh-spent life; where me thought I could doe my spirit no greater favour, than to give him the full scope of idlenesse, and entertaine him as he best pleased, and withall, to settle him-selfe as he best liked: which I hoped he might now, being by time become more setled and ripe, accomplish very easily: but I finde [that] contrariwise playing the skittish and loose-broken jade, he takes a hundred times more cariere and libertie unto himselfe, than hee did for others; and begets in me so many extravagant Chimaeras, and fantasticall monsters, so orderlesse, and without any reason, one hudling upon an other, that at leasure to view the foolishnesse and monstrous strangeness of them, I have begun to keepe a register of them, hoping, if I live, one day to make him ashamed, and blush at himself.

Montaigne, 'Of Idlenesse', *Essays*, *c.* 1571

Therefore I say unto you, Take no thought for your life, what ye shall eat, or what ye shall drink; nor yet for your body, what ye shall put on. Is not the life more than meat, and the body more than raiment?

Behold the fowls of the air: for they sow not, neither do they reap, nor gather into barns; yet your heavenly Father feedeth them. Are ye not much better than they?

Which of you by taking thought can add one cubit unto his stature?

And why take ye thought for raiment? Consider the lilies of the field, how they grow; they toil not, neither do they spin:

And yet I say to you, That even Solomon in all his glory was not arrayed like one of these.

Wherefore, if God so clothe the grass of the field, which today is, and tomorrow is cast into the oven, shall he not much more clothe you, O ye of little faith?

Therefore take no thought, saying, What shall we eat? or, What shall we drink? or, Wherewithal shall we be clothed?

St Matthew 6:25–31


It was a chosen plot of fertile land,
    Emongst wide waues set, like a little nest,
    As if it had by Natures cunning hand
    Bene choisely picked out from all the rest,
    And laid forth for ensample of the best:
    No daintie flowre or herbe, that growes on ground,
    No arboret with painted blossomes drest,
    And smelling sweet, but there it might be found
To bud out faire, and her sweet smels throw all around.

No tree, whose braunches did not bravely spring;
    No braunch, whereon a fine bird did not sit:
    No bird, but did her shrill notes sweetly sing;
    No song but did containe a lovely dit:
    Trees, braunches, birds, and songs, were framed fit,
    For to allure fraile mind to carelesse ease.
    Carelesse the man soone woxe, and his weake wit
    Was overcome of thing, that did him please;
So pleased, did his wrathfull purpose faire appease.

Thus when she had his eyes and senses fed
    With false delights, and fild with pleasures vaine,
    Into a shadie dale she soft him led,
    And laid him downe upon a grassie plaine:
    And her sweet selfe without dread or disdaine,
    She set beside, laying his head disarm'd
    In her loose lap, it softly to sustaine,
    Where soone he slumbred, fearing not be harm'd,
The whiles with a loud lay she thus him sweetly charm'd.

Behold, O man, that toilesome paines doest take,
    The flowres, the fields, and all that pleasant growes,
    How they themselves doe thine ensample make,
    Whiles nothing envious nature them forth throwes

Out of her fruitful lap; how, no man knowes,
They spring, they bud, they blossome fresh and faire,
And decke the world with their rich pompous showes;
Yet no man for them taketh paines or care,
Yet no man to them can his carefull paines compare.

The lilly, Ladie of the flowring field,
The Flowre-deluce, her lovely Paramoure,
Bid thee to them thy fruitlesse labours yield,
And soone leave off this toylesome weariest oure;
Loe loe, how brave she decks her bounteous boure,
With silken curtens and gold coverlets,
Therein to shrowd her sumptuous Belamoure,
Yet neither spinnes nor cardes, ne cares nor frets,
But to her mother Nature all her care she lets.

Why then dost thou, O man, that of them all
Art Lord, and eke of nature Soveraine,
Wilfully make thy selfe a wretched thrall,
And waste thy joyous houres in needless paine,
Seeking for daunger and adventures vaine?
What bootes it all to have, and nothing use?
Who shall him rew, that swimming in the maine,
Will die for thirst, and water doth refuse?
Refuse such fruitless toile, and present pleasures chuse.

> Edmund Spenser, from *The Faerie Queene*, II, vi, 12–17, 1596

# Indolence

## The Castle of Indolence

*The Castle hight of Indolence,*
*And its false luxury;*
*Where for a little time, alas!*
*We lived right jollily*

O mortal man, who livest here by toil,
Do not complain of this thy hard estate;
That like an emmet thou must ever moil

Is a sad sentence of an ancient date:
And, certes, there is for it reason great;
For, though sometimes it makes thee weep and wail,
And curse thy stars, and early drudge and late,
Withouten that would come an heavier bale,
Loose life, unruly passions, and diseases pale.

In lowly dale, fast by a river's side,
With woody hill o'er hill encompassed round,
A most enchanting wizard did abide,
Than whom a fiend more fell is nowhere found.
It was, I ween, a lovely spot of ground;
And there a season atween June and May,
Half prankt with spring, with summer half imbrowned,
A listless climate made, where, sooth to say,
No living wight could work, ne carèd even for play.

Was nought around but images of rest:
Sleep-soothing groves, and quiet lawns between;
And flowery beds that slumbrous influence kest,
From poppies breathed; and beds of pleasant green,
Where never yet was creeping creature seen.
Meantime unnumbered glittering streamlets played,
And hurlèd everywhere their waters sheen;
That, as they bickered through the sunny glade,
Though restless still themselves, a lulling murmur made . . .

A pleasing land of drowsyhed it was:
Of dreams that wave before the half-shut eye;
And of gay castles in the clouds that pass,
For ever flushing round a summer sky:
There eke the soft delights, that witchingly
Instill a wanton sweetness through the breast,
And the calm pleasures always hovered nigh;
But whate'er smacked of noyance, or unrest,
Was far far off expelled from this delicious nest.

The landskip such, inspiring perfect ease;
Where INDOLENCE (for so the wizard hight)
Close-hid his castle mid embowering trees,
That half shut out the beams of Phoebus bright,
And made a kind of checkered day and night.
Meanwhile, unceasing at the massy gate,

Beneath a spacious palm, the wicked wight
Was placed; and, to his lute, of cruel fate
And labour harsh complained, lamenting man's estate . . .

'Outcast of Nature, man! the wretched thrall
Of bitter-dropping sweat, of sweltry pain,
Of cares that eat away thy heart with gall,
And of the vices, an inhuman train,
That all proceed from savage thirst of gain:
For when hard-hearted Interest first began
To poison earth, Astraea left the plain;
Guile, Violence, and Murder seized on man,
And, for soft milky streams, with blood the rivers ran.

'Come, ye, who still the cumbrous load of life
Push hard up hill; but, as the farthest steep
You trust to gain, and put an end to strife,
Down thunders back the stone with mighty sweep,
And hurls your labours to the valley deep,
Forever vain: come, and withouten fee
I in oblivion will your sorrows steep,
Your cares, your toils; will steep you in a sea
Of full delight: O come, ye weary wights, to me!

'With me, you need not rise at early dawn,
To pass the joyless day in various stounds;
Or, louting low, on upstart fortune fawn,
And sell fair honour for some paltry pounds;
Or through the city take your dirty rounds
To cheat, and dun, and lie, and visit pay,
Now flattering base, now giving secret wounds;
Or prowl in courts of law for human prey,
In venal senate thieve, or rob on broad highway.

'No cocks, with me, to rustic labour call,
From village on to village sounding clear;
To tardy swain no shrill-voiced matrons squall;
No dogs, no babes, no wives to stun your ear;
No hammers thump; no horrid blacksmith sear,
No noisy tradesman your sweet slumbers start
With sounds that are a misery to hear:
But all is calm as would delight the heart
Of Sybarite of old, all nature, and all art . . .

'What, what is virtue but repose of mind?
A pure ethereal calm that knows no storm,
Above the reach of wild ambition's wind,
Above those passions that this world deform,
And torture man, a proud malignant worm!
But here, instead, soft gales of passion play,
And gently stir the heart, thereby to form
A quicker sense of joy; as breezes stray
Across the enlivened skies, and make them still more gay.

'The best of men have ever loved repose:
They hate to mingle in the filthy fray;
Where the soul sours, and gradual rancour grows,
Imbittered more from peevish day to day.
Even those whom fame has lent her fairest ray,
The most renowned of worthy wights of yore,
From a base world at last have stolen away:
So Scipio, to the soft Cumaean shore
Retiring, tasted joy he never knew before . . .

'O grievous folly! to heap up estate,
Losing the days you see beneath the sun;
When sudden, comes blind unrelenting fate,
And gives the untasted portion you have won
With ruthless toil, and many a wretch undone,
To those who mock you gone to Pluto's reign,
There with sad ghosts to pine, and shadows dun:
But sure it is of vanities most vain,
To toil for what you here untoiling may obtain.'

James Thomson, from *The Castle of Indolence*, 1748


To George and Georgiana Keats
*Friday, 19th March* [1819] – This morning I have been reading *The False One*. Shameful to say, I was in bed at ten – I mean, this morning. The 'Blackwood's Reviewers' have committed themselves to a scandalous heresy; they have been putting up Hogg, the Ettrick Shepherd, against Burns: the senseless villains! The Scotch cannot manage themselves at all, they want imagination; and that is why they are so fond of Hogg, who has so little of it. This morning I am in a sort of temper, indolent and supremely careless; I long after a stanza or two of Thomson's *Castle of Indolence*; my passions are all asleep, from my having slumbered till nearly eleven, and weakened the

animal fibre all over me, to a delightful sensation, about three degrees on this side of faintness. If I had teeth of pearl, and the breath of lilies, I should call it languor; but, as I am, I must call it laziness. In this state of effeminacy, the fibres of the brain are relaxed, in common with the rest of the body, and to such a happy degree, that pleasure has no show of enticement, and pain no unbearable frown; neither Poetry nor Ambition, nor Love, have any alertness or countenance; as they pass by me, they seem rather like three figures on a Greek vase, two men and a woman, whom no one but myself could distinguish in their disguisement. This is the only happiness, and is a rare instance of advantage in the body overpowering the mind.

from *The Letters of John Keats*,
ed. Richard Monckton Milnes, 1848

There is sweet music here that softer falls
Than petals from blown roses on the grass,
Or night-dews on still waters between walls
Of shadowy granite, in a gleaming pass;
Music that gentlier on the spirit lies,
Than tired eyelids upon tired eyes;
Music that brings sweet sleep down from the blissful skies.
Here are cool mosses deep,
And through the moss the ivies creep,
And in the stream the long-leaved flowers weep,
And from the craggy ledge the poppy hangs in sleep.

Why are we weighed upon with heaviness,
And utterly consumed with sharp distress,
While all things else have rest from weariness?
All things have rest: why should we toil alone
We only toil, who are the first of things,
And make perpetual moan,
Still from one sorrow to another thrown:
Nor ever fold our wings,
And cease from wanderings,
Nor steep our brows in slumber's holy balm;
Nor harken what the inner spirit sings,
'There is no joy but calm!'
    Why should we only toil, the roof and crown of things?

Lo! in the middle of the wood,
The folded leaf is wooed from out the bud

With winds upon the branch, and there
Grows green and broad, and takes no care,
Sun-steeped at noon, and in the moon
Nightly dew-fed; and turning yellow
Falls, and floats adown the air.
Lo! sweetened with the summer light,
The full-juiced apple, waxing over-mellow,
Drops in a silent autumn night.
All its allotted length of days,
The flower ripens in its place,
Ripens and fades, and falls, and hath no toil,
Fast-rooted in the fruitful soil.

Hateful is the dark-blue sky,
Vaulted o'er the dark-blue sea.
Death is the end of life; ah, why
Should life all labour be?
Let us alone. Time driveth onward fast,
And in a little while our lips are dumb.
Let us alone. What is it that will last?
All things are taken from us, and become
Portions and parcels of the dreadful Past.
Let us alone. What pleasure can we have
To war with evil? Is there any peace
In ever climbing up the climbing wave?
All things have rest, and ripen toward the grave
In silence; ripen, fall and cease:
Give us long rest or death, dark death, or dreamful ease.

How sweet it were, hearing the downward stream,
With half-shut eyes ever to seem
Falling asleep in a half-dream!
To dream and dream, like yonder amber light,
Which will not leave the myrrh-bush on the height;
To hear each other's whispered speech;
Eating the Lotos day by day,
To watch the crisping ripples on the beach,
And tender curving lines of creamy spray;
To lend our hearts and spirit wholly
To the influence of mild-minded melancholy;
To muse and brood and live again in memory,
With those old faces of our infancy

Heaped over with a mound of grass,
Two handfuls of white dust, shut in an urn of brass!

Dear is the memory of our wedded lives,
And dear the last embraces of our wives
And their warm tears: but all hath suffered change:
For surely now our household hearths are cold:
Our sons inherit us: our looks are strange:
And we should come like ghosts to trouble joy.
Or else the island princes over-bold
Have eat our substance, and the minstrel sings
Before them of the ten years' war in Troy,
And our great deeds, as half-forgotten things.
Is there confusion in the little isle?
Let what is broken so remain.
The Gods are hard to reconcile:
'Tis hard to settle order once again.
There *is* confusion worse than death,
Trouble on trouble, pain on pain,
Long labour unto agèd breath,
Sore task to hearts worn out by many wars
And eyes grown dim with gazing on the pilot-stars . . .

Let us swear an oath, and keep it with an equal mind,
In the hollow Lotos-land to live and lie reclined
On the hills like Gods together, careless of mankind.
For they lie beside their nectar, and the bolts are hurled
Far below them in the valleys, and the clouds are lightly curled
Round their golden houses, girdled with the gleaming world:
Where they smile in secret, looking over wasted lands,
Blight and famine, plague and earthquake, roaring deeps and fiery
    sands,
Clanging fights, and flaming towns, and sinking ships, and praying
    hands.
But they smile, they find a music centred in a doleful song
Steaming up, a lamentation and an ancient tale of wrong,
Like a tale of little meaning though the words are strong;
Chanted from an ill-used race of men that cleave the soil,
Sow the seed, and reap the harvest with enduring toil,
Storing yearly little dues of wheat, and wine and oil;
Till they perish and they suffer – some, 'tis whispered – down in
    hell

Suffer endless anguish, others in Elysian valleys dwell,
Resting weary limbs at last on beds of asphodel.
Surely, surely, slumber is more sweet than toil, the shore
Than labour in the deep mid-ocean, wind and wave and oar;
Oh rest ye, brother mariners, we will not wander more.

Alfred Tennyson, Choric Song from 'The Lotos-Eaters', 1842


This picture ... represented a woman, considerably larger, I thought, than the life. I calculated that this lady, put into a scale of magnitude suitable for the reception of a commodity of bulk, would infallibly turn from fourteen to sixteen stone. She was, indeed, extremely well fed; very much butcher's meat – to say nothing of bread, vegetables, and liquids – must she have consumed to attain that breadth and height, that wealth of muscle, that affluence of flesh. She lay half-reclined on a couch – why, it would be difficult to say; broad daylight blazed round her. She appeared in hearty health, strong enough to do the work of two plain cooks; she could not plead a weak spine; she ought to have been standing, or at least sitting bolt upright. She had no business to lounge away the noon on a sofa. She ought likewise to have worn decent garments – a gown covering her properly, which was not the case. Out of abundance of material – seven-and-twenty yards, I should say, of drapery – she managed to make inefficient raiment. Then for the wretched untidiness surrounding her there could be no excuse. Pots and pans – perhaps I ought to say vases and goblets – were rolled here and there on the foreground; a perfect rubbish of flowers was mixed amongst them, and an absurd and disorderly mass of curtain upholstery smothered the couch and cumbered the floor. On referring to the catalogue, I found that this notable production bore the name 'Cleopatra'.

Charlotte Brontë, from *Villette*, 1853


[*Saturday 31 July*]

My own Brain

Here is a whole nervous breakdown in miniature. We came on Tuesday. Sank into a chair, could scarcely rise; everything insipid; tasteless, colourless. Enormous desire for rest. Wednesday – only wish to be alone in the open air. Air delicious – avoided speech; could not read. Thought of my own power of writing with veneration, as of something incredible, belonging to someone else; never again to be enjoyed by me. Mind a blank. Slept in my chair. Thursday. No pleasure in life whatsoever; but felt perhaps more attuned to existence. Character & idiosyncracy as Virginia Woolf completely sunk out. Humble & modest. Difficulty in thinking what to say. Read automatically, like a cow chewing cud. Slept in chair. Friday. Sense of physical tiredness; but slight activity of the brain. Beginning to take notice. Making one or two plans. No power of phrase making. Difficulty in writing to Lady Colefax. Saturday (today) much clearer & lighter. Thought I could write, but resisted, or found it impossible. A desire to read poetry set in on Friday. This brings back a sense of my own individuality. Read some Dante & Bridges, without troubling to understand, but got pleasure from them. Now I begin to wish to write notes, but not yet novel. But today senses quickening. No 'making up' power yet; no desire to cast scenes in my book. Curiosity about literature returning: want to read Dante, Havelock Ellis, & Berlioz autobiography; also to make a looking glass with shell frame. These processes have sometimes been spread over several weeks.

from *The Diary of Virginia Woolf*, 1926

### The Three-Toed Sloth

The three-toed sloth is the slowest creature we know
for its size. It spends its life hanging upside-down
from a branch, its baby nestling on its breast.
It never cleans itself, but lets fungus grow
on its fur. The grin it wears, like an idiot clown,
proclaims the joys of a life which is one long rest.

The three-toed sloth is content. It doesn't care.
It moves imperceptibly, like the laziest snail
you ever saw blown up to the size of a sheep.
Disguised as a grey-green bough it dangles there
in the steamy Amazon jungle. That long-drawn wail
is its slow-motion sneeze. Then it falls asleep.

One cannot but envy such torpor. Its top speed,
when rushing to save its young, is a dramatic
fourteen feet per minute, in a race with fate.
The puzzle is this, though: how did nature breed
a race so determinedly unenergetic?
What passion ever inspired a sloth to mate?

Fleur Adcock, from *Selected Poems*, 1983

# The Harm of Work

I think that there is far too much work done in the world, that immense harm is caused by the belief that work is virtuous, and that what needs to be preached in modern industrial countries is quite different from what always has been preached. Everyone knows the story of the traveller in Naples who saw twelve beggars lying in the sun (it was before the days of Mussolini), and offered a lira to the laziest of them. Eleven of them jumped up to claim it, so he gave it to the twelfth. This traveller was on the right lines. But in countries which do not enjoy Mediterranean sunshine idleness is more difficult, and a great public propaganda will be required to inaugurate it . . .

I want to say, in all seriousness, that a great deal of harm is being done in the modern world by belief in the virtuousness of WORK, and that the road to happiness and prosperity lies in an organized diminution of work.

First of all: what is work? Work is of two kinds: first, altering the position of matter at or near the earth's surface relatively to other such matter; second, telling other people to do so. The first kind is unpleasant and ill paid; the second is pleasant and highly paid. The second kind is capable of indefinite extension: there are not only those who give orders, but those who give advice as to what orders should be given. Usually two opposite kinds of advice are given simultaneously by two organized bodies of men; this is called politics. The skill required for this kind of work is not knowledge of the subjects as to which advice is given, but knowledge of the art of persuasive speaking and writing, i.e. of advertising . . .

If the ordinary wage-earner worked four hours a day, there would be enough for everybody, and no unemployment – assuming a certain very moderate amount of sensible organization. This idea shocks the well-to-do, because they are convinced that the poor would not know how to use so much leisure.

In America, men often work long hours even when they are already well off; such men, naturally, are indignant at the idea of leisure for wage-earners, except as the grim punishment of unemployment; in fact, they dislike leisure even for their sons. Oddly enough, while they wish their sons to work so hard as to have no time to be civilized, they do not mind their wives and daughters having no work at all. The snobbish admiration of uselessness, which, in an aristocratic society, extends to both sexes, is, under a plutocracy, confined to women; this, however, does not make it any more in agreement with common sense.

The wise use of leisure, it must be conceded, is a product of civilization and education. A man who has worked long hours all his life will be bored if he becomes suddenly idle. But without a considerable amount of leisure a man is cut off from many of the best things. There is no longer any reason why the bulk of the population should suffer this deprivation; only a foolish asceticism, usually vicarious, makes us continue to insist on work in excessive quantities now that the need no longer exists.

Bertrand Russell, 'In Praise of Idleness', 1935

## Industrious Suit-Cutter 'Fined' 10s 6d

Mr Ernest Prosser, aged 45, of Lessingham Avenue, Wigan, has been fined half a guinea by his trade union – because he worked too hard. Mr Prosser is a cutter at the factory at Walkden of Montague Burton, Ltd., the tailoring firm: the fine has been imposed by the Walkden branch of the National Union of Tailors and Garment Workers.

In July the Walkden branch made a by-law restricting the number of suits a cutter could cut in a week. Recently Mr Prosser found that he had cut two suits above his maximum weekly output of 46, and he was called to a meeting of his branch. The outcome of this meeting was a letter to Mr Prosser on February 6, which read: 'The findings of the branch committee meeting, which you attended, are that, according to a cutter's by-law made on July 23, 1953, and which it is claimed you have broken, they impose a fine of 10s 6d, which you are asked to pay within the next four weeks.'

Mr Prosser said yesterday that he was given 'a good dressing-down' by the branch committee. 'I shall pay the fine,' he added, 'but I think a warning would have been sufficient punishment.' Mr Prosser is the first cutter to be fined under the by-law.

*Manchester Guardian*, 20 February 1954

## An Urge to Work?

The fascination of the Oblomovka atmosphere, way of life, and habits extended to Verkhlyovo, which had also once belonged to the Oblomovs; except for Stolz's house, everything there was imbued with the same primitive laziness, simplicity of customs, peace, and inertia. The child's heart and mind had been filled with the scenes, pictures, and habits of that life long before he set eyes on his first book. And who can tell when the development of a child's intellect begins? How can one trace the birth of the first ideas and impressions in a child's mind? Perhaps when a child begins to talk, or even before it can talk or walk, but only gazes at everything with that dumb, intent look that seems blank to grown-ups, it already catches and perceives the meaning and the connexions of the events of his life, but is not able to tell it to himself or to others. Perhaps Oblomov had observed and understood long ago what was being said and done in his presence: that his father, dressed in velveteen trousers and a brown quilted cotton coat, did nothing but walk up and down the room all day with his hands behind his back, take snuff, and blow his nose, while his mother passed on from coffee to tea, from tea to dinner; that it never entered his father's head to check how many stacks of hay or corn had been mown or reaped, and call to account those who were guilty of neglecting their duties, but if his handkerchief was not handed to him soon enough, he would make a scene and turn the whole house upside down. Perhaps his childish mind had decided long ago that the only way to live was how the grown-ups round him lived. What other decision could he possibly have reached? And how did the grown-ups live at Oblomovka? Did they ever ask themselves why life had been given them? Goodness only knows. And how did they answer it? Most probably they did not answer it all: everything seemed too clear and simple to them. They had never heard of the so-called hard life, of people who were constantly worried, who rushed about from place to place, or who devoted their lives to everlasting, never-ending work. They did not really believe in mental worries, either; they did not think that life existed so that man should constantly strive for some barely apprehended aims; they were terribly afraid of strong passions, and just as with other people bodies might be consumed by the volcanic action of inner, spiritual fire, so their souls wallowed peacefully and undisturbed in their soft bodies. Life did not mark them, as it did other people, with premature wrinkles, devastating moral blows and diseases. The good people conceived life merely as an ideal of peace and inactivity, disturbed from time to time by all sorts of unpleasant accidents, such as illness, loss of money, quarrels, and, incidentally, work. They suffered work as a punishment imposed upon our forefathers, but they could not love it and avoided it wherever and whenever they could, believing it both right and necessary to do so. They never troubled themselves about any vague moral and intellectual problems, and that was why they were always so well and happy and lived so long. Men of forty looked like boys; old men did not struggle with a hard, painful death, but, having lived to an unbelievably old age, died as if by stealth, quietly growing cold and imperceptibly breathing their last. This is why it is said that in the old days people were stronger. Yes, indeed they were: in those days they were in no hurry to explain to a boy the meaning of life and prepare him for it as though it were some complicated and serious business; they did not worry him with books which arouse all sorts of questions, which corrode your heart and mind and shorten life. Their way of life was ready-made and was taught to them by their parents, who in turn received it ready-made from their grandparents, and their grandparents from their great-grandparents, being enjoined to keep it whole and undefiled like Vesta's fire. Whatever was done in the time of Oblomov's father, had been done in the times of his grandfather and great-grandfather and, perhaps, is still being done at Oblomovka.

Ivan Goncharov, from *Oblomov*, 1859,

tr. David Magarshack, 1954

IRINA: Today I woke up, got out of bed and had a wash. And then I suddenly felt as if everything in the world made sense, I seemed to know how to live. I know everything, dearest Doctor. Man should work and toil by the sweat of his brow, whoever he is – that's the whole purpose and meaning of his life, his happiness and his joy.

How wonderful to be a workman who gets up at dawn and breaks stones in the road, or a shepherd, or a schoolmaster who teaches children or an engine-driver. Heavens, better not be a human being at all – better be an ox or just a horse, so long as you can work, rather than the kind of young woman who wakes up at noon, has her coffee in bed, and then spends two hours getting dressed. Oh, that's so awful. You know how you sometimes long for a drink on a hot day – well that's how I long to go to work . . .

TUZENBAKH: This great urge to work, heavens, how well I understand it. I've never done a hand's turn all my life. I was born in St Petersburg – that bleak, idle place – and grew up in a family that never knew the meaning of work or worry. I remember how I used to come home from my cadet school. The footman would pull off my boots while I'd make a thorough nuisance of myself, watched by my mother who thought I was just wonderful and couldn't see why others took a rather different view. They tried to protect me from work. Only I doubt if their protection is going to prove all that effective. I doubt it. The time has come, an avalanche is moving down on us and a great storm's brewing that'll do us all a power of good. It's practically on top of us already and soon it's going to blast out of our society all the laziness, complacency, contempt for work, rottenness and boredom. I'm going to work and in twenty-five or thirty years' time everyone will work. Everyone.

Anton Chekhov, from *The Three Sisters*, 1901,

tr. Ronald Hingley, 1968

It seemed to me that I was doing more than my fair share of the work on this trip, and I was beginning to feel strongly on the subject.

It always does seem to me that I am doing more work than I should do. It is not that I object to the work, mind you; I like work; it fascinates me. I can sit and look at it for hours. I love to keep it by me; the idea of getting rid of it nearly breaks my heart.

You cannot give me too much work; to accumulate work has almost become a passion with me; my study is so full of it now, that there is hardly an inch of room for any more. I shall have to throw out a wing soon.

And I am careful of my work, too. Why, some of the work that I have by me now has been in my possession for years and years, and there isn't a finger-mark on it. I take a great pride in my work; I take it down now and then and dust it. No man keeps his work in a better state of preservation than I do.

But, though I crave for work, I still like to be fair. I do not ask for more than my proper share.

But I get it without asking for it – at least, so it appears to me – and this worries me.

George says he does not think I need trouble myself on the subject. He thinks it is only my over-scrupulous nature that makes me fear I am having more than my due; and that, as a matter of fact, I don't have half as much as I ought. But I expect he only says this to comfort me.

In a boat, I have always noticed that it is the fixed idea of each member of the crew that he is doing everything. Harris's notion was, that it was he alone who had been working, and that both George and I had been imposing upon him. George, on the other hand, ridiculed the idea of Harris's having done anything more than eat and sleep, and had a cast-iron opinion that it was he – George himself – who had done all the labour worth speaking of.

He said he had never been out with such a couple of lazy skulks as Harris and I.

That amused Harris.

'Fancy old George talking about work!' he laughed; 'why about half an hour of it would kill him. Have you ever seen George work?' he added, turning to me.

I agreed with Harris that I never had – most certainly not since we had started on this trip.

'Well, I don't see how *you* can know much about it, one way or the other,' George retorted to Harris; 'for I'm blest if you haven't been asleep half the time. Have you ever seen Harris fully awake, except at meal-time?' asked George, addressing me.

Truth compelled me to support George. Harris had been very little good in the boat, so far as helping was concerned, from the beginning.

'Well, hang it all, I've done more than old J., anyhow,' rejoined Harris.

'Well, you couldn't very well have done less,' added George.

'I suppose J. thinks he is the passenger,' continued Harris.

And that was their gratitude to me for having brought them and their wretched old boat all the way up from Kingston, and for having superintended and managed everything for them, and taken care of them, and slaved for them. It is the way of the world.

Jerome K. Jerome, from Three Men in a Boat, 1889

These vagabonds count, he says, on the hospitality which the Apostle enjoined, and the pleasure of unexpected arrival, so that all kinds of exquisite relishes will be brought out, and many chickens give up the ghost under the knife. Their feet are weary with the hardness of the way, and they would like them bathed; but they would rather have their inwards drenched with infinite refilling of the cup than the fomentation of the feet, and when the table has been cleared by their starving host, and the crumbs swept up, they shamelessly insist on their mighty thirst, and if by any chance there is no goblet handy, they'll mix it up in the same plate, and when they are stuffed and sodden to the pitch of vomiting, they say it is all their hard life. And before they go to bed, more exhausted after their labours at table than by their journey, they tell all the toils of the way, and beguile still more relishes and still more cups from their host; as for the reason of their wandering, a pilgrimage, we'll say? or perhaps captivity. Soon they enquire as to the whereabouts of any neighbouring monk or monastery. And there they'll go, as men wearied, men to whom the whole world is closed, who can find nowhere a place of rest and refreshing for the soul, nowhere a complete observance of discipline: do they not well to wander? Wherever they go the traveller's thirst demands goblet hurried on goblet; pilgrims for their bellies' sake rather than their souls'. Two days pass: the supply of relishes diminishes: on the morning of the third day the host betakes himself, not to the kitchen, but to the ordinary toil of the day: our friend begins to meditate another visit. Suddenly he starts up as though impelled from behind: already he sees a fresh dinner on the horizon: not far off from that same monastery he finds another, he halts for a little rest. Behold him now come from the Italian frontier, and a good fresh tale all about pilgrimage or captivity, entering the house with humbly bowed head, and lying hard till all the poor host's poverty goes into the pot and on to the table: that host will be a well-picked bone in a day or two. Three days, and himself and his monastery and his habits and his discipline will be found displeasing: the knapsacks full of dry bread are strapped up again: the unhappy donkey recalled from his lean pasture, which would have pleased him well

237

enough if two days' hospitality had not displeased his master. Once again he is loaded up with tunics and cowls, for you can always strip your host by declaring you've only rags to cover you. Farewell, say you to your host, and away, where other feats already beckon. Beaten, thumped, poked, the poor donkey humps along, and then stands stock still, and its ears are beaten, efforts on its rear being in vain. Pushed and pulled, it gets along somehow: one must be in time for dinner. Once arrived, hear the hearty voice crying: 'Benedicite!' and hardly inside the monastery, what a thirst! ... They go to bed, always for these a strange bed: in the morning, their bones tired with the fatigues of the road, they cannot rise, even though strong and hearty at table the night before. But matins once safe over, they get up, groaning and exhausted. A little wine warms them, and just a morsel of bread: they creep about the monastery, bowed with their infirmity, though their step livens wonderfully out of sight ... Day after day, walking, begging, sweating, whining, on they go, rather than stay in one place, there to toil, and there abide: humble at their incoming, arrogant and graceless at their outgoing, as if no monastery had morals or discipline holy enough for them. For ever wandering, they know not when the last weariness will come upon them: nor do they know what place will give them burial.

Helen Waddell, from The Wandering Scholars, 1927

# Time Out

Sweet mother, I have no strength to work my loom:
the slender love-goddess has worn me out
with longing for a boy.*

Sappho of Lesbos, sixth century BC, Fragment 102,<br>tr. Gillian Spraggs, 1994

## Naming of Parts

To-day we have naming of parts. Yesterday,
We had daily cleaning. And to-morrow morning,
We shall have what to do after firing. But to-day,
To-day we have naming of parts. Japonica
Glistens like coral in all of the neighbouring gardens,

*or, girl

238

And to-day we have naming of parts.

This is the lower sling swivel. And this
Is the upper sling swivel, whose use you will see,
When you are given your slings. And this is the piling swivel,
Which in your case you have not got. The branches
Hold in the gardens their silent, eloquent gestures,
    Which in our case we have not got.

This is the safety-catch, which is always released
With an easy flick of the thumb. And please do not let me
See anyone using his finger. You can do it quite easy
If you have any strength in your thumb. The blossoms
Are fragile and motionless, never letting anyone see
    Any of them using their finger.

And this you can see is the bolt. The purpose of this
Is to open the breech, as you see. We can slide it
Rapidly backwards and forwards: we call this
Easing the spring. And rapidly backwards and forwards
The early bees are assaulting and fumbling the flowers:
    They call it easing the Spring.

They call it easing the Spring: it is perfectly easy
If you have any strength in your thumb: like the bolt,
And the breech, and the cocking-piece, and the point of balance,
Which in our case we have not got; and the almond-blossom
Silent in all of the gardens and the bees going backwards and forwards,
    For to-day we have naming of parts.

                          Henry Reed, from 'Lessons of the War', 1946

*Office Party*

    This holy night in open forum
       Miss McIntosh, who handles Files,
    Has lost one shoe and her decorum.
       Stately, the frozen chairman smiles

    On Media, desperately vocal.
       Credit, though they have lost their hopes
    Of edging toward an early Local,
       Finger their bonus envelopes.

The glassy boys, the bursting girls
  Of Copy, start a Conga clatter
To a swung carol. Limply curls
  The final sandwich on the platter

Till hark! a herald Messenger
  (Room 414) lifts loudly up
His quavering tenor. Salesmen stir
  Libation for his Lily cup.

'Noel,' he pipes, 'Noel, Noel.'
  Some wag beats tempo with a ruler.
And the plump blonde from Personnel
  Is sick behind the water cooler.

          Phyllis McGinley, from *Times Three*, 1932


# Upon the Unemployed


## *Work Without Hope*

### Lines Composed 21st February 1825

All nature seems at work. Slugs leave their lair –
The bees are stirring – birds are on the wing –
And Winter slumbering in the open air,
Wears on his smiling face a dream of Spring!
And I the while, the sole unbusy thing,
Nor honey make, nor pair, nor build, nor sing.

  Yet well I ken the banks where amaranths blow,
Have traced the fount whence streams of nectar flow.
Bloom, O ye amaranths! bloom for whom ye may,
For me ye bloom not! Glide, rich streams, away!
With lips unbrightened, wreathless brow, I stroll:
And would you learn the spells that drowse my soul?
Work without Hope draws nectar in a sieve,
And Hope without an object cannot live.

          Samuel Taylor Coleridge

## *Tom's Garland*

### upon the Unemployed

Tom – garlanded with squat and surly steel
Tom; then Tom's fallowbootfellow piles pick
By him and rips out rockfire homeforth – sturdy Dick;
Tom Heart-at-ease, Tom Navvy: he is all for his meal
Sure, 's bed now. Low be it: lustily he his low lot (feel
That ne'er need hunger, Tom; Tom seldom sick,
Seldomer heartsore; that treads through, prickproof, thick
Thousands of thorns, thoughts) swings through. Commonweal
Little I reck ho! lacklevel in, if all had bread:
What! Country is honour enough in all us – lordly head,
With heaven's lights high hung round, or, mother-ground
That mammocks, mighty foot. But no way sped,
Nor mind nor mainstrength; gold go garlanded
With, perilous, O nó; nor yet plod safe shod sound;
                    Undenizened, beyond bound
Of earth's glory, earth's ease, all; no one, nowhere,
In wide the world's weal; rare gold, bold steel, bare
                    In both; care, but share care –
This, by Despair, bred Hangdog dull; by Rage,
Manwolf, worse; and their packs infest the age.
  Gerard Manley Hopkins, 1887


## *Toads Revisited*

Walking around in the park
Should feel better than work:
The lake, the sunshine,
The grass to lie on,

Blurred playground noises
Beyond black-stockinged nurses –
Not a bad place to be.
Yet it doesn't suit me,

Being one of the men
You meet of an afternoon:
Palsied old step-takers,
Hare-eyed clerks with the jitters,

Waxed-fleshed out-patients
Still vague from accidents,
And characters in long coats
Deep in the litter-baskets –

All dodging the toad work
By being stupid or weak.
Think of being them!
Hearing the hours chime,

Watching the bread delivered,
The sun by clouds covered,
The children going home;
Think of being them,

Turning over their failures
By some bed of lobelias,
Nowhere to go but indoors,
No friends but empty chairs –

No, give me my in-tray,
My loaf-haired secretary,
My shall-I-keep-the-call-in Sir:
What else can I answer,

When the lights come on at four
At the end of another year?
Give me your arm, old toad;
Help me down Cemetery Road.

Philip Larkin, from *The Whitsun Weddings*, 1962


## Let All Go By

My sledge and anvil lie declined
My bellows too have lost their wind
My fire's extinct, my forge decayed,
And in the Dust my Vice is laid
My coals are spent, my iron's gone
My nails are Drove, my Work is done.

Churchyard epitaph, 1746

## *Idleness*

God, you've so much to do,
To think of, watch and listen to,
That I will let all else go by
And lending ear and eye
Help you to watch how in the combe
Winds sweep dead leaves without a broom;
And rooks in the spring-reddened trees
Restore their villages,
Nest by dark nest
Swaying at rest on the trees' frail unrest;
Or on this limestone wall,
Leaning at ease, with you recall
How once these heavy stones
Swam in the sea as shells and bones;
And hear that owl snore in a tree
Till it grows dark enough for him to see;
In fact, will learn to shirk
No idleness that I may share your work.

Andrew Young from *Speak to the Earth*, 1939

# Acknowledgements

Many people have helped me with this anthology. In particular I wish to thank: Gillian Bate, Louis Billington, James Booth, Judith Bryce, John Chapple, Peak Yuen Chiam, Bill Duffin, Mary Griffiths, Robin Hamilton, Jean Hartley, Elaine Hobby, Edwin Keal, Angela Leighton, Andrew Motion, Ron Shaw, Clifton Snaith, Gillian Spraggs, Patsy Stoneman, Cammy Thomas, Kelsey Thornton, Gilian West, Ralph Willett, Rowley Wymer.

I am also grateful to Julian Loose and Justine Willett of Faber and Faber Ltd for their courteous and patient advice and assistance.

For permission to reprint copyright material I am grateful to the following (extracts listed in the order in which they appear in the book):

Extract from *Candide or Optimism* by Voltaire, translated by John Butt, copyright John Butt, © John Butt, 1947 reproduced by permission of Penguin Books Ltd. 'Toads' by Philip Larkin, reprinted from *The Less Deceived* by permission of the Marvell Press, England. 'Ain't I A Woman', by Sojourner Truth, reprinted from *Black Sister: Poetry by Black American Women 1746–1980*, edited by Erlene Stetson, published by Indiana University Press. Extract from *The Idylls* by Theocritus, translated by Anthony Holden, © Anthony Holden 1974, reproduced by permission of Rogers, Coleridge & White Ltd. Extract from *Machievell: The Chief Works and Others*, translated by Alan Gilbert, 1965, by permission of Duke University Press. 'Hay for the Horses' by Gary Snyder, by permission of the author. 'Death of a Gardener', by Phoebe Hesketh, by permission of the author. Extract from *The Odyssey*, translated by E. V. Rieu, © the Estate of E. V. Rieu, reproduced by permission of Penguin Books Ltd. 'Hedger' by Ivor Gurney, copyright Robin Haines, Sole Trustee of the Gurney Estate 1982. Reprinted from *Collected Poems of Ivor Gurney*, edited by P. J. Kavanagh (1982) by permission of Oxford University Press. Extract from *Sir Gawain and the Green Knight*, translated by Brian Stone (Penguin Classics, 1959, second revised edition 1974), © Brian Stone, 1959, 1964, 1974, reproduced by permission of Penguin Books Ltd. Extract from *Memoirs of an Infantry Officer* by Siegfried Sassoon, by permission of the publisher, Faber and Faber Ltd. 'The Literary Life' by Robert Lowell from *Notebook*, 1970, by permission of the publisher, Faber and Faber Ltd.

Derek Mahon, 'I am Raftery' from *Poems 1962–1978*, © Derek Mahon 1979, reprinted by permission of the publishers, Oxford University Press. 'The Novelist' by W. H. Auden from *Collected Poems*, edited by Edward Mendelson, by permission of the publisher, Faber and Faber Ltd. *The Letters of Gustave Flaubert 1830–1857* edited and translated by Francis Steegmuller, reprinted by permission of the publishers, Harvard University Press, Cambridge, Mass., © 1979, 1980 by Francis Steegmuller. 'What the Chairman Told Tom' by Basil Bunting, from *Collected Poems*, 1978, © Basil Bunting, reprinted by permission of the publishers, Oxford University Press. Extract from *Hector Berlioz* by Humphrey Searle, 1966, with permission of the publisher, Victor Gollancz. Extract from *A Treatise Concerning the Arte of Limning* by Nicholas Hilliard (MS La.III.174) by kind permission of Edinburgh University Library. 'Eu sou carvao' by Jose Craveirinha, translated by Russell G. Hamilton, *Voices from an Empire: A History of Afro-Portuguese Literature* by kind permission of University of Minnesota Press. Extract from *Beloved* by Toni Morrison, 1988, by permission of the publishers, Random House UK Ltd. Extract from *Writings in Time of War* by Pierre Teilhard de Chardin, translated by Rene Hague by permission of the publishers, Edition du Seuil, France. 'How the first Helandman of God' (Adv. MS.1.6, ff.162v.) by permission of the Trustees of the National Library of Scotland. Extract from *The Birth Machine* by Elizabeth Baines, reprinted by permission of The Women's Press Ltd. 'Lullaby' from *The Mirror of the Mother* by Michele Roberts, 1986, by permission of the publishers, Methuen London Ltd. Extract from *Letters from Russia* by Le Marquis de Custine, translated by Robin Buss, © Robin Buss 1991, reproduced by permission of Penguin Books Ltd. Extract from *The Letters of Mrs Gaskell*, edited by J. A. V. Chapple and Arthur Pollard, 1966, by permission of the publishers, Manchester University Press. Extract from *Working-Class Wives* by Margery Spring Rice, © Margery Spring Rice 1939, reproduced by permission of Penguin Books Ltd. 'Two Women' from *Selected Poems* by Carol Rumens (Chatto and Windus Ltd), 1987, reprinted by permission of the Peters Fraser & Dunlop Group Ltd. 'Woman Work' from *And Still I Rise* by Maya Angelou, Virago Press, 1986, by permission of the publisher. 'Dusting' from *Thomas and Beulah*, by Rita Dove, 1986, by permission of the Carnegie Mellon University Press © 1986. Extract from *L'Assommoir* by Emile Zola, translated by Leonard Tancock, © Leonard Tancock 1970, reproduced by permission of Penguin Books Ltd. 'Charm of the Churn' from *Carmina Gadelica: Charms of the Gaels*, translated by Alexander Carmichael, 1992, by kind permission of the publishers, Floris Books. 'Churning Day' from *Death of a Naturalist* by Seamus Heaney by permission of the publisher, Faber and Faber Ltd. Extract from *The Diaries of Hannah Cullwick* edited by Liz Stanley, Virago Press Ltd, 1984, by permission of the publisher. Extract from 'To

University of California Press. 'Doctor' from *Enough of Green* by Anne Stevenson, © Anne Stevenson 1977, reprinted by permission of Oxford University Press. 'An Ancient Gesture' from *Selected Poems* by Edna St Vincent Millay, by permission of the publishers, Carcanet Press Ltd. Extract from Peter Quince at the Clavier' by Wallace Stevens. 'The Three-Toed Sloth' from *Selected Poems* by Fleur Adcock, © Fleur Adcock 1983, reprinted by permission of Oxford University Press. Extract from *Oblamov* by Ivan Goncharov, translated by David Magarshack (Penguin Classics 1954), translation © David Magarshack 1954. Extract from *The Three Sisters* from *The Oxford Chekhov* translated by Ronald Hingley vol III (1964), © Oxford University Press, reprinted by permission of Oxford University Press. 'Naming of Parts' from *Collected Poems* by Henry Reed edited by Jon Stallworthy (1991), © the Executor of Henry Reed's Estate 1991, reprinted by permission of Oxford University Press. 'Toads Revisited' by Philip Larkin from *Collected Poems* edited by Anthony Thwaite, by permission of the publisher Faber and Faber Ltd. 'Idleness' from *Speak to the Earth* by Andrew Young, by permission of Alison Young.

Faber and Faber Ltd apologize for any errors or omissions in the above list and would be grateful to be notified of any corrections that should be incorporated in the next edition or reprint of this volume.

# Index of Authors

Adams, W. E. 87–8
Adcock, Fleur 115, 231
Angelou, Maya 81–2
Anon (Old Testament, Genesis) 3–4, 167
Anon (Old Testament, Proverbs) 72
Anon (*Carmina Gadelica*) 88–9
Anon (China, Chou Dynasty) 169–70
Anon (Ancient Greece) 127
Anon (England, trad.) 200
Anon (England, 14th c.) 33–4
Anon (Scotland, 16th c.) 58–9
Anon (Wales, 16th c.) 83–4
Anon (England, 1746) 242
Anon (England, *c.*1820) 61
Anon (England, *c.*1830) 183–5
Anon (England, 1849) 99–100
Anon (Germany, 1933) 8
Anon (England, 1954) 233
Anon (USA, no date) 120–22
Auden, W. H. 41–2
Austen, Jane 3

Bagnold, Enid 97–9
Baines, Elizabeth 67–9
Barbauld, Anna Laetitia 84–5
Barnes, William 89–90, 174–5
Barrie, J. M. 130–32
Barrow, Mrs 152–3
Belloc, Hilaire 161–3
Bennett, Arnold 100–101, 149–51
Berlioz, Hector 47–9
Betjeman, John 119–20
Bishop, Elizabeth 178–9
Blake, William 128–9
Bradstreet, Anne 110
Brontë, Anne 107–9
Brontë, Charlotte 230
Browning, Elizabeth Barrett 110–11, 145–6
Bunting, Basil 45
Burnett, James Compton 136–7

Carter, Angela 163–4

Cather, Willa 153–5
Chang, Jung 157–60
Chaucer, Geoffrey 25, 58, 72–4
Chekhov, Anton 235
Chu-i, Po 168–9
Cobbett, William 205–6
Coleridge, Samuel Taylor 240
Collier, Mary 203–5
Comte, Auguste 194–5
Connolly, Cyril 139
Craveirinha, José 52
Crompton, Richmal 163
Cullwick, Hannah 91–2
Custine, Marquis de 74

Defoe, Daniel 30–32
Deloney, Thomas 181–3
Dickens, Charles 61–3
Dickinson, Emily 7, 74–5
Disraeli, Benjamin 146
Douglass, Frederick 27–8
Dove, Rita 82–3
Doyle, Sir Arthur Conan 51
Duck, Stephen 201–3
Duffy, Carol Ann 93–4

Eggley, Ann 144–5
Eliot, George 50–51, 137–9, 210–12
Elizabeth I, Queen 17
Engels, Friedrich 208–9
Erinna of Telos 127–8
Evelyn, John 59–61

Fielding, Sarah 105–7
Finch, Anne, Countess of Winchilsea 116
Flaubert, Gustave 43–4
Forster, J. 146–8
Franklin, Benjamin 5, 46

Galt, John 179–81
Gaskell, Elizabeth 75–6
Gilman, Charlotte Perkins 17–18

# General Index